You are about to read the autobiography of the man known as George "Machine Gun" Kelly, one of the few major criminal legends who lived long enough to tell his own story.

Pat,

May you enjoy success + happiness in all that you do.

Jim Dobbins

Jan. 23, 2015

MACHINE-GUN MAN
The True Story of My Incredible Survival
into the 1970's.

Publisher: UCS PRESS
3531 W. Glendale Ave., Suite 202
Phoenix, Arizona 85051

Cover design by Wayne Horne

Back-cover photo reprinted with permission of Phoenix Newspapers Inc.

Printed in the United States of America

First Printing: 1988

NOTE: The names of some individuals in this book have been changed.

Library of Congress Cataloging-in-Publication Data

Kelly, George, 1906-1975.
Machine-gun man.

1. Kelly, George, 1906-1975. 2. Crime and
criminals—United States—Biography. I. Dobkins,
Jim, 1943-   . II. Jordan, Ben. III. Title.
HV6248.K4l3A3 1988   364.1'5'0924 (B) 87-30071
ISBN 0-943247-04-7

MACHINE-GUN MAN

The True Story of My
Incredible Survival into the 1970's.

by

George "Machine Gun" Kelly

as told to

Jim Dobkins and Ben Jordan

ABOUT THE WRITERS

Jim Dobkins and Ben Jordan are a unique writing team. Jordan was Dobkins' ninth grade English teacher at Phoenix Union High School in 1958-59. "It was," Dobkins reports, "simply a case of the student catching the writing bug from the teacher." Jordan's book credits include LEATHERJACKETS, SKY JUMPERS, and DIRT-TRACK TWISTER, teen action novels published in the 1960's. Jordan and his wife, Naomi, have residences in Phoenix and Prescott, Arizona. Dobkins, who lives in Phoenix with his wife, Marty, is a writer-editor-publisher. His credits include co-authorship of WINNIE RUTH JUDD: THE TRUNK MURDERS, non-fiction, and THE ARARAT CONSPIRACY, a novel; also, the screenplay for the dramatization SOMEONE WHO CARES.

In memory

of

Paul Hughes

(May 1, 1916-January 20, 1979),

the man responsible

for getting the writers

together with

"Machine Gun" Kelly.

CONTENTS

INTRODUCTION

I met John quite by accident. I was working at a television repair shop as a bookkeeper when the owner and his wife were involved in a family dispute. The police were called, the wife pressed charges, and he was then locked up in the county jail.

Feeling sorry for her husband the next day, Sarah wanted to arrange for his release. She asked me to go with her to post bail for Curtis. Neither of us had ever been to a bail bondsman before. John worked for the bail bondsman. I had no idea that he was still incarcerated in a Federal Penitentiary, being allowed to work outside during the day on a work-release program. Nor would I have ever dared dream then that John had actually robbed two banks in the Dallas-Fort Worth area while on the work-release program. He had bought his way into the job using some of the proceeds of the heists.

John was quite a bit older than me, but just how much older I couldn't be sure. It seemed like at times John went through some sort of metamorphosis so that he could pass as being anywhere between the ages of fifty to seventy.

Upon our first meeting I did not pay much attention to John, but he apparently did to me. Being just twenty-two at the time, pregnant, and shattered from a broken heart, I wanted nothing to do with men.

Since I had signed on Curtis' bond, John had access to my work phone number. He started calling me at work, asking me to meet him for dinner. I was put off by this at first, but John was very persistent. I finally agreed to meet him for dinner just to get him to quit calling; however, I stood him up. This made me feel bad because I had not been raised to treat people that way. I called John the next day, apologized, and agreed to reschedule the dinner meeting. Not wanting him to know where I lived, I would not allow him to pick me up at home. Little did I know, but John had already had me followed. He already knew as much about me as my closest friend.

He dropped a bombshell on me at dinner, telling me that he knew I was going to be his woman. His words exactly. Not girl friend, lover, wife or whatever, but his woman! He sure had his nerve coming on like he did. I told him I had no intention of getting involved with anyone, especially some guy who was old enough to be my dad. No way was I looking for a father figure.

John ignored everything I threw back at him. He said he was serving the last of his thirty-something years in prison; he was working on the work-release program, and it would be two months before he would be free. Then, in that deep, gravelly bass voice of his, he proposed that he set me up in a very nice apartment, no strings attached, until his release. If I wanted to leave at that time, I could do so.

John did set me up in a very nice apartment: white carpet, brocade furniture, and a fireplace. For a man convicted of violent crimes, he was very gentle. He did not push himself on me either sexually or visitation-wise.

Meanwhile, the FBI and officials at the Fort Worth Correctional Institute where John was an inmate had been monitoring developments. I was told to go to the FBI office. There I was asked how I knew John. Did I know of his past? Why was I moving in with him? I was told that John had spent over thirty years in prison for murder, bank robbery, larceny, theft, and kidnapping. They also told me that they could not allow -- and I stress, <u>allow</u> — me to live with John. They said they were afraid something would happen to me, especially like waking up dead.

Well, I've never been one to be told what to do or how to do it. I thanked them for their information and concern, and politely told them to go butt a stump.

John moved in upon his release. Things went well at first. He did not pressure me for anything more than I was willing to give or could give.

Then, after the accident, things changed.

While visiting my grandparents, I slipped and fell down a flight of stairs. I was seven months pregnant and lost the baby. John took it as hard or harder than I did. He'd been talking about wanting to have a little red-headed baby girl just like me. And, according to the doctor, that is exactly what I lost — a red-headed baby girl.

The combination of the accident and the constantly being spied on took its toll on both of us. Also, John began making threats about what he would do if I ever left him. He made it clear — and I believed him — that in such event he would hang the members of my family from the telephone pole outside their home.

I became convinced that we should relocate. I thought that if I could get John far enough away from my family that they would be safe and I could gradually get away from him. So we left our apartment and headed for Phoenix where I would meet an old cellmate of John's — the man who would have an influence on John's return to his old way of living.

It was on the way to Phoenix that John finally told me his true identity. From our very first meeting, he had given me the nickname "George." This had not meant anything to me other than as a sign of affection from him. He used to leave notes addressed to "George" all over our apartment telling how much he cared for me. On our trip he asked if I had ever been curious about who George was. This did it. My curiosity was indeed aroused higher than Mt. Everest. He already had me pegged for the nosy person that I am.

John asked if I had ever heard of George Kelly and I said no. Then he asked if I had ever heard of "Machine Gun" Kelly. Well, there isn't a person either my age or older who hasn't heard of "Machine Gun" Kelly.

At first I didn't believe John, but the more research I did on him and or George Kelly, the more convinced I became that John was or could be George Kelly.

After a brief stay in Phoenix, John and I decided to move to Los Angeles. There we found employment through the newspaper. Larry Erickson, who hired John, was to become one of the most positive influences on his life during our stay in southern California. Larry and his wife, Liz, became our closest friends. They invited us to church with them and to their Bible study classes. Having been raised in church myself, I welcomed the opportunity. I could tell that John only agreed to go out of curiosity and to keep me off his back.

Brother Hal Rapp was the pastor at Bethany Foursquare Church in North Hollywood, and still is today. If I have ever met a man I believed was close to God and tried his best to live as God would have us to live, that man would have to be Brother Rapp.

John was immediately drawn to Brother Rapp. I'm sure this was because John saw in this down-to-earth preacher a man who actually practiced what he preached. John's life began to turn around. Not only did we attend services three times a week, but we also attended any extra activities sponsored by the church. John and Larry would sometimes leave for work early just to have time to stop at the church and pray.

John became a born again Christian and in April, 1974, was

9

baptized by Brother Rapp in the church. Then John asked Brother Rapp to marry us. He did perform the wedding ceremony; however, we did not go through the formality of buying a marriage certificate and filing it with the State of California.

It was during a private counseling session involving just Brother Rapp, John and me that John cleared his conscience, confessing his crimes of violence and identity as "Machine Gun" Kelly.

I wish we could have continued to live under Brother Rapp's influence. Instead, we moved back to Phoenix, John took up with his old cellmate from McNeil Island, and I became the getaway driver for three bank robberies.

Despite everything that happened, John was a very sensitive, thoughtful human being concerned about me as an individual. I'm sure that he loved me beyond any reasoning or thoughts of what he did to the two of us. He seemed to have no conception of right or wrong. Everything was either black or white with him. You either had what you needed or you didn't, in which case, you took it. He had no concern over our personal safety or our future. He only saw and lived for today. Tomorrow didn't seem to matter because, as he said, it is never guaranteed.

I believe my experiences with John have made me a stronger person than I was before I met him. Those experiences have also made me realize that I am a person with a right to my own feelings and thoughts. John started out by trying to dictate my feelings and thoughts. I wouldn't allow this to happen today. To be honest with you, the person that I have become would not have caved in to the kind of demands that John made when we first met.

As to whether or not I believe John's claim that he was indeed George "Machine Gun" Kelly, I am sure that he was. Alias George Kelly. Alias George Barnes. Alias John Webb. I met him as John and still think of him as John. That never bothered him because he knew that I believed him. If he were alive today, I'm sure it would not be a big deal to him one way or another what you believe after reading his story. His main concern in telling his story to Jim Dobkins and Ben Jordan was simply that they tell the story the way he told it to them. He did not want them changing the basics of his story in any way. They haven't. I am grateful to them for keeping true to his request.

Sure, I still have questions about the man who gave me the last name of Webb. For example, why has George "Machine Gun" Kelly been so sloppily documented by government and other records? I've researched out at least three different years of death, three different states in which he died, and at least a half-dozen years for his date of birth.

Why did the FBI warn me not to live with him?

Why is there a man in Texas now using a driver's license with the same number that was on John's Texas license? I called the Department of Public Safety and was told that driver's license numbers were never reissued even in the event of the death of the original license number holder.

Why has George "Machine Gun" Kelly's physical stature grown from five-feet-nine to six-feet-one between reports made in the 1930's to accounts published in the 1970's and later? You can check this out for yourself. Just look up the crime books published in the early 1930's. You'll find Kelly's real height. Then look up crime books published in the 1970's. I am amazed at how tall a person can become after he has achieved adulthood.

I repeat. Yes, I believe John was George "Machine Gun" Kelly, and I know where his body is buried. But what I'd like to ask the government and the readers of this book, is who are buried in the other graves?

Cynthia Webb
May, 1988

MACHINE-GUN MAN

The True Story of My
Incredible Survival into the 1970's.

"The only problem is, they buried some poor sucker from Leavenworth whose name wasn't even close to Kelly. It sure isn't my carcass rotting away under that stinking Texas dirt!"

1. Birth Of A Book

I'll bet Paul Hughes, author and public relations man who lives in Phoenix, Arizona, is still kicking himself for not taking the time to help me write this book. Cindy, my 24-year-old wife, went to his office and asked if he would be interested in writing the life story of George "Machine Gun" Kelly. That visit on January 6, 1975, sure set the ball rolling. But Hughes wasn't the man who would put down that story. He told Cindy that he just didn't have the time to take on such a project, but he knew another Phoenix author who might be interested.

So Cindy ended up calling Jim Dobkins, who had just co-authored WINNIE RUTH JUDD: THE TRUNK MURDERS.

I almost told Cindy to chuck the whole idea. After all, I'd lived nearly sixty-nine years without anyone telling the whole truth about my life. What good would it do now? But my Texas Lamb Chop is a very stubborn woman. She reminded me once more about how I had the right to tell my own story and reap any profits that would come my way. Why should I keep sitting back, letting others keep capitalizing on my past reputation? Hell, there was even a disc jockey in Los Angeles who was calling himself "Machine Gun" Kelly. He was the No. 1 D-J in Southern California — and at my expense the way Cindy saw it.

Cindy's reasoning did have some logic to it. I let her have her way. But the reason I let her go ahead didn't have the same kind of thinking behind it that she'd thrown at me. I'll get right to the point. I'm a dying man. Any life left in me is just about all drained away. Being all locked up like I am, telling my life's story is the only way I have left of helping Cindy hold her head above water financially.

I owe her that much. It was all my doing that got her involved in those three bank robberies in Phoenix. Just like it was all my doing that got me cooped up in this Federal detention cage here in Florence, Arizona.

But I'm getting ahead of myself. You'll just have to wait until later in this book to find out how I almost walked away with $200,000 cold cash from a bank in west Phoenix. Let me get back to explaining how Cindy got Jim Dobkins involved with my autobiography — isn't that a nice sounding word? Say, that makes me an author. Hey, Karpis! I'm an author! I just hope I live to see this in print.

Anyway, Cindy convinced Paul Hughes that somebody ought to check into the matter and see if I'm the real McCoy. Like most folks, he'd been of the impression that I kicked the bucket long ago. But you just can't always believe the garbage that is spit out of Washington, D.C.

You'd get a headache if you examined all the death reports filed on me. You'd have to choose which agency to believe. Would you believe the records that claim I died on Alcatraz in 1946? Would you believe the Leavenworth and Federal Bureau of Prison records that say I died at Leavenworth in July of 1954? And what about the various FBI statements that I died in 1954 and 1956 at Alcatraz?

Wouldn't it be easier to believe J. Edgar Hoover when he admitted during a 1958 speech that I was at that time safely tucked away on McNeil Island?

Then there's that "Machine Gun" Kelly grave over there in the Cottondale Cemetery in Wise County, Texas. I'm sure the big show, the fancy funeral and all, impressed a lot of people — the event certainly got splashed in a lot of newspapers around the country. The only problem is, they buried some poor sucker from Leavenworth whose name wasn't even close to Kelly. It sure isn't my carcass rotting away under that stinking Texas dirt!

It seemed that Paul Hughes grew up in Oklahoma during the years I was on the rampage. He even went to East Central State Teachers College in Ada — that was in the mid-1930's — when Kathryn's step-daughter, Pauline, went to school there. He knew the story that Cindy told him was a mighty big mouthful to attempt to swallow and digest all in one sitting, yet he had one of those deep-down feelings that she was being truthful. That's why he suggested that Cindy contact Dobkins. Several years earlier Jim had worked with Hughes' son, Mark, at THE ARIZONA REPUBLIC newspaper. He knew Jim had a nose that liked to sniff into the unusual.

Well, my Texas Lamb Chop had to do some powerful talking to convince Jim to at least consider the possibility that I wasn't some stir crazy old con imposter. During a phone conversation and follow-up visit at her house trailer in Tempe, she discussed many of the facts of my life.

Things like how my identity was changed by the government in 1954 to John Webb and the events leading up to President Nixon's signing of my clemency papers in 1973. That Tempe visit stretched into four hours. Cindy was loaded for bear. She showed Jim old and fairly recent photos of me, including photos of two of my sons and my daughter. There are certain physical characteristics which have stayed with me most of my life. The photos showed this. Jim was hooked. He had to have a face-to-face meeting with me. That was arranged for Friday, January 10, at the Federal Detention Center in Florence, where I was being held pending disposition of three bank robbery charges against me.

Meanwhile, on the evening of January 8, on his way home from that visit with Cindy, Jim stopped by to see Ben Jordan, another Phoenix author. Ben had been Jim's freshman English teacher at Phoenix Union High School seventeen years earlier, and had gotten Jim interested in writing.

Jim told Ben the story of his phone conversation with Cindy and their meeting and wanted to know if he would like to help write a book about "Machine Gun" Kelly. A partnership between the teacher and student was formed. I'm sure it was Jim's way of saying thanks to Ben for starting him down the road of writing.

Cindy accompanied Jim to that January 10th meeting with me. He registered in as a personal friend. The guard had no idea he was letting in a writer to interview me. Anyway, he motioned for Jim and Cindy to wait for a heavy, barred glass door to be opened electronically by another guard who was stationed in a bullet-proof glassed-in room directly inside the main holding area. As soon as that door had opened and then closed behind them, Cindy guided Jim through a bare office area where there was only a desk and a chair, then on through the entrance into the visiting room.

This room was light blue and was thirteen-and-one-half-feet long and eleven feet wide with a nine-foot-high ceiling. The room was split down the middle with a partition of four panels of bullet-resistant glass, which reached to the ceiling from a three-foot-high foundation of heavy cement blocks. A thick board shelf jutted out on both sides of the partition at the base of the panels. This shelf could be used as an arm rest or for writing purposes.

You probably wonder how I can give such minute details. Well, I'd been seeing Cindy almost every day since they'd sent me to Florence. With my background, my line of work, you get into the habit of noticing every little detail of everything around you. You just never know when such information might prove beneficial.

Folks have been known to try escapes. I've got at least eleven escape attempts on my jacket.

Our only means of communication during these visits was through telephone receivers on each side of the glass partition. Both prisoners and visitors sat in molded fiberglass chairs and each had access to a receiver to talk into and listen with. Back of the visitor section was the control room where a guard had complete command of both prisoners and visitors.

Of course, with the tremendous phone receiving equipment they had in that joint, it was often hit-and-miss as to whether you got a receiver that worked. Most of my visits with Jim, only two of the four receivers on each side of the partition worked worth a damn. Then on weekends we'd usually get caught in the wetback rush. Many of the prisoners were illegal Mexican aliens, and when they got visits, it was like Pancho Villa's family reunion. You couldn't hear anything except a bunch of wailing Mexican women. They're good people, but when they visit their men they know only one way to talk, at the top of their lungs. Hell, some of them could carry on a two-way conversation through a brick wall without any receivers!

The point I'm trying to make is that during those weekend wetback rushes, Jim and I had to read lips if we expected to get any work done. Then there were a number of visits cut short when my face would turn blue and I'd be pulled back into my isolation cell for a shot of adrenalin to keep me alive.

I was kinda excited over the prospect of meeting Jim. Cindy had warned me to be on my good behavior; but that's my baby, always trying to get me to reform.

Well, when that steel door to the prisoners' half of the visiting room swung open and I stepped through and looked at Jim, I could almost read his mind. I was pretty good at such things because I was in my natural environment while he was out of his. He saw me as a powerfully built man, who could easily have been anywhere from his late fifties to early seventies. I was wearing a brown, cotton, short-sleeve shirt which hung outside my brown duck trousers. I knew I didn't present a very good picture because my shirt was stained with sweat, and it was open to the fourth button.

I'm sure he didn't take me for no weakling because I have a barrel-like chest and big arms because I've done pushups during much of my prison life. My down next to my scalp was gray because I hadn't had a chance to touch it up with a new dye job.

He looked my face over good, studying my heavy eyebrows and the two parallel lines which run the whole length of my forehead. And I'm sure he found my large W. C. Fields nose interesting. It had gone through so many beatings that it was beginning to look like the beak on a punch drunk boxer.

I've often been told that my eyes got immediate attention, even though their lids are drooping as if it's a struggle to keep them open. But since they're deep-set and penetrating, they take on an obscure color. Some might call them light steel blue and others have sworn they're milky gray with even a shade of green.

I might add that I have a one-of-a-kind voice, a gravel bass ranging somewhere in tonal quality between the voices of the late Illinois Senator Everett Dirkson and the actor Richard Boone. I've never had a problem letting people know that my voice carried authority.

Before I sat down I knew Jim was also measuring me with his eyes. At the time I would hit around two-twenty and a shade under five-nine.

Cindy told him to pick up the phone receiver from its cradle, then she lifted the one in front of her. I had to place a receiver to each ear so I could carry on a conversation with both of them at the same time. We were lucky; there were no other visits going on.

That was the first of sixty-eight interviews I had with Jim which lasted through March 31, 1975. The round-trip from Jim's house to Florence was 156 miles, making him travel 10,608 miles in his beat-up 1968 Javelin. Just the total trip alone took him close to three hours. Our daily visits lasted from ninety minutes to four hours and the actual visiting time amounted to one hundred and eighty hours before we were finished.

I knew from the start that Jim was out to prove that I was a fake. But I gave him names to contact such as relatives, cellmates and my children, and not too many weeks had passed when I knew he was believing what I told him and to him I was George "Machine Gun" Kelly.

He wasn't able to bring recording equipment into the visiting room so he took reams of notes during the interviews. He told me that when he left the Federal Detention Center he would drive up the road a ways, pull off by a palo verde tree, and get out his tape recorder. He would recreate the interviews on tape, then stop off on his way back to his house and turn them over to Ben and his wife, Naomi, who typed them up. Ben would then organize the materials into chapter drafts.

I made Jim promise that he would let me tell my whole story in my own way and that he and Jordan wouldn't change anything. What you are going to read here are true facts as I remember them about my life, not as John Webb but as George "Machine Gun" Kelly.

"I wasn't raised normal. I was treated like a stepchild. You remember Cinderella, how she was treated?"

2. Born Different

It took nearly five weeks of visits before I would openly discuss my early childhood. I did not want to pain myself with the memories. To the best of my ability, I was born on July 18, 1906, in Shelby County, Tennessee. That was nine months after my mom went alone to a dance and came home with me. I figure that's the way it happened. A guy named Kelly ran around with my mom. I figure that's who she danced with. Mr. Barnes figured it that way, too. I think he conceded the fact that I was not his son and he treated me that way.

Frankly, I don't know if my mom and Mr. Barnes were married when I was born. Coming or going, anyway I looked at it, I always thought I was a bastard from an unknown source. But everybody, including that guy Kelly, eventually conceded and took for a fact that I was Kelly's son.

Growing up as a boy I was pretty much passed around from pillar to post, like playing cards being shuffled. Most of the time, maybe seventy-five per cent of the time, I lived with my mom and George Allen Barnes in Memphis. Now and then I was shipped out to Denver to spend stretches with my dad. So it might truthfully be said that I had growing roots in both Tennessee and Colorado. I was well traveled between those states.

My dad was a rounder. Him and a guy by the name of Slaughter used to run around. He was a ladies man; had a different wife every time I'd see him, at least it seemed that way. As I recall, he did civil engineering work and over a period of years worked in Memphis, Denver and in Dallas.

Emma Barnes was my mom's name. She wasn't very big, maybe about five-four, but kinda heavy on the top side. Her family had come from Chicago early enough for her to have mostly grown up in the Tennessee farm country. She was a reddish brunette, an Irish protestant and phony religious. I don't think she ever had much education. She certainly wasn't happy. If she was, it never showed. What showed was that she was lonely most of the time. And she did know how to attract men with her body. I expect she learned that long before I was born. Mr. Barnes

19

was an insurance man and he was gone a lot on trips. When he'd leave, other men would come. For a while I wanted to believe my mom wasn't different from other moms.

I have a hunch that at six I had the knowledge, maturity of boys twelve or fourteen. I was not close to my mother. I was never close to Mr. Barnes or to my dad. I was close to myself. I have always been a private person. You'll never find anybody who had more of a private life than I had. At a very early age I accepted that I was me and that was about the size of it. I learned to take evaluation of me, any situation and anyone involved and keep my conclusions to myself. I was completely detached.

A lot of things about my life I blotted out all these years. Like at Christmas, I got an apple, an orange and two nuts. That's how much they cared. It's not that they couldn't do for me. Mr. Barnes had three children of his own. They always got more. Such incidents like that stick with me. I let other incidents wash off.

If my mom loved me, she had a hell of a way of showing it. Nobody liked me. I didn't like anybody. I didn't because I was an off-breed. I was a misfit. Nobody understood me. You hear kids today saying that nobody understands them. Well, that's the way I felt. How else could I feel? I reacted different because I was treated different. I wasn't raised normal. I was treated like a stepchild. You remember Cinderella, how she was treated?

I don't know how many times I've had dreams of that apple, orange and two nuts. I never would've known what a new toy was if I didn't see one of Mr. Barnes' kids playing with one. I couldn't forget that. I never said anything or asked questions. I just waited. I knew that some day I'd get mine. I didn't know how, except that I would sooner or later find a way. The way didn't really matter since no one cared about me or what happened to me. Love was something I didn't know about. Nothing could tie me down.

When I was five or six, I remember a woman being at our house. Her son was to hang that day in the state pen. At the time of his execution, she was weeping and screaming out. I remember the neighbor ladies talking. One of them called me weird. They were talking in a hush-hush tone when I heard it. I was listening from the porch. My mom tried to console the woman. "You can't go on like this," she told her. "He was the one who got into trouble. You gave him a good home. They proved that he killed the man, now he has to pay the price. My boy will probably end up the same way. I dread to think what he will be like in ten years."

I will never forget that conversation. As I slipped off the porch

20

the last thing I heard was another woman saying, "Yes, poor Emma, that's the way George will end up."

I ran away from the porch. I ran until my chest felt like it was going to break. When I couldn't run anymore I began to cry. I sat down on a big rock in the middle of a pasture and cried until no more tears would come. I made a promise to myself right then and there that no one would ever make me cry again. No matter what anybody said about me or did to me, I was going to shut them out. Even my mom might as well of been a stranger after that. She was just somebody who happened to live most of the time under the same roof.

When I started to school I caught on to the subjects rapidly and never had to study. Sometimes the teacher would compliment me and even send notes home to my mom. She never saw the notes. I tore them up and scattered them in the wind or in the weeds. I just kept passing from grade to grade. I believed very early that I was a genius. I'd go to school, never study, never concentrate and get A's.

I only met one man that was smarter than me: Frank, Charles F. Urschel, he was stone brilliant. But my meeting him was a lot of years ahead of me. I crossed and burned one hell of a lot of bridges before Urschel. Yet I don't know if my experiences with the kidnapping were more frustrating or if my childhood was more frustrating. There wasn't much to laugh about on either account.

The most humorous thing that ever happened in my childhood, when we lived in Memphis, was the time the goose took a liking to my mom. Every Christmas we'd get a goose. Mr. Barnes had a portable pen in the garage and we'd keep the goose in the pen. This one goose got to be real friendly with Mom, and she couldn't kill it. Neither would she allow it to be killed.

In February when the ground wasn't as hard and it wasn't so cold, Mom was out digging so she could plant some bulbs. The goose was always following her around. It wanted to get at some worms in the place where Mom had been digging. She kept nudging the goose away, and it kept sticking its head back and getting in the way.

Finally, after she had given it a good nudge, she was bent over, putting some bulbs in and covering them with dirt. The goose went up behind her and bit her on the butt. Like it was a reflex, Mom whirled around with the shovel. She only meant to scare the goose so it would back away and leave her alone. Instead, the shovel caught the goose just below its head. The head came off and the goose thrashed around on the ground until the blood had all run out.

Mom grabbed the goose and went screaming into the house. Mr. Barnes was home and he just laughed. That night, when we all sat down to eat baked goose, Mom cried and refused to eat. That was the funniest episode I ever saw at home.

"There was a sharp scream. I could no longer see Earnie May. I did see the clerk hurry over to her when moans, groans, and heavy gasps for breath filled the room."

3. The Drugstore Dandies

When I was a small boy of eight but big enough to pass for a twelve-year-old, I had two pets. Each was a character like myself. The first was a little dog of questionable ancestry named Amber, a stray that had taken up with me during one of my wanderings across the open fields. We became inseparable as we tramped around the neighborhood together.

Amber was really the first true friend I had, the only one with whom I could share my thoughts and still receive a friendly lick of understanding.

From the beginning there was an argument around home whether Amber could come inside the house. The answer was an absolute no, especially from Mr. Barnes, but I trained the dog to wait beneath my bedroom window; the dog would jump and I'd catch him and lift him inside.

After a few months, it happened. Mom began finding dog hair on the sheets; she surprised me one morning before I had a chance to raise the window and let the dog out. She told Mr. Barnes how I'd disobeyed his orders.

I never found definite proof why Amber came up missing, but I suspected Mr. Barnes killed the dog and buried him. This suspicion gave me another reason for hating the man. I was going to bide my time and get even. There was nothing to be gained by bringing up the subject of the dog's disappearance. I knew what the answer would be.

My second pet was an alley cat which had been thrown into an incinerator. I was in the area when I heard the screams of the cat and saw three boys running away from the scene. By the time I'd rescued the frightened animal, its feet were badly burned and most of its hair was singed off. I managed to fold the cat in my arms so it wouldn't scratch me, then ran toward home. I passed a neighbor woman who was working in her yard. "What in the world has happened to that cat?" she asked.

"Some boys tried to burn it alive," I told her. "Good thing I happened by and heard it screaming."

"Well, bring the poor thing to the back door. I'll get some salve and bandages; we'll see what we can do for it."

We doctored the cat, then I took it home, put it in a box in the garage and fed it. The burns healed and the animal stayed around for three years, but it also disappeared. I began to wonder if my whole life was going to be built around developing attachments only to have them chopped off by strange circumstances.

I began to look forward to the time when I would be on my own and not have to rely on others for food and a room. The big question in my mind: "Am I going to become a thief? Others are always taking my possessions away from me and never giving anything in return. Even my parents don't think enough of me to give me a few pennies for candy. If I get any I have to steal it." And that I did!

One morning on the way to school I passed a grocery store and saw some small boxes of fresh fruit arranged in a display rack on the sidewalk in front of the store. The display was in plain view of the owner inside the store. A few extra boxes had been set on an old wooden table. Right away I began to plan how to get some of the fruit without being caught. I walked by the table a few times before I decided that if I kicked the right outside leg hard enough the whole thing would cave in and the apples and peaches would roll all over the sidewalk. I could then stuff my pockets and shirt full of the fruit and get away without being seen.

One last time I walked by the table and glanced through the plate glass window. No one was around. When I approached the table leg, I gave it a hard kick, the same kind I'd used many times to send a tin can tumbling end over end. The leg caved in; fruit tumbled to the sidewalk. I fell to my knees and began stuffing apples into pockets. I'd just picked up a luscious looking peach when someone grabbed me by my shirt collar, yanked me to my feet and spun me around. Suddenly I was looking into the angry eyes of the store owner.

"I've been watching you," the enraged man said. "I ought to box your ears and give you a good butt kicking, you little thief." He gave me a hard shove. If I hadn't been so quick, I would've dug a ditch with my nose. The guy began screaming. "Don't ever let me catch you around here again or you'll pick splinters out of your butt for a month!" I got away with two large apples.

I knew it was too late to go on to school so I decided to climb up in an old abandoned railroad engine that was on a siding and enjoy my apples. I thought over and over about what the man had said.

It wasn't the first time I'd been called a thief. Sure, stealing was wrong but I never felt guilty about it. I just had to be more careful in my planning. The man said he'd been watching me. Well, from then on I was going to <u>know</u> when I was being watched and outsmart the watcher.

Even as a boy I knew every policeman in my part of town and decided I didn't like them. They were supposed to be protectors over women and children and sometimes me, but I confess that I never met one that was any good. Sooner or later they'll let it show that they are little lord gods themselves. It always comes out that they're dogs.

I often got into fights as a boy. Most of them were not of my choosing. I was a loner and wanted to be left alone, but I seemed to attract the attention of older and bigger boys, especially those who had a bully streak.

After two or three fights, the word went out that George Barnes didn't fight with his fists. The brother of one of the girls who liked me found this to be very true. He tried to make friends with me. I ignored him and told him to beat it. The big bully accused me of being a sissy and only wanting to be around girls. He gave me a push. "Go home and play with your dolls."

That did it! I looked around for something to change the shape of his head. I spotted a rake with curved steel teeth. Someone had been raking leaves and left it there. Grabbing the rake handle in both hands, I swung it at the boy but missed. On the second swing he dodged forward, the handle caught him on the side of the head and broke. The third swing made contact and the handle broke again, leaving a long gash just below the hairline. Stunned, the big boy put his hand to his forehead, drew it away when he saw the blood. Although unsteady on his feet, he managed to turn and stumble away. The boy's name was Sealey, and he never made another attempt to be friendly with me, even though he saw me many times after that morning.

Several months later, while I was swimming in the Rice Plant pond, a group of boys came up, took off their clothes, and dived in. I'd selected a spot which was around twenty-five feet in diameter and very deep. I'd been practicing my diving when the other boys arrived. They told me to get lost, that they wanted the whole place themselves. I told them that it was big enough for all of us and I wasn't leaving.

"You are going or I'll give you a ducking you won't forget," one of the boys said.

"Just leave me alone," I replied and began to swim to the far bank, away from my clothes. I heard a splash but didn't bother to look around. Then suddenly I was grabbed by the legs and dragged under. I came up coughing. As soon as I got my breath I watched for the boy to surface. When he did, I got a half-nelson around his neck and held him under until he stopped kicking. Then, turning him loose, I swam over to where my clothes were and climbed out onto the bank.

"Where's Harry?" one of the others demanded.

"How should I know. He tried to drown me so I left him on the bottom."

I watched as the big boy dived in and brought Harry to the surface. He didn't offer any resistance whatsoever. The other boys pulled him up onto the bank and began applying artificial respiration.

Even though I didn't get along very well with boys, I was attractive to girls. They found me interesting. I could laugh and joke with them and be a good sport. My first little girl friend was Earnie May Story, a skinny little dishwater brunette who lived four doors down the street. She was a year older and one grade ahead of me in school. While I was stockily built and strong for my age, Earnie May was tall and slender, very athletic, could run like a deer and didn't hesitate to take me on in a wrestling match or trade licks with me even though she usually lost.

She was an individualist, too, and often had run-ins with her parents because they refused to give her an allowance and very little spending money. "It's not because they can't afford it," she told me soon after we began to chum around together. "They're just so darned tight with their money."

Because of our total rebellion against parental authority and our lack of pennies to spend for candy and pop on a hot summer day, we began to scheme how we could steal and not get caught. I was usually the brains behind some of the strange plots we came up with. But Earnie May contrived one idea that I'd never thought of.

"I'll go in the store first and stand a little ways from the candy counter, then you come in. When I get the clerk's attention, then you go into action. You've never seen me throw a whopper."

I followed her into the drugstore, glanced her way for an instant, then walked over to the glassed-in counter that held all the different colored candy. There was a sharp scream. I could no longer see Earnie May. I did see the clerk hurry over to her when moans, groans, and heavy gasps for breath filled the room. I wanted to see for myself Earnie May's whopper, but she'd warned me to take care of my end.

The clerk shouted, "She's having a fit! Someone get a doctor!" That was when I pushed back the sliding door of the candy counter and began to stuff my pockets and shirt full of jawbreakers, licorice, mints, and hard and soft candy. On the way out of the store I picked up a harmonica, and had not gone half a block before Earnie May caught up with me.

"Boy, you should have seen that clerk's face when I stopped kicking. I opened my eyes and said that I was all right. 'I guess it's the heat,' I told him. You know he wasn't going to let me go before he called Mom to come and get me. I wasn't about to give him my name. I did give him a fake phone number. When he went to call, I beat it."

I laughed. "I got the candy. Let's go to the old engine and make ourselves sick. See, I picked this up, too. I can play it almost as good as you can throw a fit."

"I'll believe that when I hear you."

She believed me real quick. I had taught myself to play "The Tennessee Waltz", "I'm An Old Cowhand", "Deep In The Heart Of Texas", "Home On The Range", "Clemintine" and some other songs. The harmonica drove away my loneliness; it was my friend.

Between songs, we talked about things we would do when we got older and away from home. I got off on the subject of robbing trains while I was trying to work the rusty levers of the old engine. I'd read a book about how Jesse James and his gang pulled off some of their robberies. The large amounts of money they made in their hauls intrigued me. I captured Earnie May's attention and she begged for details.

After I'd related all the facts that I could remember she said, "Boy, I bet one of my whoppers would sure come in handy back then. Let's try pulling off a big job like that some time."

Later we did try to steal a train. It happened when we were walking through the railroad yard on our way to climb up into the cab of the old engine. A train crew had left their engine completely unattended on a siding not too far from a cafe. Little puffs of steam escaped as it breathed its slow hot gasps in the noonday sun. I dared Earnie May to climb aboard with me and see if we could get the sleeping giant to go rolling down the track. Earnie May was all for it.

I pulled every lever I could reach; nothing happened. Finally I became disgusted and jumped for the rope I was sure would ring the bell. Sure enough, the bell worked, clanging so loud that it signaled three surprised trainmen from the cafe. Two of the men caught us and roughed us up. They threatened to throw us in jail if we ever got close to their engine again. This little experience made us even more determined to steal an engine. I began to plan my strategy, to pick out spots where we could "short stop" an engine on the outskirts of town, but we never got to fulfill this ambition.

Our next run-in with railroad personnel happened a few weeks later. We discovered a pond in a wooded area not too far from the tracks. The pond was railroad property and signs were posted to keep out. As we were poking around in the water with sticks, and skipping flat rocks across the pond's surface, I spotted a big fish in the clear shallow water. I began to take off my clothes so that I could try and catch the fish with my hands. When Earnie May asked me what I was going to do, I explained that fish had a hard time breathing in muddy water and I was going to see if it would come to the top for air.

"In that case you'll need help. Wait for me," she called.

Both of us waded into the water stark naked and began to churn up the muddy bottom with our feet. One large fish did surface right in front of me. I grabbed it and tossed it on the bank. Then Earnie May let out a yell when she was able to scoop up another fish. We had become so interested in our new found sport that we were totally unaware when two men drove up in a car. One shouted, "Hey, come out of there you two! Can't you read? This is railroad property and you're trespassing." He gathered up our clothes and gave them to his companion who drove away.

We waded out of the water, feeling silly standing around naked. In a few minutes the other man returned with the police and we spent the night in the local detention facility.

The next morning when we were released and back home, Mr. Barnes gave me one of the hardest lickings I'd ever received. I managed to grab the heavy leather strap and jerk it out of his hands. "Don't you ever lick me again," I warned. "If you do, you'll be sorry!"

When I was twelve and Earnie May thirteen, I got my last beating. We were riding through the city park on our bicycles where there were several tame ducks. It was necessary that we turn aside to keep from hitting the ducks. One factor in my nature was never to give in to anyone or anything. When one of the ducks

28

refused to move as I approached, I ran right over its back and killed it. While that duck was still kicking, Earnie May, not to be outdone, ran over another one.

We jumped off our bikes and decided to clean and roast them right there in the park. Several picknickers watched as we tried to remove the feathers from the birds. Someone called the police and once again we were taken to the detention home and held there over night.

When I got out, Mr. Barnes had the strap ready. He took me to the garage and gave me five or six licks across the back while threatening to cut me to shreds if I ever got into any more trouble. His remarks drove me into a rage and, although he was much bigger than me, I managed to jerk away and grab a two-bladed ax that was hanging on two nails on the garage wall. I turned on Barnes, with the ax held high, and backed him into a corner.

"I warned you the last time you whipped me never to do it again. If you ever lay another hand on me, I'll cut your head off." I twisted the leather strap out of his hand, then walked over to a heavy board which was leaning against the garage wall. With the toe of my shoe I flattened the board, bent over and chopped the strap into little pieces, threw them into Barnes' face and stalked away.

This incident caused me to become more isolated from both my mother and Barnes. I never spoke to them other than to answer their questions. I got my own meals and became quite proficient at frying eggs and bacon, preparing oatmeal and anything that was available. I could kill, dress and fry a chicken, then eat most of a small one by myself at one sitting. When I brought a chicken home that I'd stolen, no questions were asked. Neither did I invite anyone else to join me when I sat down to eat it.

Since Earnie May and I were together often and had complete freedom of going and coming it was inevitable that we experiment with sex. It was soon after the garage incident that I got around to having my first real sex experience with Earnie May.

She had slipped out of her house to be with me one night. We made ourselves comfortable under the hedge and once more were trying to achieve satisfaction. This time we were having considerable success and Earnie May was in full cooperation. Suddenly the porch light flashed on. We never did get to finish that job. Earnie May's mother was calling us a couple of animals and I was trying to get my clothes on straight. She declared that if she ever caught me with her daughter again she would have me locked up and see that the key was thrown away.

But her threats didn't stop us. We went right on seeing each other.

"The bottom of my rib cage felt like it was on fire, but I wasn't going to drop the brick yet. I had a purpose for it. After I used it, there'd be only one chance with the crowbar. If that failed, Bill Pruitt would kill me."

4. The Sex Menu And The Neighbor's Wife

After me and my stepfather locked horns in the garage, Mr. Barnes began to put the pressure on Mom to keep me out of his sight. He wouldn't admit it outright, but the ax incident had frightened him. He knew that if he'd made a wrong move that morning, after he'd tried to whip me, I would have followed through on my threat, "I'll cut your head off!" Mr. Barnes was going to leave me alone in the future, regardless what kind of trouble I got into.

Mom decided that the best way to keep the peace was to move my sleeping quarters to a room which had been added on to the rest of the house and was completely isolated. It had its own private entrance, and I could come and go as I pleased without anyone being aware of my presence. A hot plate was installed so I could fix my own meals.

Mom had become estranged from me and wanted to see as little of me as possible. If two or three days passed that she did not see me, she never worried. Her usual remark when asked about my whereabouts: "Oh, he's fine. He's big enough to take care of himself, and he usually does."

By the time I'd reached the age of thirteen, I was well-traveled, especially between Denver and Memphis. Mr. Barnes had to spend months in each place and he would take his family with him.

I've been old all my life. Never knew what it was to be a boy, to think like a boy or act like a boy. My parents saw to that. They never had anything to do with me, so I learned to shift for myself.

Herman Kelly, the brother of my real father, owned two drug-stores which were located in each of the two cities where I lived. After I turned thirteen, Mom contacted Uncle Herman and begged him to give me a job so I could be kept occupied before and after school and on weekends. Then maybe I would stay out of trouble. In Memphis I attended school at Lauderdale Elementary, a one-room school which went from the first through the

31

eighth grade. While in Denver I went to Curtis Adams School. I would hurry to Kelly's Pharmacy early in the morning, sweep the place out, then put new stock on the shelves. After school I would act as a soda jerk and do everything else I was asked to do. Kelly's Pharmacy was located in the old part of the city where the houses and stores were in a run-down condition. Nothing was ever said about a salary, and when no money was given, after I'd been there for a week, I asked Uncle Herman about it. The fifty-five-year-old, heavy-set man looked at me for a long time before he spoke. "Your mother said I would be doing you and her a favor if I took you in and taught you the business. Just forget about money and make me a good hand. You'll never regret it."

As far as Herman Kelly was concerned, the matter was closed, but it wasn't closed for me. I did everything I was asked to do, never failed to report to work on time and I was furious when Uncle Herman would shout at me as if he didn't know my name. "Hey, you, do this!"

Mom had made a bargain with the man, yet I felt I was entitled to some compensation for my long hours. I began to steal anything in the store I felt would be of use. I cheated on the counter money, and ate ice cream when I grew hungry for it. My uncle wasn't giving me a fair shake; therefore, I was entitled to anything I wanted in the store. The change, which I failed to ring up on the cash register, was used to buy delicacies I could prepare on the hot plate in my room. I came to like the adventure of cooking and preparing my meals. This hobby was to last me all my life, when I was able to do my own cooking. I never took a backseat to anyone when I played the role of chef.

My new bedroom offered me the opportunity to see Earnie May Story in complete privacy. No longer did we have to seek hiding places under bushes to have sex. Now we had a comfortable bed which we used almost every night. Earnie May enjoyed the set-up so much that she confided in her girl friend, Sally Capps, who was two years older than me. Sally was anxious to learn about sex and found a willing teacher in yours truly who took care of both girls at the same time, two or three nights a week. She, in turn, asked me if she could bring two other girls whose names were Dorothy and Frances. I didn't object, so some nights there would be three girls in bed. The girls would climb out their bedroom windows after their parents had gone to sleep. They would stay until two and three in the morning and then slip back to their own homes.

One night me and my harem almost got caught. A father and mother came looking for their daughter and began banging loudly on the door, making threatening promises if the girl did not appear at once. Meanwhile, their daughter was in the process of climbing out the window.

The very next day I rigged up a series of tin cans with rocks in them, strung on hidden wires. When someone approached the entrance, and did not know how to evade the wires, the cans would sound a warning. The bedroom window was quickly raised; the girls would slip outside behind the shelter of tall bushes and escape while their parents were becoming entangled in the wires, and waking up the neighborhood by rattling the cans. When they would finally reach the door and demand entry, I would open it and invite them in to look around and prove that I was the only one in the room. The parents began to hate me. My clever actions and words made them appear foolish and even sorry that they had disturbed me, yet they knew I was guilty.

The girls talked about me at school and my reputation spread. Boys regarded me with awe, but knew they could not be friends with me. I could have my pick of almost any girl. Sally Capps soon became my favorite. She was a little over four-feet tall, and I referred to her as my midget. My, how she did enjoy the activities of the bed! She talked me into eliminating all the other girls. Things went fine until her mother followed her to my place and put a stop to Sally's escapades.

My fame as a Don Juan spread in wider circles. One of the girls broke the news to my seventh grade teacher, a woman by the name of Miss Roach. One day at the close of school it was raining hard, and I had lingered behind waiting for the downpour to slacken. Miss Roach called me back into the classroom, locked the door and told me what she had heard. "I'm envious of those girls," she said. "I would like some of that fun myself."

She was hungry for sex and didn't hesitate to prove it. I learned a lot besides English and history from Miss Roach. She became downright indignant when I didn't remain after school to catch up on my homework. Of course, the inevitable happened — Miss Roach became pregnant. The community accused her of having my child, but she had too much experience. I'm sure I wasn't the father.

I went back to Denver in November with my mother and Mr. Barnes. I worked in Herman Kelly's other drugstore, doing the same chores without pay. My sleeping room was an extension which had been built onto the garage. All I had to do to set up housekeeping was to take my hot plate with me. The little girls up and down the block I'd played with as a young boy, were now teen-agers and were ready to resume where they'd left off.

My sexual activities caused me to have my first serious brush with the law.

One day at quitting time the pharmacist handed me a small package. "This is for Mrs. Bill Pruitt who lives in your neighborhood. She's waiting for it. Just drop it off at this address." He pointed to the typed label. I realized it was only two houses down from my house, across the street. I knew that an older boy, close to my age, lived there; also, I'd seen a smaller boy about six or seven playing in the yard.

I parked my bike and climbed the three steps to the porch, which was bordered with evergreen bushes growing across the front of the house. I knocked hard on the front door, then had to wait for several minutes before it was opened. The woman who greeted me apologized for making me wait, and said that she had been in the back. She invited me in while she got the money to pay for the prescription. Again she was gone for a long time. When she returned she was wearing a housecoat. As I turned to look at her, the housecoat parted. I saw that she had nothing on underneath. She gave a little giggle as if the whole thing was an accident, but only smiled at me. "It's cold outside. I bet you'd like some hot chocolate. Come into the kitchen and I'll make you some. I'm here all alone; the rest of the family's gone to a movie."

I drank the chocolate and listened to a tale similar to the one I'd heard from Miss Roach in Memphis. Mrs. Pruitt claimed that she had been awakened by my tin can trap. The whole neighborhood was gossiping how I'd been seducing the girls up and down the block. She led me to a bedroom and motioned for me to join her.

I studied the woman. She was around thirty-five, not bad looking; neither was she pretty. She was of medium height and well built. I'd seen her husband in the yard several times when I'd ridden by on my bike. He was well over six-feet tall, a big fellow. Some things I just didn't understand about women, including my own mother. Weren't any of them ever satisfied with a normal relationship between themselves and their husbands?

From that evening on for the next two weeks, I met Mrs. Pruitt at prearranged times, while her husband was out of the house and she could get rid of her boys for an hour. She refused to go to my room at night, afraid that some of our neighbors would see and

34

recognize her. One afternoon while we were together, her youngest son slipped into the house and caught us in bed. He told his dad about us.

I always parked my bike in back of the drugstore. When I left each night after work I never bothered to switch on the back light. I knew exactly where the bike was and could find it in the dark. One afternoon I received a phone call from Mrs. Pruitt warning me to never come to her house again. The information didn't bother me. Now I could go back to girls my own age.

It was a Saturday night. I'd worked late and was tired. I pushed open the back door of the drugstore, stepped into the darkness and heard the door spring shut as it locked behind me. I was reaching for the handlebars of my bike when I was grabbed in a vice-like grip around my chest. Suddenly I was almost smothered by a big hand clamping down over my nose and mouth. I was dragged away from the door, out into the darkness, then spun around and my arms were pinned behind me. A big ape-like form loomed up in front of me. Only then was I aware there were two men.

"I'll teach you to come to my house when I'm not home, you little bastard!"

By this time my eyes were adjusted to the darkness. Bill Pruitt was glaring down at me. "I'm going to work you over so your own mother won't know you!"

I felt a crushing blow slam into my face and heard the cracking of my jaw. Before I blacked out, I felt other blows battering my sides, chest and head. The man holding me was too strong. I couldn't wiggle free to defend myself. The heavy smell of liquor on their breaths almost gagged me before complete blackness.

I'd no idea how long I'd been lying on the ground, before I started coming to. It took me several moments to remember where I was and what had happened. Finally I managed to get to my feet. Something terrible was wrong with my jaw. I couldn't close my mouth without placing my fingers on my chin and pushing. My ride home was hell, especially when I took a deep breath, but I knew I had to get there.

As I rode by the Pruitt house the lights were on in the living room, but I didn't stop. I went straight home, parked my bike and began to make plans. I remembered the ax incident with Barnes, but Bill Pruitt was too big and strong. I didn't want to take the chance. Suddenly I remembered a crowbar under the house.

I breathed in quick gasps as I got down on my hands and knees to search for the long metal bar. Finally I felt the cold steel and dragged it out. I thought I'd pass out again, but managed to get to my feet. I couldn't let myself black out now. I had a job to do. After it was done I'd come home and get Mom to call a doctor. On the way to Pruitt's I picked up a brick and weighed it in my hand. A sharp pain shot across my chest. The bottom of my rib cage felt like it was on fire, but I wasn't going to drop the brick yet. I had a purpose for it. After I used it, there'd be only one chance with the crowbar. If that failed, Bill Pruitt would kill me.

When I reached the edge of the yard, I bent over and crept to the bushes that grew about four-feet high at the edge of the porch. When I straightened from my crouched position I was right in line with the living room window. I drew back my arm and sent the brick crashing through it. Stooping down again, I took a firm grip on the crowbar, balancing its weight in my hands, and waited.

The porch light came on. Bill Pruitt barged out the front door, slamming the screen up against the wall of the house. He paused on the porch to look around, then almost stumbled down the front steps, weaving in a drunken stupor. He turned his back to me and started toward the opposite corner of the house. I straightened and swung the crowbar like I would a baseball bat. The steel bar caught Pruitt on the side of the head. There was a sound much like a ripe watermelon popping open, after a knife is shoved into it.

I watched him turn, then in slow motion, his legs caved in and he stretched out in the yard. Another man came through the door and I heard him ask Pruitt what had happened. "Why are you on the ground? Did you fall down the steps?" I watched him come down and take a look at Pruitt.

I raised the crowbar, ready to swing. Then, as if he'd sensed my presence, he spun around, looked at me and started running down the street. I was still watching him disappear in the darkness when I heard the screen door open. I turned as Mrs. Pruitt walked out on the porch. She looked at me and gasped, "What in the world happened to you?"

"Your damned husband and his friend tried to kill me tonight out behind the drugstore after I got off work. I just laid your old man out with this." I raised the crowbar so she could get a good look at it. "Pruitt's friend held me while Pruitt beat me. He just now ran down the street. Go call the police if you want to. I'm going home."

I was explaining to Mom what had happened when the police arrived. She begged them to take me to the doctor before they locked me up, if that's what there were going to do. They did take me to the hospital where I was examined. It was discovered that my right jaw was broken along with some ribs. My mouth had to be wired shut before I was able to travel. I was taken to Canon City, which was about twenty-five miles outside Colorado Springs, and put in the custody of an old couple who were in charge of a detention home inside a tall fenced-in area. I stayed there for three weeks.

When the police came for me, they said they were taking me home. The man who had held me while Pruitt beat me up, had been arrested in Boulder. He confessed his part in the beating. He was a Canadian thief called Kanuk.

As the weeks passed I was able to get around again. I rode by Pruitt's on my bicycle. His head was bandaged, and he was propped up with pillows, sitting in a wheelchair on his front porch. As I went by on the sidewalk, Pruitt made strange noises which brought his wife running. They both stared at me, as if they expected me to attack.

I would've liked to push the son-of-a-bitch down the steps even if he had turned into a vegetable. He'd probably have thanked me for finishing the job. Anyway, he died a couple of months later.

I never had any more relations with Mrs. Pruitt. A month after her husband died, Barnes was sent back to Memphis. I went with him. I've been asked if I was sorry for what I did. Why should I be? He got exactly what he deserved.

"His fork and bite of pie clattered to the empty plate; his eyes rolled up in his head; his face turned the color of the table cloth, red."

5. Last Family Reunion

A few months after Mr. Barnes had taken his family back to Memphis, Herman Kelly, my not-so-generous uncle, had returned to check on his drugstore during June, 1920. The Barnes' family decided to have a reunion and, knowing that Herman was in town, they invited him to join them for dinner.

I had just taken my last exams in the seventh grade and was relieved because that segment of my life was over. I still was not certain what I was going to do with my future. There was one thing for sure, I wasn't going to work for Herman for the rest of my life if I didn't get paid for it. I'd been thinking a great deal about that lately and finally decided that I must go into action. I was not yet fourteen years old but powerfully built for my age. I knew that I could pass for sixteen, and I was anxious to get out on my own.

As I watched my uncle eat, I became madder than hell. Those years I'd worked for him, he hadn't as much as said, "Kiss my butt." Never offered me one red cent. It was time to collect. Without excusing myself, I got up from the table and went to my room. No one even glanced at me or bothered to ask what I was going to do. Fine! I'd catch them completely off guard.

I fished around in the old chest of drawers where I kept socks and underwear until I found a .45 pistol which I took from a hardware store just before we left Denver. I wanted to be prepared if I ever got into any more trouble. I checked the pistol to make sure it was loaded, then slipped it into my shirt just above my belt buckle, and walked back into the dining room.

I took my seat again and finished eating a piece of apple pie. Herman Kelly was eating his second piece of pie. I waited until he started to take his last bite before I pulled the pistol out from underneath my shirt. I got to my feet, and in one quick movement shoved the muzzle of the .45 against the tip end of Herman Kelly's nose. His fork and bite of pie clattered to the empty plate; his eyes rolled up in his head; his face turned the color of the table cloth, red.

"What is the meaning of this?" he stammered.

"I'll tell you the meaning," I said. "I've worked for you all these months without pay. Yesterday, I saw a brand new Dodge car. I want it. You're buying it for me. It'll cost you five hundred dollars."

Herman Kelly got all shaky and looked over at Barnes. "What are we going to do?"

Barnes returned the glance. "What do you mean we? I'm not involved."

Herman Kelly's voice cracked. "Wh...wh...what if we don't get it for him?"

"I think he'll kill you," Barnes said in a matter of fact way. He was probably remembering the time I'd threatened him with the ax. The crowbar incident was also still fresh in his mind. "Yes, I think he'll kill you," he repeated.

"You mean to sit there and say we can't do a thing about this?"

"That's right," Barnes agreed. "If I were you I'd spend the five hundred dollars, that is, if you think your life is worth that much."

An hour later Herman Kelly, Barnes and I went to the Dodge showroom and bought the car. It was a 1921 model, a new line that had just come out. The cars back in those days came out earlier than they do now.

That was the last family reunion I ever had. You can also say that's the first time I ever used a gun to get one of my requests realized.

"I put cigar ashes on the doorknobs, on the window sills, on the steps, all over. And when I came back and any of the ashes had been disturbed, I didn't go in again."

6. The Perils Of Rotgut

When I left home, I knew that it was for good. I could never go back again. I also knew that I was going to lead a life of crime. I remember those early years with no real regrets because they were filled with more adventure and daring exploits than most people could hope to live in several lifetimes.

In July, 1920, after my uncle had bought the Dodge for me, I went to Broken Bow, Oklahoma, because I'd heard the prospects for bootlegging were good there. I was only there a couple of days when I got my first bootlegging job, delivering booze. The first car I drove was outfitted for hauling corn whiskey. There was a fifty-gallon drum bolted to the trunk and two fifty-gallon drums inside the car. I liked this car but didn't have it very long—it was passed on to someone else because it was hot. It wasn't very smart to keep the same car for a lot of runs.

A whole series of cars followed this one which I either bought or stole. I owned at least five Whippets, a Cad, several Buicks and even a twelve-cylinder Auburn. It was equipped to haul over four hundred gallons. It had tanks under the fenders, under the running boards, and even the seats were tanks. There was also one big tank in the trunk. I'm sure that car could carry over four hundred gallons, maybe as much as eight hundred when it was completely full.

I used to change cars often, after a few runs. Sometimes I only took one or two runs because I didn't feel certain cars had what I would need if I got in a tight spot. A fellow called Iowa was one of the best partners I ever had when it came to preparing cars to make some of those wild runs. He didn't use a lot of welding; he had bolts and straps holding tanks together. And he could tune a car so it would take off like a rocket or purr like a kitten.

I used to take whisky from the bootleggers. I'd go around the back way and rob them. I had a lot of commitments to fill and I filled them. Most of my booze went into Dallas. When I was sixteen, I got busted. I told the officials that I was twenty-six and they believed me. I fooled them completely. When I was fourteen, I told them that I was twenty-four. Everybody thought

I was a lot older than I really was. In the work I did I matured rapidly. I had bootlegging busts at different times in Tulsa, Memphis, Oklahoma City, Dallas, even in New Mexico.

In this bootlegging business you're either buying or selling, always trying to reach a higher market. I had ambition which was the main thing the run of the mill bootleggers lacked. I was going to rise above everything, and I wasn't going to let anybody stop me. It wasn't very long before other bootleggers were working for me. I had a reputation of fair dealing. Even if I did all the work myself, I'd split the shares equally. They knew I was fair, and anybody who didn't work for me was fair game. I was always out front where the action was, directing the fireworks. I did this mainly because I had faith in only one person, myself. If I'm directing things, I know they'll go right.

Early in my bootlegging activities, even though I was still a teenager, I had developed the habit of getting very little sleep. It might sound strange, but I always slept with curiosity; I wanted to know what was going on. I used to sleep at irregular hours, at irregular intervals. I knew that if I got too much sleep, it would become a health hazard; but I wanted complete control over everything I did. Later this one factor saved my life.

When I look back, it's amazing, as dangerous as bootlegging was, and the fact I robbed other bootleggers and then sold what I got, it's a wonder I wasn't killed. Believe you me, there were plenty out there who wanted to put a bullet through me. But I only got shot one time when I was in the business. It happened in a backwoods area, not far from Tahlequah, Oklahoma. I had taken some whisky away from someone. I stopped my car along a wooded area because I had the feeling that I was going to be ambushed and wanted to be ready.

I was just getting out of the car on the left side and had put my foot down to step to the road when a bullet struck the left part of my foot. I quickly got back in the car, crawled across the front seat and out the other side, picking up my machine gun all at the same time. Whoever had fired at me turned chicken and disappeared into the woods, and I wasn't about to go after him with my foot bleeding and hurting like it was. I never did find out who'd taken the shot at me, but it's a pretty safe bet to assume he was an unhappy customer. When I say an unhappy customer, I mean another bootlegger who was not strong enough to take his catch away from me after I'd stolen it from him.

I got to my destination and was taken to see a doctor in Joplin,

Missouri. He was about six-feet-eight or nine. He had hands that could hold a basketball with his thumb and pinky finger. I'm telling you, he was the biggest doctor I'd ever seen — tall and real stocky. When you think of a doctor, you think of a guy with delicate hands. His were as big as hams.

My foot had become all swollen and a little infected, but he took care of me as if I were his favorite customer even if I hobbled into his office leaning pretty heavily on the shoulder of a whore I'd picked up in one of the cribs. It didn't make any difference to him — I was somebody who needed help and he gave it to me.

I grew to know that bootleggers were a different kind of people. Most of them were all wrapped up in selling their wares, doing the same thing over and over. Their main concern was keeping up their own supply of booze — that was more important than stepping up in life. Back then it didn't take much to make a living and keep happy. But that wasn't enough for me. I wanted to make it big.

My work was more dangerous than robbing banks. I was robbing someone who was making an illegal living as it was. I had three different cars shot out from under me. Then there were the roadblocks where the law would park their cars long ways across the road. Hell, I didn't see any sense in crashing into those cars and killing myself. If I didn't have time to turn back or go around the roadblock, I'd give up.

Usually all they'd do was take my load away from me, give me a warning and turn me loose. But if they were other bootleggers, I was in bad trouble. These guys didn't fool around so I'd get out of there. The whole idea behind it was competition. I had a bounty on me at all times. People were looking for me. I got into several gun battles where a couple of guys got killed.

I was always on guard when I stayed in a hotel or a rooming house. I knew those guys didn't stop looking for me on the road; they'd come looking for me anywhere they felt they would have the advantage. I could smell them out like a rat. I put cigar ashes on the doorknobs, on the window sills, on the steps, all over. And when I came back and any of the ashes had been disturbed, I didn't go in again.

How I got to be called a society bootlegger is because I delivered for a while for Mary Louise, better known as Texas Guinan. She had a speakeasy for higher class people up in Chicago. Because she became such a sore thumb, she was killed on the steps of her place there. I think it was done by Dutch Schultz, but I'm not sure.

One thing for certain, she always wanted good booze, and since I was the taster, I always saw that she got the best.

I always had a special name for everybody. The agents who used to go into the sloughs and bayous to hunt for stills—I called them the swamp killers. They popped me a time or two. I used to ride shotgun sometimes. There would be three or four cars strung out, five minutes apart. This was for protection. If there was any shooting up ahead, the others could stop. One time I got popped while riding in a car that didn't have any booze on it. Maybe you think those guys weren't shook up, coming up empty handed like that.

The law was really crooked in those days. I must have been busted a dozen times by crooked law people over a period of about three years. These busts were in Oklahoma, Arkansas, Tennessee, and Texas. It usually went like this: I'd get busted and taken into the sheriff's office. The sheriff would take my booze and sell it. He had his own business going. Then I'd usually pay a fine to the judge; he'd set the bond and I'd pay the fine, and he'd keep the money. This went right through the judicial system.

You asked how I got my first machine gun. Of course you know that it was the newspapers that added "Machine Gun" to my name after I'd shot up a few places which I'll tell you about later. I got my first two Thompsons through a deal on my first bootlegging job just before I left home. There was this gyp joint about a block outside the city limits in Memphis. I guess you'd call it a honky tonk because dancing along with all the other things went on there. A hooker I knew who worked there told me that one of her customers let the secret out where a large stash of whisky was buried. She knew I was leaving town and was broke. Of course, she wanted part of the cut.

Well, I went to this place she described and saw that the spot had been covered over with rubbish, branches, and twigs. I cleared it all away and really hit pay dirt. I began to uncover burlap bags stuffed with pint bottles which were all wrapped up in newspapers to keep them from rattling and breaking. By the time I'd finished my digging I'd unearthed nine of these bags which held over four hundred pints. The hooker had even told me the guy to contact to make the sale and he told me where to buy the guns. I left Memphis in style and often think the guy who had buried the whisky got one hell of a surprise when he went back to dig it up because I had left everything just as I'd found it.

The first place I shot up was in 1922 — a gas station and store combination run by an older couple. The man must have been in his late fifties or early sixties. I didn't think he was giving me fast enough service so I shot the place up. This was the only thing I ever did that made me feel bad because the man had been good to us. I bought about half of my gas there.

But the machine gun wasn't the only weapon I used. During my early robberies and criminal activities, I used a .45 and also had a chopped off buffalo gun that would leave a mighty big hole in what it hit. I will have to admit that the Model 21 Thompson was my all time favorite weapon. It rapidly achieved the two most important functions that a reliable gun should achieve — it scared 'em and it killed 'em.

I entered the Navy in early 1923 under the name of George B. Barnes. This probably could be verified in St. Louis where military records are kept. I lied about my age. I was actually only sixteen — just shy of seventeen — and didn't have anyone to sign for me. My contract with Uncle Sam was illegal, which was to play an improtant role later on.

The only reason I went into the Navy was I'd done something pretty bad. I'd robbed a load of whisky from the wrong people who wanted to kill me. I thought the safest place was to be in the Navy where I could let things cool off. I went to Great Lakes for boot camp, then was shipped to San Diego. I was in the middle of the pack for most of the training activities except on the gunnery range. I could take a 30-06 or a .45 and shoot with the best of them; and I could hold my own with the standard rifle they used, too.

Let me tell you something, I could handle a gun with the best before I went into the Navy. Those stories they wrote about me learning to shoot while I was in the Navy were just a lot of hogwash. I could shoot a dime out of a man's hand at forty feet long before I went into the service.

The Navy didn't offer anything at all except to keep me out of circulation. I stayed in longer than I'd planned. When I decided to get out, I make a stink about how my papers weren't properly filed; that no adult had signed for me. It took them forever processing all those simple papers, but I got out after seven or eight months.

When I did get out I went right back into bootlegging. The heat was off and that bootlegger wasn't as anxious to kill me as he had been before.

"I've thought a lot about that time. If we had gotten a lot of money in that robbery, I probably wouldn't have returned to bootlegging; I wouldn't have met Kathryn; I wouldn't have gotten involved in a lot of things."

7. The Falling Out Of George And Earnie May

How did I get started robbing banks?

Well, it was another way to make money in a hurry, a by-product that blossomed into something much more profitable than bootlegging, and it was a lot safer.

I always thought if you wanted money, you went to the bank for it. Long before I was twelve, I had that in mind.

When I robbed a bank, I only had the law after me instead of the bootleggers AND the law. My very first job was with a fellow named Cotton Tabors. I don't recall too much about it other than we were just passing through Memphis on our way to Oklahoma, and we stopped and robbed a bank in Ft. Smith, Arkansas. As I say, we were just passing through and Cotton asked me if I'd like to help him rob the bank and I said yes.

I robbed banks long before I met up with Kathryn, in spite of what the news media would have you believe. There was a childhood sweetheart, who had been one of the girls in my harem, that craved any kind of excitement. I guess you'd say that she was my first partner in crime, especially when it came to robbing banks, but one incident I remember put a stop to our association.

Earnie May Story and I were going through Mississippi when I saw a bank located on the corner. I cased the place and counted ten people working inside. That was a lot of people back then. There were also four customers. I went back outside and gave Earnie May her instructions. When we went inside, I had my machine gun under my overcoat. Earnie May was carrying a pistol. There was a wooden check stand right in the middle of the floor. As I went through the door, I thought the stand would be the ideal place to get on so I could keep an eye on the whole building inside, and have everything under control as I gave the orders.

I moved a cement ashtray stand that was full of sand; I moved it right up next to the check stand so I wouldn't have any problem getting on top. As I straightened to my full height on my high perch, I opened my overcoat and produced my machine gun and drew down on everyone. I yelled, "Everybody, hands up! Hands up! Put them over your heads and lock your fingers!"

My command was polite but firm. I had just given the command and was sweeping the whole place with my machine gun, when the wooden stand collapsed. As I fell, my head hit the side of the ashtray. Believe you me, I saw stars. That fall almost knocked me out. Somehow I managed to get in a sitting position. I still had the machine gun in my hands. I yelled, "The next one that makes a move will get it. I'll kill everyone of you!"

Just before I'd fallen, I saw Earnie May over by the cashier's cage. She had her pistol in her hand and was getting ready to take care of her end of the job. I guess when I fell, she turned around to see what was happening; and when I gave the command, "The next one who makes a move will get it," that must have triggered her laugh button. She laughed so hard she wet her pants.

Four times I shouted at her, "Get your ass back there and get that money!" Every time I said it she laughed that much louder. She couldn't do a thing but stand there and laugh like a braying jackass. I couldn't get through to her, but I did have sense enough to know those people weren't going to stand still much longer. I shouted, "Come on, let's get out of here!"

That was our last robbery together. After that episode, I wouldn't have her help me rob a candy store. This one incident was a big stumbling block in our relationship. I've thought a lot about that time. If we had gotten a lot of money in that robbery, I probably wouldn't have returned to bootlegging; I wouldn't have met Kathryn; I wouldn't have gotten involved in a lot of things.

Looking back at it now, as mad as I was, Earnie May was lucky that I didn't kill her on the spot. Even after I dragged her out of there and threw her in the car, she was laughing so hard she couldn't talk. To me, it was no laughing matter.

"I should have had sense enough to know that something terrible was going to happen if she continued to down all that rotgut, but I was too busy formulating my own plans."

8. A Case Of Coors

I first met Lila Mae Coors when she was about twelve. We were close to the same age. She would come to Memphis during the summer to live with some relatives. Then she surprised me by returning during the Christmas vacation and when school started again, she enrolled and continued to live with her relatives.

She was a blonde and had big features. There was nothing delicate about her. She was big boned, tomboyish, and could hold her own with anyone. I guess the reason we hit it off so well was she was an individual like me. My other girl friends didn't like her too well because she was dominating. She took charge of them and whether they liked it or not, they did what she wanted to do.

I'd have to say that she was very much an introvert—kept things to herself. No one knew what she was thinking. She could be in a school room with forty kids and see no one but me.

Lila Mae couldn't participate in my almost nightly harem activities. She was the only one in the group of girls I ran with who couldn't be out after eight o'clock at night. The relatives she lived with had burglar proof screens, and she couldn't slip out like the other girls. But she used to come down to the drugstore on Latham Street where I worked and get ice cream sodas. And sometimes we'd go to the movies on Saturday. Sometimes there would be two, three or even four girls with me. We were always together and I never associated with anyone else. Nobody sat in our seats, even if we weren't there. It was right near the front and in the center of the theater.

I had an on-and-off relation with Lila Mae that extended over a number of years. She was a dominating girl, and as I've already said, she was the boss when other girls were around. If they didn't do what she told them to do, she would box them around. I guess you'd say she had a mean streak. Since she couldn't participate at night in the harem, we made up with our sex activities after school at my place. She'd come over for a brief period right after school, before I went to work at the drugstore. I'm here to tell you, that gal really thrived on sex. For the next ten years we never lost track of each other.

It was during the winter of 1926-27 when Lila Mae and I planned a kidnapping which included her Uncle Adolphus. She came to see me in the Dallas area; then we went to Denver to make our final plans. At that time there must have been at least twenty members of the Coors family associated with the brewery. It seemed like half of the population of Golden, Colorado were Coors — fourth cousins, ninth cousins, whatever — everybody seemed to be related to the Coors.

Lila Mae and I couldn't get to the old man himself. His name was Adolph, so we got a by-product, her Uncle Adolphus. He was one of the cousins. Too bad we couldn't have picked off Adolph; we'd have gotten big money for him. But the way it wound up, in kidnapping Adolphus, we were getting someone who wouldn't be missed.

The actual kidnapping was easy. We simply drove down the main street in Golden, in the afternoon. Lila Mae was with me, and when she saw her uncle crossing the street, she called him over and we took him for a ride. Right away I saw that he was a thin, bony, even scrawny old guy, already broken physically. Not that he was in such bad condition, but he was already going downhill. I would say that he was at least in his early sixties.

We ended up taking him outside Kit Carson, Colorado, which is near the Kansas border, to an old deserted mining camp. I remember that the camp was about thirty miles southeast of Turkey Creek, a darned good location to do business. I figured that I'd be smart and work it so that Lila Mae's mother would be the contact. We tried to make her the middleman in the deal.

We started out by asking one hundred thousand dollars for Adolphus, but finally wound up coming down to forty thousand. It turned out that I couldn't make any personal contact. They couldn't care less on the Coors Board of Directors whether the old man froze in the creek or what. They knew that Lila Mae was in the car with the kidnapper. I talked to Lila Mae's mother on the phone and tried to get her to go ahead and act as a go-between. She just snapped at me.

"I know what you kids have done, and I know who I'm talking to. You tell Lila Mae that you'd better bring Adolphus back. When you do, I'm going to give her a whipping she'll remember for the rest of her life. I've told her time and again she was crazy for messing around with you."

Lila Mae's mother was Adolphus' sister, and apparently there wasn't too much love lost in the family for Lila Mae, particularly since she'd been running around with me for several years off and on.

I quickly found that negotiations were impossible when I tried to deal with the Board of Directors of the Coors Brewery. They just put the matter in the Executive Board and held it there. In later years I was convinced that the main reason why the DENVER POST downed me so much was because the paper was controlled by the Coors family.

Strange how you start building air castles when you're very young. Well, I did this in regard to Denver. I wanted to make it my retirement home. That in itself was crazy because I knew I'd never stop to retire while I was on the run from robbing banks, kidnapping, killing and living my kind of life. But it was all there in the back of my mind — Denver would be my retirement home, even though I knew I'd never retire.

At the mining camp where we took Adolphus, there was an old tool shed; and not far from the tool shed was the entrance to a mining shaft. The camp was about one-half mile from a well-traveled road and was ideal for what we needed it for. If Lila Mae had acted halfway right, our whole scheme would have worked. While I spent my time planning how to negotiate and collect the ransom money, even though my price had dropped down to forty thousand, Lila Mae spent most of her time cozied up to a five gallon metal gas can which was filled with corn liquor. I should have had sense enough to know that something terrible was going to happen if she continued to down all that rotgut, but I was too busy formulating my own plans.

We had Adolphus chained to a post in the tool shed. I should say that the chain was attached to the post and Adolphus was hand-cuffed to the chain. I used an old pair of cuffs I'd taken off a policeman a few months earlier.

Adolphus and Lila Mae weren't hitting it off too well, especially when she got drunk on the corn liquor. Suddenly she'd scream, "He's leering at me, that sonofabitch! If he doesn't stop it, I'll mash his face in!" She got so mad at him that she unloosened the chain in the tool shed and dragged the old man outside and chained him to a bush. I stayed out of it, thinking it was some kind of family argument that was going on between them.

After we'd been holed up at the mining camp for several days, I decided I'd have to leave Lila Mae and her uncle and pick a spot between Colorado Springs and Golden and make one more attempt to make phone contact with the old man's family. We had to complete negotiations and get some type of ransom payment or get rid of Adolphus because the running battle that he and Lila Mae were having was about to run me up the wall. I hated to leave them alone, but there was nothing else I could do. It wouldn't be very logical or feasible to take either one or both of them along; and it was almost physically impossible to keep running back and forth from where we were. Sooner or later I'd be spotted.

I told Lila Mae that I was going to leave and would be gone for whatever time period would be necessary for me to complete negotiations, or until I was convinced it was going to be impossible to go any farther with my dealings with the family. She was too drunk to care what I intended to do.

As a safety first measure, I took Adolphus into the mine shaft. Even though it was winter, it was hot in there during most of the time because of the nature of the shaft. I left two blankets by him, and of course he had his clothes on. I knew he'd be out of the rain and wind. He was already burned by the sun. But in my wildest thoughts, I didn't think what Lila Mae might do to him while I was away.

Two days I tried to score, but all my attempts seemed to fall on deaf ears. As I was driving back to the camp, I began to make plans what we could do with Adolphus. We'd tie him up in the middle of the highway and leave him there. Some motorist would stop and take care of him. I'd had my belly full and was going to wash my hands of the whole mess.

It was in the middle of the afternoon when I drove into the camp. Lila Mae had worked herself into one hell of a drunk. I found her sprawled on the floor of the tool shed, and when I walked in, she just looked up at me and in her worst drunken manner said, "That sonofabitch has been grinning at me."

I never felt so disgusted in my life. She looked like something that had just crawled out from underneath a rock. I left her and went into the mine shaft to see Adolphus. What I saw made me want to vomit. Lila Mae had used a razor on him, probably soon after I'd left. The sides of his mouth were slit almost back to his ears on each side of his face. She had also laid open his chest.

Flies can breed very rapidly in an open wound, especially when the temperature was like that in the shaft. It actually got hot in there during the afternoon. Maggots and worms were crawling and working in and out of those cuts on his face. His eyes were sunk in and the old fellow was off in a coma. When I examined the gash in his chest, I saw that the maggots were there also.

50

When I pried his mouth open with a stick, I almost dirtied my pants. His mouth was full of worms. I heard a low gurgling sound coming from inside his throat. I knew he didn't have long to live. My God, what a mess he was in! He had defecated all over himself.

I knew there was only one thing to do—the humane thing. I shot him twice in the head with my .45 and then drug him over to the place where the track ended. I knew the hole was about thirty feet deep. It was covered with heavy boards. I removed them and pushed the old man's body down the shaft and very carefully replaced the boards. Frankly, I didn't have any feelings about Adolphus one way or another. It did surprise me that Lila Mae had been that cold, to cut him up as she had done.

After I made sure that the camp looked like no one had been there, I got Lila Mae loaded into the car and we headed out. As I drove down the highway I started thinking that maybe we should stop by the money drop point just one more time. I really didn't think there would be any money there, because I'd stopped by several times during the week that we'd had Adolphus. But what the heck, there was always the chance that they'd changed their minds.

I just kinda fooled along, because I wanted it to be good and dark when we arrived on the road going out of Colorado Springs, near the Turkey Creek bridge. Long before we reached the drop point, it started raining a regular flood, but Lila Mae didn't know anything about it. She had passed out on the front seat. I drove by the place without slowing down, looking over the scenery very carefully, to make sure no one was dumb enough to be out there in the rain waiting for me. About a mile down the road, I turned around, went back and stopped at the exact spot where I had told them to leave the money under an old car body that was at the edge of a field which bordered the highway.

When I tipped the car body and reached into the open place, my fingers closed over a canvas bag. I grabbed it and ran back to the car. I'd left the motor running so I got out of there in a hurry, keeping a sharp lookout in my rear-view mirror to make sure no one was following us. Finally we came to a graveled road which branched off the highway. I pulled onto it and drove three or four miles before I parked in a deserted spot.

Lila Mae was still out. I snapped on my flashlight, opened the bag and began to count the money. There was forty thousand dollars, mostly in twenty dollar bills. That night we slept in the car. I didn't sleep much for thinking of all that money. I got to wondering what we'd do with all of it. Lila Mae sure as hell couldn't be trusted with it because she'd get drunk and tell someone where we'd got it. I had to come up with something. Two days later the whole thing was solved for us. I tried to pass a twenty dollar bill in Gallup, New Mexico. In just a little while the whole town was swarming with law. I knew then that the money was marked in some way. It was useless to us. Of course I knew an outlet for it, but there was too great a risk getting caught. We left Gallup by way of a country road, and that night on the New Mexico prairie, we burned forty thousand dollars, minus one twenty dollar bill.

The botched kidnapping of Adolphus Coors made me start thinking of pulling off a perfect kidnapping, a kidnapping that would net me enough money and enough publicity to last for a long time. One thing I knew would have to be done different the next time around — I'd have to come up with some way of establishing firm ground rules right from the first kickoff. The people who were to pay would have to understand the exact terms of the ransom and how the money was to be delivered. There wasn't going to be any more marked money. I had holes that needed to be plugged up. I thought about them a lot. This thinking was in the back of my mind all the time from then until I pulled off the Urschel kidnapping six years later.

There were two other almost kidnappings between that time and the Urschel affair. I called off the planned kidnapping of C. H. Crump of Memphis at least four times. I finally junked that idea because I felt I had a better one with Urschel. Crump was sort of a Huey Long individual. He had so many contacts and associates, I figured that he would be a valuable person for someone else to want back. At other times I thought about kidnapping Mary Louise, Texas Guinan, even though I'd done a number of bootlegging assignments for her. She was big business; therefore, I thought it would be good business to kidnap her. She was a controller and had partners who I thought would pay off. They did not have as many contacts as Mary Louise had, and because of that, I thought they would pay to get her back. But this exploded when Dutch Schultz — I'm pretty sure he did it— had her killed on the steps of her swanky place in Chicago.

All these big plans were running through my mind. Why shouldn't I dream big? I was only twenty years old. I wasn't even a full-fledged gangster yet.

"Three bullets had lodged in my guts in the colon area, a little up from the pelvis on my right side. The fourth bullet — the one that entered my jaw — passed out through my neck. How in the hell I managed to live through it, I'll never know."

9. The Birds Were Gone

Several weeks had passed since I and Lila Mae had kidnapped her Uncle Adolphus. We were hiding out in a mountain cabin in Colorado during the early part of the winter of 1927. There is no way I could forget that experience.

It was cold and there were several inches of snow around. Every few hours I'd go outside the cabin and start the car to make sure it was running OK. I wanted it to be ready to roll in case we needed it in a hurry because I knew the woods were being combed pretty thoroughly for us. Each time I started that car, a whole flock of birds would fly out from underneath where they had been roosting to keep warm.

Well, I went out this one morning, not too long after daylight, to start the car. There were no birds. At first I didn't think much about it; then I got to thinking something was missing. I'd already climbed back into bed when it suddenly dawned on me that I wasn't hearing a single bird. I knew something was wrong. Someone or something had scared them off. We had company and I had to find out who.

I walked into the living room and was just reaching for my gun when I felt something rip into my back which slammed me up against the wall. Then I was hit again and I realized someone was shooting at me. I got it a third time before I fell to the floor and managed to pull out a pistol I was carrying.

Believe me, I didn't know where the shooting was coming from, I was so mixed up. Then I figured it was from the front porch and whoever was doing the shooting had a clear view of me through the window. When I fell, they must have thought they got me because this guy came through the front door and was getting ready to shoot me in the head when I let him have it. He fell sideways into the room and I moved in the other direction.

Another guy came through that front door, blazing away and I caught a bullet in the jaw, but I got him in the chest. A third guy, who was close behind the second one, fell into the room and lay still. To this day I think he was faking, but he didn't make a move after I passed out and Lila Mae drug me to the car through the snow and boosted me into the back seat and headed out of there. She knew enough to go to Colorado Springs where I had an old crony whose wife had a beauty shop. Lila Mae had met them on previous occasions.

After they got me inside, the man and his wife made several phone calls. I had come around and was giving instructions. I told them about Dr. Drake. I'd heard about him. After many calls, they contacted him. He told them what to do and said he would meet us in Tulsa.

They began using cotton swabs and alcohol to clean out the wounds. Then they started swabbing out the holes with mercurochrome, and this hurt like hell. Three bullets had lodged in my guts in the colon area, a little up from the pelvis on my right side. The fourth bullet — the one that entered my jaw — passed out through my neck. How in the hell I managed to live through it, I'll never know.

It took nearly two full days to reach Tulsa; my guts were burning every mile of the way. After Dr. Drake examined my wounds and had cleaned them, he decided it would be best to leave my gut wounds open for a couple of weeks to make sure they drained properly so infection wouldn't set in. Later he put some kind of a net, a wire mesh, over the worst wound in the stomach area. Since then I've had that wire mesh replaced twice and it's time to have it done again. He also had to do some work on my jaw which had been shattered.

This meeting with Dr. Drake was the beginning of a long and valuable friendship because over the next several years he made himself available when I or one of my men needed him. He wasn't the smoothest doctor around, neither was he the most sober, but he was available for a price, and he would move quickly when we paid. There were never any questions asked. He couldn't care less how anyone got shot up as long as we paid him so he would have funds to sustain his appetite for good whisky. He wasn't anything like another doctor I had dealings with before I met Dr. Drake.

Right after Lila Mae and I had done away with her Uncle Adolphus, I had one hell of a toothache that was about to drive me up the wall. We went into Colorado Springs and looked through the telephone directory, trying to find a dentist. We decided on one and drove to his address. He was getting ready to leave. He took a quick look in my mouth and said that I needed to have the troubled spot X-rayed, but he just didn't have time to do it then. Abruptly he left me and I followed him out to his car, asking him to pull the tooth right now. "Come back tomorrow," he said over his shoulder. He climbed in underneath the steering wheel and was reaching for the ignition key when I jammed my .45 in his face.

"You're pulling this tooth right now or I'll kill you where you're sitting."

He turned as white as a sheet, climbed out of that car and hurried back into his office. His wife was his assistant, and she got pretty scared, too, but I got my tooth pulled and he wouldn't accept a cent for his services.

The next time I needed Dr. Drake was in 1928 when I came down with scarlet fever. I was one sick person for several weeks, running a high fever most of the time. That's when I lost a lot of my hair. The reason that I recall that it was in 1928 was because that was the year Hoover was elected President. I identify with that.

I was laid up in a backwoods area of Oklahoma because I couldn't go to a hospital. At that time everybody wanted to kill me — niggers and all. I knew that if the bootleggers didn't get me, the law would, so I couldn't take a chance in a public hospital. I got word to Dr. Drake to come and take care of me. He did.

This time I had a good chance to study the old alcoholic. The only thing to say about him was he was an old punch drunk, drunk — a short guy with stooped shoulders and a Hitler style mustache. He didn't have any medical license left. It had all been stripped from him years earlier. And his practice wasn't just confined to one area — it was where he was needed, providing the ones in trouble had his price. If you were too far away, he would tell you on the phone that he'd meet you halfway and it was up to you to live until you got there.

We always got word to Dr. Drake through the Francis Katz Drugstore Chain. There was a Katz Drugstore on Missouri Street in the old Spanish section of Kansas City. We'd also connect him through another drugstore in Memphis. He was an expert on bullet wounds, and members of my gang were always getting lead poison.

A fellow by the name of Bill Williams was either getting it in the guts or in the butt, and sometimes in the legs. One time he had a flesh wound in the leg. The bullet had gone right through the fleshy part of his leg without hitting any bone or big veins. I cleaned it out for him before we took him to Dr. Drake. I ran a piece of cotton through the wound and out the other side.

We always carried a little homemade first aid kit with us filled with such items as morphine, cotton, gauze, swabs, bandages and alcohol. I also had some gunpowder along so when one of us got hit, I'd sprinkle a little of it on the wound and then set it afire to cauterize the wound. Sure, it would hurt like hell, but it always did the job.

"You learn very quickly that at least half of the work done in a penitentiary is carried out by the prisoners themselves. After you make the right contacts, you can do pretty much what you like to do."

10. The Leavenworth Connection

It was in early 1930 before I finally ran into a situation in which I could not bribe the arresting officers.

Some federal agents claimed that I had been selling liquor to the Indians in Oklahoma. They were right. I had been. I'd sell them the rejects because they'd drink anything from caribou piss on up. I was surprised that I couldn't put up bail and walk away. This was the first time that all deals were off. These federal people wouldn't do business with me.

I was taken to the County Jail in Oklahoma City where I spent five months before being transferred to the "Big Top" in Leavenworth, Kansas. I served here one year of a three-year sentence.

During the seventeen months that I was out of circulation I had a chance to do some serious thinking. I got word by the prison grapevine that several men who had worked with me had suffered from bad cases of lead poisoning inflicted by the law. I also remembered those who had been killed before I'd been put in prison. The realization that I was vulnerable; that I, too, could be shot down, began to bother me for the first time.

I'd already pulled off nine successful bank robberies and was now known as "Machine Gun" Kelly. Most of the other prisoners admired me for what I'd done and the reputation I'd already built. I was not a braggart, but obviously, I thrived on my reputation. I conducted myself in a way which led people to think me to be much older than I really was. The fact that I'd shot a few people, plus having cultivated the ability to get along easily with most anybody, helped me to have the run of the prison.

I was put in a ten-man cell, which was not very large, but still had enough room to house five two-man bunks. I was assigned a top bunk, and my bunk mate was a man named Bill Walden, who was serving time for armed robbery of a post office. We hit it off from the beginning, and it wasn't long, because of my affable nature, likable personality and outgoing friendliness—I'm not bragging; just stating the truth — that Walden got me involved in the more desirable activities prison life had to offer. Through Walden's

57

influence, I was assigned to work in the Records Room at Leavenworth.

You learn very quickly that at least half of the work done in a penitentiary is carried out by the prisoners themselves. After you make the right contacts, you can do pretty much what you like to do.

My assignment was referred to as "kiss-ass work", and I had the opportunity to put the snatch on certain records lying around, including my own. When I went through mine, I saw that they had me being born in 1906; I changed that year to 1911. This was the beginning of the many different birth dates which were attributed to me over the years. My work on my records added a lot of confusion. I didn't feel it was anybody's business what my real age was.

In later years I became very sensitive about my age. At every opportunity I would convince people that I was many years younger than I actually was. In fact, it got to a point where they just gave me a birth date and a year which no one was sure of.

It was during that first term at Leavenworth that I began my study of fingerprints. I became an authority on the subject. Some of this knowledge came in handy later at Alcatraz. Also, during this first term at Leavenworth I became self-conscious about two of my physical characteristics.

I used to practice keeping my eyes wide open. I knew I had droopy eyes and I hated them. They were also deceiving in regard to their color. Some would say they were green; others would swear they were milky blue; then there were those who claimed they were gray. I also had a droopy lower lip, and I began sucking it in while concentrating on keeping my eyes wide open. I was afraid these two things might help somebody identify me at a wrong time. My focusing attention on them went on for many years, and even to this day I still find myself struggling to keep my eyes wide open and that lip from sagging.

I'd already built up some valuable connections in St. Paul and Kansas City. My vacation in Leavenworth gave me opportunities to make more connections. I planned to make use of them when I was released. My Records Room work helped me devise ways to forge passes. This knowledge helped me set up the escape of Thomas Holden and Francis Keating. By doing this, plus my association with "Jelly" Nash, I got in thicker with the "right" people.

I had already done a couple of dumps, maybe three or four, and had known some of the people in the St. Paul area. Sure, I helped three guys escape. I made up outside gate passes. The passes and signatures were definitely forged. At Leavenworth there were a lot of outside work details such as the piggery, grass details, paint details, and the repair of the houses at the penitentiary where the employees lived. All of these had to have passes to get through the gates to reach the houses and places outside the prison complex. The workers would walk to the main gate in groups while the guards watched them. Individuals would call up to the sally port tower to get that guard's attention so he would look down and see their passes. When satisfied, he would signal to have the gate opened. He knew exactly what to look for and was very careful in his inspection of passes.

Then there were specific work detail lists which were made up in the Records Room. By juggling these lists and doctoring them, I was able to help three of my friends escape. I remember how it all started.

A convict from Texas named Charlie Hammond and I were working in the photography section of the Records Room. I knew Hammond had many good contacts, so I catered to him. Several times during the course of many months, "Jelly" Nash, I and Hammond discussed how easy it would be to forge a trusty pass, get the man's name on a work detail list, then have him walk out the gate and disappear. We all thought it would be a cinch. I even encouraged Nash to try it after I laid all the ground work.

"Nope, I'm not ready to leave this place yet. I'll let you know when the right time comes," Nash said.

Even though we called Nash "Jelly", he was a rugged individual and somewhat vicious, seldom good natured. I didn't argue with him. But Keating and Holden were ready to try my plan. Each of them had served only a few months of a twenty-five-year sentence for train robbery. I managed to get their photographs on the right cards and arranged for them to be dressed in trusty raincoats over their prison uniforms, and their names on the right lists for work details.

They walked right out with their groups, the guard checked their passes and decided that everything was OK; he allowed them to go through the gate. By prior arrangements Keating and Holden went to a haystack in a field, located at the edge of town. There they found civilian clothing, which they changed into, then hitch-hiked to Kansas City and went back to work as usual.

A few months later Nash felt it was finally time for him to go.

He'd worked hard and got himself established as a trusty, assigned to do work around the home of the deputy warden, taking care of the grounds. After we got everything ready, he simply made arrangements with another convict, who was being released from prison, to pick him up during the night in a car. The other convict did and they just drove away.

Nash got involved with pretty fast company. Some didn't trust him. They thought if he ever got caught, he might squeal on them in order to get a lighter sentence, so he was eliminated. I'll tell you about that later.

I never had any serious thoughts about escaping from Leavenworth. I was a short-timer from the start. I only had a year to do, why ruin a good thing? I had built up connections which would help my own causes when I walked out a free man.

"I was never Kathryn's dupe. I did what I wanted to without asking or telling her, and she was never behind anything that I did. I've never read two printed pages in any book or magazine about me that were true. The accounts were always tainted with a little truth and the rest was a lot of garbage."

11. Kathryn The Publicist

I was released from Leavenworth in 1931. Feeling my oats, I made a beeline for Tulsa, Oklahoma, where a major purveyor of bootleg whisky, a man by the name of Anderson, had his head-quarters. Even though I'd made some excellent connections in other places besides Tulsa while I was in the penitentiary, I thought it best to return to my old stomping grounds. I'd made some bootleg runs for Anderson two years earlier, and one person had stuck in my mind, Anderson's girl friend, a hooker named Kathryn.

Kathryn was a gyp-joint whore, but she was a good looker and I wanted her. I knew she had access to what I needed: whisky, machine guns and money. I also knew that she had heard of me, and since she was image-conscious, I had exactly the image she wanted, a man with a reputation and power. I wasn't too disturbed, knowing that Kathryn had been with a number of men; she had even been married three times, the last one to a man named Charley Thorne, who had killed himself. In later years, J. Edgar Hoover implied in a magazine article that Kathryn had probably killed him and then made it look like suicide.

When I arrived in Tulsa, I made myself available to Kathryn. I talked her into helping me take all of Anderson's whisky, his money, and anything else we could turn into quick cash. We split for Ft. Worth where Kathryn had excellent connections. From that time on over the next two years she got me at least fifteen machine guns.

I guess a pointed way to describe Kathryn would be to say she was an extrovert and insane. I never knew her age because we never discussed our ages; but I would say she was two or three years older than I was. She was the only person who ever seriously gave me recognition. She put me out front and made me feel good, especially at first, but she carried her little game too far. You'll know what I mean before I finish describing this very complex person. She would build up situations to try to make me jealous.

Then if she became angry at someone she'd say, "George will kill you and you know it!"

She wanted everyone to think I was a killer, a number one gangster. I'd never tried to build such an image of myself before. Frankly, I didn't go for it but she got a charge out of it. When I'd return from an operation, I'd hear all kinds of tales she had told about me, most of which had been hatched in her imagination. She made everything I did or was going to do real big. Several times she'd get a weak type of person who she wanted to impress or to upset and she'd flatly say that I was going to kill him. I guess in her sick mind, she was hoping that one of these guys would be provoked into challenging me. Hell, she wanted it to be a situation where I'd either kill or get killed. I don't think she gave a damn which would happen, as long as she could be in the limelight.

Finally she did fill a guy with this kind of drivel and he jumped me, and asked me to repeat some of the things I'd been saying about him. I'd never seen the man before in my life, but when he began throwing out his insults, I killed him. This was a new ball game for me. I never threatened anybody; Kathryn threatened everybody. She did that publicly more than once. Like the time during the Urschel trial, she popped a guard up the side of the head. It was never in my defense, yet I was crazy enough to think so at times.

She was a tough bitch, a rapid talker, one of those kind who knew every subject that was brought up. I guess we were all a little like that back in the early thirties, but she was worse than most. She would tell people that she was the first one to start calling me "Machine Gun" Kelly, but she wasn't. No other person tagged me with that name. Come to think of it, I introduced myself to Kathryn as "Machine Gun" Kelly to impress her, knowing that she had heard of me.

I was never Kathryn's dupe. I did what I wanted to without asking or telling her, and she was never behind anything that I did. I've never read two printed pages in any book or magazine about me that were true. The accounts were always tainted with a little truth and the rest was a lot of garbage. The output never had an end; the writers speculated from situation to situation, not knowing what went on in between. Nobody knew about my life back then, the real things about my life, not even Kathryn.

She didn't go along on most of my trips. I only lived with her one week out of a month. The rest of the time she went her way and I went mine. I'd go off and rob six or seven banks, and she wouldn't be along, but when I returned from a swing around Dallas, Ft. Worth and Wise County, she'd start pumping me for information. I'd tell her what I wanted her to know and no more, then she'd add her imagination and start spreading a lot of bull. She enjoyed doing this but I'd stay in the background and let her have her kicks.

She was really no more colorful than any other smart whore. Our sex life was compatible, and nothing more. She would make a play for anyone wearing pants as long as he had a certain amount of lawlessness and notoriety.

Between Kathryn's activities of publicizing my exploits, and her writing letters to Philip Lord, who had the Gang Busters radio program, I began to get blamed for robberies and killings which I couldn't possibly have committed simply because they were done in different geographical locations. Let me give you an example. One time I was in Tulsa when two banks were robbed in Kansas City. I got credit for both of them. The papers and the news broadcast on the radio told how "Machine Gun" Kelly was up to his old tricks, robbing two banks in the same place.

As soon as I heard and read about those two bank robberies, I got mad and decided to do something about it. I hurried on over to Kansas City, picked up Verne Miller and another guy and robbed a couple of banks. I felt as long as I got credit for something, I might as well not disappoint my public.

Back to Phillip Lord and his Gang Busters program. I used to listen to them quite a bit, and I heard a lot about myself on them. I knew Kathryn was feeding Lord some of the garbage I was dishing out to her. Some of it made me mad, then sometimes I'd laugh my head off, thinking how anyone could be so damn stupid. But it all went into the mill of giving "Machine Gun" Kelly a name. I guess I became a by-word in just about every American home that listened to that program.

I will have to say one good thing about Kathryn. She could sure as hell polish my machine guns. I'd return from a trip, and after I rested up, I'd begin breaking down my guns whether they needed it or not, and clean them. Kathryn would polish them until they really shined. She wanted those guns to look nice at all times and attract attention and make me famous. I'll have to say she was successful in carrying out this mission. We were never officially married, but according to Texas law, I guess you'd have to say we were common-law marriage partners.

63

It was during this time period that my gang was active. I used to rob banks within four hundred miles of Ft. Worth. I robbed a lot of the banks out of there — a lot of little banks all over Oklahoma and all the way down into Mississippi, but my base of operations was in the Ft. Worth area.

While robbing a bank, normally I wouldn't introduce myself, but sometimes I did. Usually one of my men would say, "This is 'Machine Gun' Kelly's gang; that's 'Machine Gun' Kelly right there," and the one I'd instructed to say that would point me out with his gun.

For a while in a swanky joint in the suburbs of Ft. Worth, I used to have a booth and no one was allowed to sit in that booth but me. I don't remember the name of the place but the man who ran it was named Green. There was a little cabinet in the corner of the booth, like a dish pantry, about forty inches tall and twenty-four inches wide and a foot deep. That cabinet was my stash; I used to store a machine gun. I'd walk in with a gun underneath my overcoat, unlock the cabinet and put away the gun without attracting attention. I never knew when I might need that gun in a hurry, so I wanted it handy.

Something else I remember which might not seem important, but it sticks in my mind. For a period of a little over two years after I got out of Leavenworth, I seldom had my own hair color. I kept it dyed with a henna rinse, using a compound mixture. This helped me to be a redhead for a while, then I'd use peroxide to bleach my hair blond. Maybe all this changing color was responsible for me losing a lot of hair from time to time. It might also have caused my hairline to change, because in different photos you'll notice that the hairline rises and falls. These things didn't bother me; they just helped confuse people who tried to describe me accurately to the authorities.

For about the first six months after I was out of Leavenworth I worked off and on for Herbert Noble, who was called "The Cat Man." I served as his bodyguard. He was called "The Cat Man" because thirteen attempts had been made on his life, and they were all unsuccessful. One night he and I were coming out of his fancy joint, The Paris Cellar, and started walking across the street toward his car. Someone shouted, "There he is! Shoot the sonofabitch!"

I spun around and saw two guys. One of them was trying to pull a gun out of his pocket. I shot him in his tracks before he cleared the cloth. The other guy disappeared. I don't think the one who got away was even armed.

I was taken to the police station, and before they could book me, I was turned loose. That's the kind of influence Noble had. He was finally gunned down one night, but I wasn't responsible for him then. I guess his time just ran out. The six months I had worked for him gave me an opportunity to make some good connections and meet some important people such as Benny Benja who is still around and now owns The Horseshoe in Las Vegas. At that time he and Noble just about controlled Dallas. People would fly in to gamble in The Paris Cellar. This was also a period when I could squat and pick out places I wanted to rob later.

Verne Miller had built up a good connection in the "hot bed" of the St. Paul-Minneapolis and Kansas City organized crime network. He became the front runner, the eradicator; he killed a number of people and I had deep admiration for the man.

But there was a gangster in the Dallas area that I had to put a notch above Verne Miller. His name was Jean Paul Norris. He had more class than anyone I've ever known. He had been accused of several killings but managed to walk away from all of them. He stayed around for an awful long time. Finally he was killed in San Antonio by the CIA in 1964. His partner was Roy Underhill. They were in the gun smuggling racket when both of them got it by the CIA.

Norris never killed anyone who didn't deserve to be killed. He was a gentleman killer, better educated than Miller. I picked up a lot of good points from Norris. I still think he was about the best eradicator I ever knew.

Harvey Bailey also crossed my path from time to time during this period. He wanted to throw in with me, but I knew if he did, he would want to call the shots. I was more of a loner than Bailey and didn't want to get myself tied down with him. I knew he was available for hire if and when I needed him.

These were dangerous but exciting years. I had a lot of narrow escapes while I was on the road being hunted down, and also while I was robbing banks. I always tried to outguess everyone and anticipate what they might do, but sometimes I got fooled, fooled badly.

One time we were driving on a country road that was graveled. We weren't too far from Dallas. There were three of us in the car and I was driving. A police car started following us and the driver was pretending to be just out looking over the countryside. But when we would speed up, so would the police car; when we slowed, so would the police car. It dogged us for several miles. Finally we came to some hills and the road started winding. I speeded up, came to a wide place and skidded around so I was headed back toward the car. When it came around a curve and the driver saw that I was headed straight for him he was caught completely by surprise. He then spun the steering wheel to miss us, went off into the steep barpit and rolled over. We turned around and as we went by, I waved and roared with laughter.

During most of my bank robberies I never had a machine gun out of my hands. The ones I used could take a lot of rough treatment, but throwing them around in the car would cause them to get out of balance. The drum had to fit exactly or it would cause the gun to jam. When this happened I'd take the gun into Ft. Worth to my own private gunsmith who would fix it in short order. He kept around sixteen guns for me there and all I had to do was leave one and pick up one or two. When we were away out in the country sometimes I'd practice on small trees. I got so I could chop one down with fifty rounds.

I designed my own leather harness made to fit me and no one else. I had straps going over my back and across my chest so I could carry my machine gun underneath my overcoat where it wouldn't be noticed. I found out very early that it was the element of surprise that upset people in banks. They became so excited that they were ready to cooperate immediately. Let me relate a few examples.

One time I went into a bank and fired four or five shots into the wall to get the people's attention. I saw this customer go completely stiff while he was standing in the middle of the floor. I told everybody to move but he just stood there. His eyes rolled back in his head; his mouth was open, gaping; his arms were down at his side, frozen in place. I couldn't penetrate him. I ran my hand back and forth across his face several times and I still didn't faze him. Finally I rocked him like he was a statue and managed to get him up against the wall and the counter. Before I left, I took a closer look at him to see if one of my bullets had glanced off and hit him. I couldn't find a hole in him. The papers the next day reported he was in a catatonic state. I felt better because the only reason I read the papers was to see if any harm had been done.

During a bank robbery in McAlister, Oklahoma, I told everybody to freeze. This stocky woman, an employee, was walking slowly across the lobby. I told her to stop, but she kept moving in slow motion. I cut loose a burst of bullets into a door that was five or six feet in front of her. She turned around slowly and looked at me. I could see that she was in a state of shock. She had on a yellow dress and it began to turn dark. Water began to run off the hem of that dress as if a faucet had been turned on. Her face turned white and she fainted where she stood. She fell backwards and hit her head on the corner of a table and started bleeding like a stuck pig. She was sitting up when we left so I know she survived. After we got in the car and was headed out, we all had a good laugh.

Then there was the time I decided to rob a small bank in the Dallas-Ft. Worth area all by myself. It was during the grand opening. The manager had just opened the front door and I was the only one waiting to get in. I showed him my machine gun and told him why I was there. He got real shaky and said, "Can I sit down, mister?"

"Why, I guess so."

He sat down in the middle of the floor not over three feet from a chair. Not one time did he take his eyes off me. He was one of the few guys who ever made me take my eyes off him, but I had work to do, a business transaction to make. He was still sitting there when I left.

But sometimes I ran up against a person who acted differently when he was scared. One time in Memphis I commandeered a car after a holdup. I'd gotten separated from the rest of my men. I jumped on the right running-board of this old car. A black man was driving. I had my machine gun strapped over my shoulder and was trying to hold on with both hands as that man swerved his car from one side of the street to the other. When he got straightened out, I tried to point the gun at him but it was in an awkward position, so I cocked my finger at him.

"You drive straight down this road and open the car up."

I glanced down at the floorboard and saw that it was loose, as if someone had been doing some work on that part of the car. Once more I looked at that black man. He was so scared that he pressed his foot down so hard that the loose floorboard tipped up and he got his foot stuck in between the gas pedal and the board. He couldn't bring his foot back, and the car started going all over the road. Suddenly it jumped a curb and went into a park and was heading straight for a tree when I jumped off. I rolled on the grass and heard the crash at about the same time. Man, I'm telling you that car literally wrapped itself around that tree. The impact threw the fellow out and he went sliding head first across the grass. I saw my backup car coming around the edge of the park, and I ran to it and climbed in. I hope the black man made it OK.

A lot of times I'd be the last person out of the bank. Because of this I'd often get caught without a car or my getaway or backup car would be a couple of blocks away and wouldn't have made their pass yet. This happened in Oklahoma. We'd robbed a bank in a little town near the Kansas line. I jumped on the running board of a car, driven by a little old lady, and I pointed my gun. I yelled at her to get moving, to pour on the gas. She calmly looked me straight in the eye and right into the muzzle of that machine gun.

"Now listen here. I don't care what you've done, and where you have to go. I'm not going over thirty." And she didn't.

Fortunately, I didn't have to ride with her very far before my pickup car caught up, but while I was with her, she caused me more turmoil than robbing the bank. When I got out, I just looked at her and said, "Lady, you're something else!"

She wasn't the least bit disturbed even if my machine gun was practically pointing down her throat. If they had hauled me into court for frightening her, I'd have beaten the charge. She and Charles Urschel were the only two people I didn't frighten.

During my bootlegging and bank robbing years, I used to start many a car without keys. How many cars have I stolen that way? Well, I can't say for sure, but it would have to be more than fifty. I've taken as many as three cars in one day, and never took less than two for most jobs.

I was always particular about the way I rode in cars. I rode on the left side, even if I wasn't driving. I figured if the car turned over on its right side, I had less chance of getting hurt. The left side was also the best side to sweep with a gun if someone pulled up and started shooting. If Kathryn was along, I always made her ride in the middle regardless whether we sat in the front or the back seat.

I told you at the beginning of this talk that Kathryn had a lot to do toward making me famous on the radio and in the newspapers. Well, I'll have to admit the publicity I got had a lot to do with some of the things I did. When I'd read about something I'd done or was supposed to have done I'd say, "Wait until the next time!" Then I'd try to do something just a little more spectacular.

For instance, if they were writing about a bank robbery, the papers would build the affair up to a higher pitch than it really was. Everybody who was in the profession of robbing banks then was on an ego trip. Yes, I'll have to admit that I had quite an ego, but their terminology was different then. I don't remember the actual term they used, but I'll have to admit that I was on an ego trip. I wanted to be known as a gangster, and I think I did a pretty good job advertising "Machine Gun" Kelly, with Kathryn's help, of course.

"When I got upset, or someone got out of line or didn't do his job right, or the motive wasn't right, I got what they called depressed. If I stomped on my hat, they were in trouble."

12. Thanks, But No Thanks, Dillinger

My greatest period of activity occurred during a fifteen-month span extending through July, 1933. My reputation was founded on the fact that I'd developed into a notorious bank robber. This made me one of the most desirable partners in robbing banks at that time. I was always the center fielder, calling the shots and leading the gang. I liked to change associations often, knowing that it was easier to survive that way.

Bank robbing was more profitable than bootlegging; however, one of my most pleasurable memories was of an experience that happened one day when I combined the two. I took a guy into Tulsa to get money to buy some whisky. He said that he had to see this banker to get the money to pay me for the load of whisky I'd just delivered.

We drove up in front of the bank and the man went in while I stayed in the car. After a while he returned with the money. I guess seeing all that money and knowing where it came from aroused my urge to get more. After all, I'd been casing that bank for the past several minutes. I said, "Wait here. I just remembered something I've got to do — a little business to transact inside."

I reached under the seat and pulled out a canvas bag I always carried for such emergencies and gave my new-made friend a big smile. "I won't be long."

I went into the bank, picked out the fellow who looked the most scared. I thought he might be the manager so had him bag the money and was back in the car within three minutes. On our return to my customer's place, I asked him to describe the bank manager. I knew then that I was right about the one who had helped me with the money. Then I was told that he's the one who'd been buying and selling whisky at a big profit. In the Tulsa paper the next day, I read where the manager was plenty upset over the amount he had lost in the robbery. As far as I was concerned, it was only a business transaction. I was used to taking whisky from makers who intended to sell it at a big profit. Well, in this particular deal I was the go-between for myself. I was selling the man back whisky that I'd taken from him. Yes, sir, that was really an enjoyable day.

I had a knack of keeping from getting out of hand. I had complete control over people who worked for me. Situations came up before we were going to pull a big job. Someone would have to blow off a lot of steam. I remember one time Alfred Bates gave me some trouble. I ended up shooting him in the hand because he refused to listen to me. It was the animal in him, the part I could reason with only by using force. If I hadn't shot him, the whole gang would have jumped me, so I quieted things down in a way everyone understood. There was no future argument.

I've always felt, that to survive, is to do the job right. If you know you have to do something, do it right then, before the other guy does it to you, like they did back in the Old West. When I ran into trouble, my solution was to shoot the other guy, knock him in the head, or do whatever was necessary. I didn't believe in arguing. I felt I had to display more animal tendencies than I really had in order to rule.

Another thing that has saved me was I've always been a cautious sleeper. I slept on my side, facing the door or window. All I had to do was to drop my foot off the bed and I would be up. A pistol was my bed partner.

I was feared by my gang members. They were afraid that I would be in a depressed state, particularly if a job didn't go as well as planned, or we didn't get as much loot as had been anticipated. When I got upset, or someone got out of line or didn't do his job right, or the motive wasn't right, I got what they called depressed. If I stomped on my hat, they were in trouble.

Twice I remember robbing banks and there was no money. The first time was in Tupelo, Mississippi. Kathryn was with me on this job and so was Charley, Bates and Iowa. There were several employees in the bank but no money. They even showed me the empty vault. I was so damned mad that I shot out all the windows of the bank to cool my frustration. I sure stomped on my hat that day. The second bank was also in Mississippi, and they had to get new windows after I'd finished with them.

One time a farm family was hiding me and a couple of my gang members. The law was very hot on our trails, and we were on the run. One of the fellows with me at the time had more animal tendencies and was more vulgar than most. This family where we were staying had two children. One was a nineteen-year-old boy who was a spastic. He was kept in a homemade pen, like a playpen. He just rolled around, retarded, had the mentality of a

71

one-year-old. The other child was a fifteen-year-old girl, also retarded, but she had the mentality of a six-year-old.

I caught this guy having sexual relations with the girl. Of course she didn't know what was happening. I told him that if he did it again, I'd kill him. He'd been on my nerves for months and there were times when he really bugged me because he was constantly bitching. If it wasn't the food, it was something else. He was just a sorry person, the kind that wanted to do things his way; he always wanted to be boss.

A couple days later I caught him with the girl again. I said, "Come on, let's go outside and take a walk." He began crawling around on the floor and started crying and pleading with me not to do anything. I said, "Well, I gave you my word; let's walk."

I had anticipated that the man would go against my instructions, that action would have to be taken. I picked up my machine gun and tossed him a machine gun. What he didn't know — the machine gun that he had was jammed. We walked down a little road to a bridge, then climbed down to a dry stream bed and walked until we reached a bend that was shaded with trees and a thicket. I turned my back and started pacing off some steps. I heard two clicks and slowly turned around and filled him full of lead. Now you may ask me if that was fair. Didn't he try to shoot me when my back was turned? I'd say what I did was as fair as could be.

I've always had a warm spot in my heart for kids, and I always liked to see them happy. One thing I've found that will make them happy is ice cream. Since I never seem to get enough ice cream, I always buy it when I'm around kids. Well, one incident involving ice cream and a little twelve-year-old girl, who had never eaten any, almost got me killed.

It happened like this. We'd robbed a couple of banks in Oklahoma and were hiding out until things quieted down. A farmer and his wife had taken us in. On this Saturday morning I got to talking to their daughter about ice cream. She didn't know what it was. I told her that I'd drive into town and get her some because a weekend without ice cream was like going without apple pie and fried chicken.

Roy Underhill went in with me to Clinton. We bought a couple of one hundred pound chunks of ice and put one chunk on the back bumper and split the second one into two pieces and put one on each side of the front bumper. Then I bought a six quart ice cream machine and all the makings including a large box of cones.

While I was doing the shopping, Roy was off looking around. The sheriff happened to pass by and recognized me. He got out of his car and was sneaking around to jump me. Well, Roy saw what he was doing and crept up behind him, jammed a pistol in his back and marched him over to our car shouting, "Look who I found trying to play cops and robbers."

We made him get in the front seat with us and took him down Route 66 for about eighteen miles then turned him loose after taking his gun. That was one mad sheriff. Roy kidded him along. "It's not every day you get dry-gulched by 'Machine Gun' Kelly."

When we got back to the farm I helped the farmer's wife make some of the best ice cream I've ever tasted. Their daughter declared that I was her friend for life.

One time when we were robbing a bank, I'd given my men their orders and they were carrying them out to the letter. I had my machine gun trained on the employees. The bank manager wanted to sit down at his desk because he felt like he was going to be sick. I let him. There was a beautiful red apple on his desk. I picked it up, shined it on my pants leg, then ate it while the other fellows were carrying out their orders.

There were two different times in my career that I had occasion to burn a lot of greenbacks. The first experience happened when I burned the ransom money from the Coors' kidnapping after I'd found the forty thousand dollars worth of bills were all marked. The second time was several years later when me and my gang were on a rampage in the early 1930's.

We were traveling in a two-car convoy, three to a car. We'd hit a bank in Oklahoma and then camped out for several nights. This one night it started raining. The top of the car I'd been riding in began to leak. I got out and joined the rest of the fellows who'd built a fire and were huddling around it under a lean-to they'd rigged up.

I examined the bag which I'd been keeping the money in from our last five or six robberies. It was soaked through so I laid it down near the fire and covered it with some wood. The fire felt so good that I stretched out and soon fell asleep. I got cold during the night and threw some wood on the fire and went back to sleep. The next morning when I woke up I started looking for the money. All I found were some curled up burned bills — nearly forty thousand dollars worth. I must have thrown bag and all on the fire when I replenished it.

Even during the latter months of my rampage as a bank robber, a bootlegger, a kidnapper, and a hired killer, I never lacked sex from a variety of women.

Oak Cliff in Dallas was my favorite whore house. I liked the people there. I gave the lady who ran the place at least twenty thousand dollars over a period of time to take care of me when the heat was on. Her name was Mrs. Johnson. She was middle-aged, weighed around one hundred and forty pounds and wasn't over five-feet-four. She hid me almost everywhere in her house except up one of her girls' skirts, but I can assure you I never wanted for sex. Mrs. Johnson had around eighteen beds in that place, and I'm telling you on a busy night I used to hear every one of those beds squeaking in unison.

The woman I thought was about the most beautiful I've ever met was the wife of a Nazarene minister. Her husband's name was Beckam. I think he was the one who formed the Stamps Quartet, a gospel singing group popular back in the thirties and forties. He and his wife had two children when I met them.

Brother Beckam gave me the pitch that I should change my life and get right with God. I've often wondered what would have happened to me if I'd have listened to him. I'll never forget how he towered over me because he was very robust and was at least six-six in height. He took me into their home so he could tell me more about God:

There I met Becky, his wife. She didn't wear one bit of makeup but still had the prettiest complexion. Her long brown hair was naturally wavy and hung clear to her waist. I guess you would say that I fell for her the first time I saw her and decided then and there I was going to make her mine. Of course she was impressed over the kind of life I'd led and kept wanting to know more and more. I had her wrapped around my finger. The next day, when her husband wasn't home, I went and got her and left town. Yes, I kidnapped her, but later she wouldn't admit it.

The first few days after I'd taken her there were tears and heart rending sobs. She tried preaching to me about the kind of life I was leading. As the days passed I won her over and she grew very attached to me. She became pregnant. After three months I decided that she was going to be too much care so we started back for Memphis. She began asking me questions why we were going back, and I flatly told her that our little affair was over. She could get the kind of love she needed at home. She told me that sex with her husband had always been just to make children and nothing else, but with me it was different. I'm sure I had opened up a whole

74

new life for Becky.

When she and I walked into her home, her husband got down on his knees and prayed right there in front of me. He thanked God for the safe return of his wife. If he hadn't been a man with so much faith, he would probably have tried to tear me to shreds. He was big enough to do it. I wanted to tell him that he should change his ways toward his wife, but that was a problem they had to solve between them. I told them both good-by and drove away.

Her children welcomed her back as if she were returning from a long trip. They probably never knew that I had kidnapped their mother because I thought she was one of the most beautiful women I'd ever known.

Not long after I'd returned Becky to her husband I headed for McAlister which is located in Pittsburgh County, Oklahoma. The county sheriff at that time was a man named Jess Summers. I'd never personally met him, but I'd gone through McAlister once before, robbed the bank and shot out its windows and other windows nearby.

The night before I was to arrive in the town, I called the sheriff and told him that I would be there the next day and suggested that he and his deputies go fishing and not be around when I got there. If they were, I'd shoot the town up worse than I did before. I went there when I said I would, robbed the bank, then left without seeing a policeman, so I guess they all went fishing.

I'm sure it wasn't because Summers was a coward; he just looked at the situation rationally and wanted to avoid bloodshed and possibly unnecessary injuries to his citizens. It was his way of cooperating. He knew that after I'd shot up the town the first time, I was a man of my word.

I was still doing a little bootlegging from time to time. I'd be hired to deliver a load of booze as far away as Cleveland and Chicago. It wasn't unusual for me to haul six or eight hundred gallons at a whack. I'd carry a few bottles of choice samples to gain entry into clubs so business would be insured later on. The going pay was from four to eight dollars per gallon, according to the grade. A club owner would buy one hundred gallons from me, then add about twenty to thirty gallons of water before selling it to his customers. This would be his profit margin.

In the winter of 1932 I was captured in Memphis. I had taken a load of whisky to a place called The Plantation. It was necesary for me to pass over Harrihand Bridge which went to West Memphis. Six policemen blocked me in and caught me by surprise. They put me in one of their cars and we were on the way to the lockup. Someone had tipped them off that I was peddling booze, but none of them knew who I was.

I'd been put between two of the policemen with the handcuff only on one wrist. Neither of them was taking any special precaution. In fact, they were very lax and started looking at the scenery. That's where they made their mistake. With my free hand I jerked out one of their revolvers and made them unlock the cuff around my wrist. Then I locked the two guys together, grabbed the ignition key and made all three of the police get out. I turned the car around and went after my own. As I drove back by a few moments later they were still on the bridge. When I waved, they refused to smile at me.

During this period I worked with several partners and had many unusual experiences with them. Some of these hit the papers and some didn't. Each man who walked through my life at this time left a memory. Some carved their names in the annals of crime while others died before they gained such notoriety. I liked to change associations often, believing that it was easier to survive that way.

If there's a spoiled piece of meat in a room and there are ten flies around, eventually all of them will land on that piece of meat. That's how it was in my operations. If I kept partners too long on too many operations in a row, there would soon be trouble. I made a full circle of the available talent. Someone would send me information about a lucrative bank through one of their men, and of course I'd have to give their man a cut of the take. Everyone in the rackets knew who I was and what I was doing. They'd send good people and I'd send people their way. I felt if their men came highly recommended, I could use them. I'd go on their reputations, too.

Someone introduced me to Harvey Bailey. As I've said, I knew about him before I was sent to Leavenworth, but I didn't meet him until I got out. I recall that meeting. We were near an old barn that had a wooden fence running away from it. I was taking some target practice. Someone told Harvey how good I was with a machine gun, how I could write my name with it on the side of a barn.

"Well, Kelly, I'd like to make a five hundred dollar bet with you that you can't knock off a row of walnuts that I'll set on the top of that fence without touching the fence."

"I'll take that bet," I smiled at him. "I'm not called 'Machine

Gun' Kelly for nothing. I've got a reputation to keep."
He lined up the walnuts and told me where to stand. At his signal I began shooting. I knocked everyone of those walnuts into splinters in short order. Not a one of my bullets had touched the fence. That was the least trouble I ever had collecting five hundred dollars.

At that time the Carpis and Barker gang was very much in the news. I never worked with them, but Bailey did. Everywhere he went he seemed to wind up in the middle of things. We did several jobs together before the Urschel kidnapping. He was always a gentleman, easy to get along with, very soft spoken. I considered myself a gentleman but sometimes I wasn't too soft spoken, especially when someone tried to cross me up and I became mad and started stomping on my hat.

To the best of my knowledge, Pretty Boy Floyd, Baby Face Nelson and John Dillinger only did two jobs together. When I was asked one time to compare myself to Dillinger I replied, "He was a man of strict precision in his activities; so was I. He depended on his own ability to survive; so did I. He felt that he would be killed; so did I. I felt that he was more brazen and more forward than I was. I didn't want the spotlight as much as he did. I like to think that he was easier to keep track of than I was. That was his downfall."

I met Alfred Bates in Ft. Worth right after I got out of Leavenworth and made some "Christmas" runs, both with booze and banks. He and I decided to go to the West Coast and knock off some banks in Oregon and Washington. We did and had a fine time. He was a little taller than I was, a happy-go-lucky kind of guy, but he had animal tendencies. I had some, too, but I ruled mine with an iron hand. When I did go berserk, I caused real trouble; I always steeled myself against trouble.

But we were living in an age when everybody was trying to out-tough everybody else. When I ran up against such a character, I first tried to reason with him; then if I thought he'd carry a grudge, I'd run him off. If I was sure none of these would work, I'd shoot him and end the trouble.

I did a number of assignments for a man by the name of Samples who headed up a political machine in Minneapolis and St. Paul. He also had his finger in the organized crime around Kansas City. There he had the mayor under his thumb and gave the man instructions to follow. Samples sent for me when he wanted someone eradicated in any one of these three cities. This was easy money and I never had any occasion to turn him down. It was just another way of building up good connections.

I teamed with Alvin Carpis on a kidnapping operation which involved putting the snatch on one of the Hamm's Brewery family. The ransom money was to be handed over in a meet outside St. Paul. As I remember, I got two cars and two thousand dollars as my part. This was relatively minor, but it taught me a lot in setting up money exchanges and getting know-how for my own big job which I was planning to pull off later.

There were lanterns to mark the route outside St. Paul. Part of the deal — that had been arranged behind the scenes — was the feds had agreed to wait just twenty minutes before going after the payoff. These lanterns were lit to show the route for the drop car more than anything else. I was five minutes behind the drop car and I knew the feds were fifteen minutes behind me. I shot out the lanterns as I drove by which really made things confusing for them.

The operation went so successfully that I never was picked up. Roger Toughy's gang got blamed for the kidnapping at first, but Carpis was eventually hauled in for it and they proved him guilty. Carpis and two of his men got life in prison for the Hamms' kidnapping. But they didn't squeal on me. Carpis later wound up on Alcatraz while I was there, and I saw him again at McNeil Island.

Shortly after this I was riding in a car with a gangster named Slaughter. Another man, who I thought was his associate, was with us. We were driving in some hilly country. Slaughter told the driver to pull over; he wanted to look at a particular drop-off point and also to relieve himself. The driver turned off on a side road that led over into the hills and continued on it until we arrived at a sheer cliff which bordered the road. Slaughter told him to stop.

All three of us got out of the car and walked over to the edge of the cliff. I was looking down at the dry creek bed far below when suddenly I was almost shaken out of my skin. The other man had whipped out a pistol, shot Slaughter and pushed him over the cliff. I watched the body turn in the air and bounce when it hit the bottom. Slowly I turned and looked at the man who was putting his gun back in a shoulder holster. Was I going to be next? A half-smile crossed his face when he said, "Well, he didn't do his job right. What else could I do?"

The Delaney Brothers snubbed me only one time. They were running a lot of the organized crime activities in Cleveland. When

I arrived on the scene they sent word for me to keep moving or they would move me out in a box. Well, I was broke when I arrived in Cleveland, and had gone there to knock over a couple of banks. I knew the Delaneys weren't in too good a standing with the brass in St. Paul. I called Samples and told him what had happened. I also told him that I would take care of the whole situation free of charge. It was a case of them getting me or me getting them.

I followed them to a building and waited outside until they came walking down the steps shoulder to shoulder. I let them have it. They never knew what hit them; it happened so quickly.

That afternoon I robbed two banks in Cleveland. Once more I mixed business with pleasure.

John Paul Chase was the most intelligent organizer and out-and-out planner I've ever known. He became intrigued with the potential of a three-gang combine with me, Baby Face Nelson, and John Dillinger serving as the individual gang leaders. His idea was to synchronize action at three different locations, make three big hauls, pool the take, and split it. He argued that by pulling off the action at a set time this would help take the heat off all of us.

I couldn't see putting all my eggs in one basket. I could have had dealings with Dillinger long before this but I refused. Why should I get mixed up with him when I was well established myself? I had a good thing going and could see no reason to complicate it. Hell, I'd robbed more banks than he had. I had the feeling that if he and Nelson were thrown together, there would be a power struggle. That I didn't need. Somehow, I felt that the power struggle was already on. I wasn't going to get caught in between.

My answer to Chase was an emphatic no.

I remember Nelson as a little guy who had a high pitched voice, but he was one hell of a man. I would say he was a man's man. Later at Alcatraz, Chase told me the story how Baby Face got his. Chase claimed that he was an eye witness, and I have no reason not to believe him.

These two agents were shooting at Nelson and almost hit his wife. This made him pretty mad. He started walking toward them and they were filling him full of lead. If they had had a cannon and had blown his legs off, those legs would have kept right on walking to them. Neslon walked seventy or eighty feet to a ditch, then stumbled back to his car, climbed in and started to drive away before he fell over dead.

Chase said, "I don't know how many bullet holes he had in him, but I'm here to tell you he was like a sieve."

I made two excursions with Alfred Bates to the West Coast. The first trip was taken in late 1931 and the second one was early in 1932. We hit around eight banks in the area on the first trip and went to the Colfax area twice, which was across the line from Tacoma.

Along with Alfred I had a crippled man with me who almost got his legs shot off before I'd met him. One time during our second trip we got into a conversation with a guy who was a personnel manager for a large restaurant. When we left his place, I was driving and almost hit a policeman who was crossing the street. He blew his whistle and pointed to the curb. I debated whether I should make a run for it or do as he suggested. Well, I knew he probably wouldn't know me if he saw me, so I pulled to the curb.

He was boiling mad when he came up to me on the driver's side. I apologized for my actions and told him that we were there for a convention, we were personnel managers and had just arrived to attend the convention. I invited him to eat at our restaurants in Portland the next time he was there. It wouldn't cost him a dime. He fell for it hook, line and sinker. Lucky for me, I'd remembered the names of three of the largest restaurants in Portland. It was lucky for all of us that our conversation with the real personnel manager was still fresh in my mind. If he had pulled us in, and they found out who we really were, they would have thrown the key away.

But I wasn't too worried. Alfred and Henry had their hands on their pistols. If the policeman had made a wrong move, he would have been dead. We drove on into Vancouver and robbed a bank.

Bates was a good partner because he was dependable and didn't scare. Regardless what happened, he remained cool and did exactly what he was told. But I'd have to say that Harvey Bailey was the best man I ever had to work with me while robbing a bank. He was probably king of the heist men in the 1920's, but I'm a little prejudiced who should have that title in the 30's. I give credit where credit is due.

I say Harvey was good, but he wasn't a leader; he wasn't capable of taking three or four good men and directing them to carry out an operation. Still, he could bulldog any bank job that was planned by someone else. He had more guts than Bates.

Verne Miller, old fiddling Miller! He was one hell of a gunman! He could also make a fiddle talk, and I liked to try. He turned up his nose at my efforts and encouraged me to stick to my harmonica.

Verne didn't like my pace either. I was going all the time. During the busiest months, we'd hit two or three banks a week, then I'd end up giving away my part of the take. Not Verne. He'd save his take for a while, then cut out and lay up with some broad for a couple of months to love and be loved. He didn't like the pressure I put him through. He claimed that robbing banks wasn't his real bag.

Toward the beginning of the summer of 1932, as I was returning from my second sweep through the Pacific Northwest, the pressure of being hunted down became tight. I decided that I'd better drop out of sight for a while. I saw a sign near Indio, California, which told of a mission located off the highway. I went to the mission and volunteered my help to work in the kitchen for two weeks during my vacation.

The man in charge claimed that I was sent by God. Anyone who would give up his vacation to help at the mission was surely a man of God. I attended all of their religious functions and was praised time and again how well I could cook. When I got ready to leave, at the end of the two weeks, they gave me a going away party and each one told me what a fine man I was.

I drove into Barstow, robbed a bank, and when I was on the main highway again, I got to thinking how hard Brother Beckam had tried to get me to give myself over to the Lord. I guess it just wasn't the right time for me to take those steps, but at least I gave it a lot of thought.

You asked me about how much money I'd taken in bank robberies up to the Urschel kidnapping. Roughly I'd say it was in the neighborhood of six hundred thousand dollars. Bank jobs then would often run from nothing up to two or three thousand dollars. Remember, there was a depression on. If we got six to eight thousand, we considered ourselves lucky. If we hit twenty-five and thirty-thousand-dollar takes, we were really in the chips.

Before Bates and I went to Oregon the first time, we decided to have a meet at a mountain cabin which was partially owned by my family on my real dad's side. The cabin was located in the mountain area between Salida and Ouray, Colorado, and had been a favorite place for gangsters who operated in the Midwest. It was a real haven and had a lot of bunk space and comfortable facilities. There was a large outhouse on one edge of the back yard and a meat locker just opposite on the other edge. I knew the meat locker was seldom used at this time, but it was sturdily built and in good shape for the years it had been in use.

Bates and I had arrived early because of a message I had received in Denver. Two gunmen were being sent out from St. Paul to the meet. When I got to thinking about who was sending them, I knew the reason. Of course, the message I had received made everything perfectly clear.

Bates and I built up a big fire in the fireplace, turned up the lanterns so everything would look nice and cozy, then we stationed ourselves so we'd have a complete view of the front door. We'd locked the back one and had pulled all the shades on the windows so there would be no surprises and only one way to get inside.

When we heard their car drive up and the doors slam, we were ready. They called our names and introduced themselves. I shouted back that the front door was unlocked, for them to come on in. When they pushed that door open wide and were framed on the threshold, Bates and I let them have it with our machine guns. They were both blown backwards and were dead before they fell into the snow.

The ground was frozen solid and we didn't have a thing to dig with. We drug them out to the meat shed and hung their bodies on meat hooks. I knew they'd be perfectly preserved in that shed for several months; no one would be using it. Bates and I had a good night's sleep knowing that we had done a good job of eliminating two unwanted hit men.

Several months later, when I returned from California after working at the mission, I picked up a hooker. I asked her how she'd like to spend a few days in Colorado at my mountain retreat. She was all for it, so we went to the same cabin. I knew I was sitting on a keg of dynamite. If the police had opened that meat locker while I was gone, they'd have the place staked out. Still the prospect of shacking up with the good looking broad was worth the chance.

We bought a lot of groceries and made ourselves at home. Sure enough, the second morning we were there, up drove a couple of troopers. I wasn't about to let them in and start asking questions. I didn't know whether they were looking for me or not. I grabbed my machine gun and told the gal to stand in the corner. When I heard them step up on the porch, I jerked the door open and came out shooting. Both of them died from lead poisoning.

That gal and I got out of there, leaving all those groceries. I even forgot to check the meat locker, but I had the feeling that I was no longer welcome at the cabin and never returned. You asked if I've ever had any pangs of remorse over what I did to those two troopers. Nope, I can't say that I have. It was either them or me. I've never regretted what I did or felt any emotion one way or the other. Those two troopers brought the number to eight that I'd killed in Colorado, beginning with Bill Pruitt, who I'd hit with the crowbar. Those were tense times. There wasn't a day when the sun would come up that I wouldn't think to myself, well, I might get mine today.

"Floyd was touched off twenty-four hours a day. Not that he wasn't good people; he was a fine physical specimen, good with his fists, a knife, a gun or a piece of pipe, but not with a machine gun."

13. The Truth About The Kansas City Massacre

Yours truly was enjoying himself in the friendly confines of Mother Ash's whore house in Kansas City, Missouri, on the morning of June 17, 1933. I got a call from Dick Galatas concerning a five thousand dollar contract to take part in efforts to either liberate or silence Frank Nash. I'd helped Nash escape from Leavenworth three years earlier.

A short time before I'd received the notice, Nash had been kidnapped by FBI agents right from under the noses of his racketeer pals in Hot Springs, Arkansas. He was put on the Missouri Pacific Flyer which was headed for Kansas City. From there he was to be transferred by car caravan back to Leavenworth.

To help facilitate the transportation of Nash, they had covered his bald head with a wig. There were two FBI agents in the total group of nine bodyguards. The two agents were F. J. Lacky and Frank Smith. Otto Reed, chief of police in McAlister, Oklahoma, was also one of the group. Nash was heavily guarded because a possible ambush was expected. The authorities were not taking any chances.

But their plans didn't include anything in the way of preventing the event which quickly became known as the "Kansas City Massacre."

I was at Mother Ash's whore house to pick up money from another job, the eradication of a squealer. A man named Galatas was to give me the money for that job. He started talking about a new one. I asked him to explain it to me. He bluntly said, "Call Samples; you'll find out."

I made the call and Samples ran it down for me. He would pay five thousand dollars for my part. He said, "Either pull Nash or kill him. If we let him get away, he's going to give up the ship and we'll all sink with it."

From what I knew of Nash at that time, he would do just that. I think Samples' fears were reinforced. There had been an indication that Nash would make a deal. The word was that they wouldn't charge him with anything new, including his escape, if he'd spill the beans on the Minneapolis-St. Paul and Kansas City operations which would bust them wide open. If he did this, my own life was in jeopardy, so I was willing to do what I could to get him back or kill him. Several months later, the activities of the Carpis and Barker gang led to the breaking up of the crime syndicate in the three cities.

We met before the shooting for a little strategy session. Those included in the meet held in the lobby of the Union Station were Pretty Boy Floyd, Adam Rachetti and myself. We spent about twenty-five minutes together while waiting for the train. It turned out to be the most brazen act I ever got involved in.

We had four cars, all told. We decided that two girls we had working on the side should bring up two more. We didn't want to put all our eggs in one basket. None of us knew what to expect when the shooting started. I sure didn't think I'd end up in the parking lot.

Charles Arthur Floyd and his sidekick, a gunman call "The Greek", were the other two paid participants. Floyd told me that he got the assignment out of Cleveland, but we were on contract by the same outfit. A leak from Nash's wife had set the ball rolling. Later I learned that Hoover of the FBI had told his men to shoot to kill if there was an ambush. Floyd and I talked all of this over in the waiting room. We decided that we weren't going to take any chances; we'd kill first.

Floyd was touched off twenty-four hours a day. Not that he wasn't good people; he was a fine physical specimen, good with his fists, a knife, a gun or a piece of pipe, but not with a machine gun. He wasn't the kind who would fall down, even when he was drunk. He could drink a half gallon and keep right on going. I'll say this to his credit: he wasn't a liar, and he wasn't a bragger. When he said he'd done something, you could believe that it was right.

I say he wasn't good with a machine gun because he didn't really aim at a target but would just start spraying as he turned in a circle. His idea was to get any police that might be coming for him. Sometimes he wasn't too careful and would hit women and children, as he did at the Union Station when the action started.

After we finished our meeting we went outside to look over the setup. Floyd ended up sitting on the running board of one of our cars when a little old lady walked up to him and said, "Aren't you Pretty Boy Floyd?"

Floyd looked up at her in a matter of fact manner and replied,

"Yes, mam."

The little old lady went on her way.

As I said a while ago, Nash's wife set the ball to rolling. Her name was Frances. Nash had been allowed to telephone her just before he was put on the train. He told her when he was leaving, how he was traveling, and what time he would arrive in Kansas City. The very fact that the FBI had allowed him to make the call convinced Samples, who was in the St. Paul area at the time, that Nash had made some kind of a deal, and if he talked, we were all in serious trouble. I think his wife was aware of what might happen. It was one of the occupational hazards back in those days.

You can rest assured that the officers were afraid they would be ambushed, but they thought it would take place before they got out of Arkansas. Not in their wildest imagination did they think anything would happen in such a busy place as the Kansas City Union Station.

Another person I saw when we went outside was Blackie Audett, an ex-con, who many years later would turn writer. He was a worthless sonofabitch. He later gained a certain amount of fame by writing a book called RAP SHEET in which he would credit someone else as seeing the event. He was afraid I'd kill him if he told the truth about me. He was sitting in a car with one of his whore girl friends to watch the show. Someone had tipped him off about what might come to pass. But from where he was sitting he sure didn't see too much what really went on. Still, in his book he claimed that Verne Miller master-minded the ambush. The FBI even were stupid enough to think the same way; they closed their books on the case when Miller was found killed a few months later. But I knew that Miller was in Oklahoma on June 17, 1933, recovering from a bad case of .45 slugs. Later, when he was killed, his previous wounds hadn't completely healed.

RAP SHEET was published in 1954, and in it Audett said that Floyd and Rachetti had nothing to do with the killings; the men involved were Verne Miller, Maurice Denning and William Weissman. This was the biggest line of bull I ever heard, but Audett was running true to form. He used to walk the yard at Alcatraz, pumping guys for information to put in a book he was going to write some day. I told him then if he ever put a word about me in his book I'd kill him. The way he got paroled from Alcatraz proves what kind of skunk he was.

An inmate told him about a train robbery he'd taken part in back in Virginia. He even told Blackie where the money was buried.

Two weeks later there were pictures in the paper and a story how Audett had led the FBI to the hiding place of the loot. He was a man who just couldn't stay out of trouble, or at least he couldn't keep from getting caught. In the 1960's I was sent to McNeil Island in Puget Sound, where I had a light stroke. When I was sent to the hospital, who was there also recovering from a stroke, but Audett. One night, when no one was around and he was asleep, I walked down to his bed and tried to smother him to death with his pillow, and was doing a pretty good job of it when a medical aide, whose name was Walter Maxted, walked in, jerked me away and put Audett on the resuscitating machine and revived him. I never really forgave Maxted for his part in saving that sorry piece of humanity.

There were hundreds of people around Union Station that morning. Taxi cabs were bringing passengers to catch the Missouri Pacific Flyer while others were coming to meet people who would arrive. There was no indication whatsoever that just in a few minutes a regular shoot-out would be staged right in the middle of town with hundreds of people as spectators.

In fact, before the shooting erupted, the men who had been left with the two cars which were supposed to transport Nash and his bodyguards, were just standing around talking. They'd even tossed their weapons onto the front seats and didn't have anything in their hands. I'd been watching them closely for several minutes. The one thing they'd done wrong was to park the cars too close together. I was glad because those who were getting in wouldn't have room to go into much action without shooting each other.

Each one of us, who had come to get Nash, knew exactly where our stations were so we wouldn't get caught in our own crossfire. We just stood or sat on the running boards of our cars as others were doing who were waiting for the train to arrive. Of course we were parked in front of the Union Station with our cars headed out. We had a clear view of the two cars that were waiting for Nash. They were forty to sixty feet from us. Floyd had told me when we were planning our positions, "We'll take them if they decide to approach their cars on our side. We don't know how far back they are in the train or which exit they'll take when they get off. You get them if they come to your side."

When the train pulled in, we had Rachetti stationed on the platform to spot them, and to see which way they were going to walk. Suddenly he came running up to me and said, "There are nine of them, too heavy for us to try to take. Nash is handcuffed to two of them, and they're armed to the teeth and headed for your side."

I told him to get the hell out of there and let us do our job. We didn't come to the station to put our tails betwen our legs and run like a yellow dog.

A man was sitting in the front seat of his car a few feet away, and when I looked at him I knew he'd heard everything Rachetti had said. He looked plenty jumpy. I was afraid he was going to blow the whistle on us. He had his back to me as he was climbing out of his car. I slipped up, grabbed his arm and tumbled him sprawling to the ground. I poked my machine gun in his face and told him to roll underneath his car and stay there. If he made a sound or tried to run, I'd blow his head off. He must have believed me because I had no more trouble with him.

The nine men had split up, and I saw five of them coming on my side. I recognized Nash who was handcuffed between a couple of big burly policemen. The other two men in the group were alert as they marched toward the pickup cars. I had already made up my mind that I was going to wait until they started to get into the cars before I went into action. I wanted to catch them at a disadvantage with their pants down, so to speak.

One of the drivers had already climbed in underneath the steering wheel. The car that Nash was being guided to was on my left. The leading policeman he was handcuffed to started to climb into the back seat, and Nash was on the verge of following him when the shooting started. The other man he was handcuffed to fell to the ground while reaching for his gun, pulling Nash and the first policeman with him.

I'd stretched out underneath a car and started spraying them with my machine gun. Before I'd stopped I was sure I'd killed Nash and the two officers he was handcuffed to. I didn't know about the other two that lay still on the ground. As I've already said, they just didn't have space between those two cars to operate. It was like shooting fish in a barrel. I knew that Floyd and his man were taking care of their side, from all the chatter of their guns.

I rolled out from under the car when I didn't see any more movement from those five bodies. I slipped around behind my car and took a look across the way. Floyd and Rachetti were still holding their machine guns as if they were looking for someone else to shoot.

We had really caught them all by surprise. I know that none of the five I'd mowed down had seen me. We hadn't given them a chance to fire a shot; they were knocked so completely of balance, fumbling, and trying to hide behind each other. The whole bloody mess was over in about thirty seconds.

I ran into the clear and was picked up by one of our getaway cars. Later we had a good laugh how those guys started falling and looking for cover. The plain clothes officers, who were supposed to be at the station in secret, must have cleared out, because no one gave us any static. It was our ball game all the way, and we didn't hit anything but home runs.

The paper printed the names of those who were killed. An FBI agent by the name of Raymond J. Caffrey headed the list. Then there were three local Kansas City detectives: William Grooms, Frank E. Hermanson, and one by the name of Reed. Of course, Fank "Jelly" Nash got his, which made the whole assignment successful. Floyd injured some innocent bystanders and two policemen who had been among the four that had split off from Nash.

Later I learned that a special agent named Smith had been with the five I'd shot at. He must have fallen first and the others had collapsed on top of him because the paper said he wasn't even injured. There's one thing for sure, he did a good job of playing dead. That meant the driver, who I thought had got away, was also shot. A special agent in charge, whose name was R. E. Vetterli, and an officer by the name of Lacky were wounded by Floyd.

After the shooting, I went back to Mother Ash's whore house and didn't leave town until twenty-four hours later. When I did leave I stuck a big cigar in my mouth, put a hat on my head, cocking it at a rakish angle and drove right by the police who were watching the main highway going out of the city.

Over eighty known gunmen were considered suspects in the shootout which became known as the "Kansas City Massacre." The FBI contented itself with Floyd, Rachetti and Verne Miller as the trigger men and prime candidates. Several eye witnesses testified that they had seen a stocky man and a foreign-looking companion riding away from the scene on the running board of a car. Later, when I was captured after the Urschel kidnapping, a warrant was issued for my arrest as a suspect in the killings, but I was never officially charged.

"My greatest mistake was that I didn't kill him after I got the ransom money."

14. The Urschel Caper

Urschel was my idea; he was my choice. I'm the one who pointed the finger toward Urschel because he was rich, independently rich. Kathryn didn't plan the kidnapping, but she did know someone who could give us information about the man. I want it understood that it was my show all the way, not Kathryn's. Hoover and the press ran that bunch of garbage into the ground.

The time I helped Carpis in the Hamms' kidnapping by shooting the lights out of the lanterns, I'd already planned the kidnapping. I knew I was going to kidnap somebody and I had in mind who it was going to be. The Urschel kidnapping could be covered in five lines: It went off exactly as planned except we had to put the snatch on two guys.

You know why it went off so well? I made it go off. I laid all the ground work and did the actual kidnapping, and I made the pickup of the ransom money. I was later told by my attorney that it was immaterial who did the kidnapping; they were after a name to capture; everything they'd put together was hearsay. They didn't care about real evidence.

I'd plenty of time planning the kidnapping, several weeks in fact. There was never any real doubt that Mrs. Urschel would arrange the payoff. I had a man riding on the same train with the man she had appointed to deliver the ransom money to make sure there was no law looking on.

Alfred Bates and I were in a hot car on our way to the Urschel home. I believe it was a Ford. I normally didn't pick up cars, at least during this particular period; I had other people do that. The second car was a Buick I'd picked up from a new car dealership somewhere near Saraya, Oklahoma. There were three people riding in that car: Bailey, Kathryn, and another person. We knew that Urschel was at his home in Oklahoma City. It was a nice summer day, July 20, 1933. This was to be the biggest haul I'd ever made and I really felt wonderful.

On the afternoon of the kidnapping, we cased the house for a couple of hours, watched traffic, and made a couple of swipes by the house. I also walked from one direction while Bates came from the other, and we looked over the lay of the land very carefully. Bailey was in the car, keeping a lookout for anyone who might be watching us from the house. At first I intended for him to help us make the snatch, but he was too tall and would be too easy to describe.

The Urschel home was a large brick, bungalow-styled house with a corner screened-in porch. We were not aware that another couple, the Jarrets, had arrived at the house before we began our surveillance, to spend the afternoon and evening with the Urschels.

It seemed like darkness was forever coming. We had planned to wait until just after eight. Bates and I were sitting in the Ford parked on the street about two hundred feet down from the entrance to the Urschel home so we could not be seen from the house. I had been checking my watch every few minutes and also keeping an eye out for any cruising patrolman. There was little traffic. Finally it was time. I turned to Bates and said, "Let's go."

I picked up my machine gun from the floorboard of the car and climbed out to the road. Both of us closed the car doors quietly and soon started our walk up the driveway. I heard voices coming from the screened-in porch and could see the tops of people's heads as we approached. We climbed the steps and Bates opened the screen for me so I didn't have to fumble with the gun. Our entrance caused four startled people, sitting at a card table, to turn and look at us in unison. I had my machine gun trained on them and it had its usual shock effect. "Which one of you is Charles Urschel?" I asked. I couldn't chance taking the wrong individual.

The two men looked at each other, and one of them said, "I'm Urschel. What's the meaning of this?"

When the man opened his mouth I knew he was lying because Urschel had been described to me very carefully. But still I wasn't going to take any chances. I marched the two women into a bedroom and tied their hands behind them and their feet to the bedposts. Then I put tape over their mouths. I told them that I was taking their husbands with me and the one thing they must not do was contact the police when they worked themselves free. They would get explicit instructions which better be followed to the letter if they ever wanted to see their husbands alive again.

I went back to the screened-in porch and Bates and I took the two men to our car. I got in the back with both of them and Bates drove. My machine gun was trained on them all the time. I sure didn't want to kill them, but neither could I afford to take any chances.

When we had driven about twenty miles and were on the

91

outskirts of Oklahoma City, I made Jarret give me his wallet. I went though it carefully after Bates had stopped the car, making sure that we were going to keep the right man. The wallet had about fifty dollars in it which I kept. I made Jarret get out of the car and start walking across country after I had given him instructions to not contact the police. If he did he would never see his friend again.

We bound Urschel's hands, then I put a wad of cloth in his mouth and covered it and his eyes with a large bandana handkerchief. My next step was to make him stretch out on the floorboard between the front and back seats. Not until I was sure he was comfortable and couldn't see a thing did I tell Bates to drive on. We gassed up about twenty miles after we had crossed into Texas. An old farmer-like individual with a distinct Texas drawl waited on us and got to talking about the weather and how badly they needed rain. Not too far from this place we switched cars. I figured we had driven one hundred and eighty miles; my watch said that it was midnight.

Bates and I took turns at the wheel while the other held a gun on Urschel. He was a gentleman all the way. Finally we reached a farmhouse which Armon Shannon owned part interest, and we spent the rest of the night there. Early the next morning we started out and drove to Paradise, Texas, which was only a wide spot in the road. Shannon's old home place was located about seven miles off the highway out of Paradise, right out in the middle of nowhere. We had no reason to believe that anyone would ever locate us.

I supervised getting Urschel out of the car and into the house. His bedroom windows were all boarded up according to my instructions, and he was tied to the bed. The gag was removed but not the bandana. I wasn't taking any chances of him looking through a crack and seeing the outside. Neither was I going to give him the opportunity to overpower anyone who came into the room.

I checked my watch. Fifteen hours had passed since we had picked Urschel up. His wife had been contacted by phone and a ransom note, which I had written, had been delivered to her house. She was in shock but seemed to comprehend what it was all about. The only instructions that weren't followed later on was she had not destroyed the ransom notes.

I want to make it clear about those ransom notes. I had written three of them in advance and had turned them over to one of my men. The first one was to be put in the mail that night so she would get it the next day; the second one was to be mailed from Joplin, Missouri, on the second day. Kathryn did not — I repeat; Kathryn did not — write either note. Later she would be convicted at our trial as a participant in the kidnapping because she had written the notes. She should have never been convicted. No one saw her because she remained on the fringe area. I'm telling the truth. Kathryn did not write those notes!

The third note was giving instructions to watch the newspaper for a certain ad. Mrs. Urschel received that note on the fourth day. I had arranged it so the ad would run every day for a week. Our next move was to have a phone call made to her. She was instructed to send two hundred thousand dollars in cash to Kansas City, Missouri, by someone she could trust. She chose a man by the name of Kirkpatrick to make the delivery. There was never any question in my mind that we wouldn't get the money. I was worried about getting clean unmarked bills.

There was no lawman on the train which Kirkpatrick took out of Oklahoma City. I wasn't taking any chances. I had Kirkpatrick watched from the time he got on that train until he arrived at his destination. While he was on the train, one of my men gave him a note with instructions to follow. The way he did it was simple. He waited until Kirkpatrick went to the dining car and was seated, then he passed by him, put the note on the table, walked to the end of the car, turned around and walked back, picking up the note as he passed.

Earlier instructions had told Kirkpatrick to check into the Muehlebach Hotel in Kansas City, but the note given to him in the dining car changed that. He was to switch to the La Salle. I personally stationed myself so that I could watch him check into the La Salle. I knew who he was because the man who had been tailing him described him to me. I gave him time to get to his room, then I called him on the phone and told him to put the money in a briefcase and take it with him as he walked toward the Muehlebach Hotel. He would be watched every step of the way, from the time he hit the street until I took the money from him.

When I saw him come out of the La Salle I was directly across the street. I hurried to the corner, crossed over so I would come down facing him. As he approached, I walked right up to him, blocking his path and looked him straight in the eyes. At the same time I started speaking. "I'll take the briefcase," I said, and I locked my fingers over his on the handle.

He was startled. He snapped, "You won't take nothing!"

I tightened down on his fingers and reached down to encircle the briefcase with my other arm. "It's for me," I said.

He tried to pull the briefcase away. "What about our deal?"

We were standing in the middle of the sidewalk and people were passing on both sides of us, but I didn't pay any attention to them, and I was going to make sure that he didn't either. I wanted them to think that we were involved in a friendly argument and nothing more.

Still looking him in the eyes and tightening my grip on his fingers I said, "Our deal will take twelve hours to deliver; the deed is intact to the property owner." My fingers tightened some more.

"I'm not going to let just anyone walk up and take this," he said.

I repeated, "It will take about twelve hours to deliver the deed with all the equipment to the property."

Finally he released his grip on the briefcase handle and I let him drop his hand. He immediately began to massage his fingers. I turned and hurried away. What he didn't know was Harvey Bailey and Alfred Bates were also on the street watching the scene. Later he would have a difficult time to describe me because my hair was bleached a peroxide blond.

I went to a phone and had word sent to Armon Shannon to have Urschel brought to a meeting point where he would be released. I later met them outside Oklahoma City where we released him on the eleventh day after the kidnapping. I recall that I had kidnapped him on the night of July 20th, but the court records later said that it was July 22nd, but it was really on the twentieth. I released him at midnight, July 31, 1933. I gave him ten dollars of his own money and told him to catch a cab and go home.

Mrs. Urschel had called the FBI chief, J. Edgar Hoover, the night that the kidnapping had taken place. She had followed my instructions and told him that she was going to abide by my wishes, so Hoover held back. The Urschel family at that time simply carried more weight than the FBI, so he did sit back and wait until the ransom had been delivered before any of his agents got on my trail. Of course, when they did get on my trail, all the forces of the FBI all over the country were called into action. The Urschels were personal friends of President Roosevelt, and the President encouraged Hoover to do everything possible to capture me.

After I had collected the two hundred thousand dollar ransom, some of the St. Paul folks were waiting. I gave them sixty-five thousand. One of the dirty things about the whole deal was later when Harvey Bailey and I were caught. They shook us down and took a lot of money from us. Not one red cent of it was the ransom money. We had collected this money on previous jobs.

The eleven-day period between Urschel's kidnapping and his release turned out to be somewhat of a legendary part of folklore created by Hoover. He built it up to not only being one of the most popular kidnappings of the whole Twentieth Century, but one of the most smoothly executed.

Despite the massive efforts of the FBI and other law enforcement agencies, I was not to be taken until fifty-six days had passed and I'd driven over twenty thousand miles, running to the Pacific Northwest. During that time I became the most widely hunted man in the United States. For almost two months I was Public Enemy Number One.

Years later, and for most of the forty years that I was to spend in prison, many times I would think over the whole Urschel case. If I were asked what I'd do differently, I would repeat the same stock answer:

Charles Urschel was the smartest man I ever met. He had a computer mind. He remembered things, even though he was blindfolded, things that I didn't remember, and I wasn't blindfolded. My greatest mistake was I didn't kill him after I got the ransom money.

"Purvis came to see us get killed, then cart us off to be buried after he got his name in all the papers. Instead he was lucky that he got away himself, alive."

15. THEY Got Away

Three weeks after the Urschel release, me and several of my associates gathered at the farmhouse in southern Oklahoma where Urschel had been held the first night after the kidnapping. The purpose of the gathering was to have a meet, to plan future strategy. But from the very beginning that meet was doomed. Events leading up to it were ominous.

We arrived at the designated place a day early, in two cars. There were five counting me and Arky in his car. Along with us were Kathryn, another gunman whose name I don't remember, and Alfred Bates.

Arky was properly named "The Weasel" because nobody trusted him, and there was good reason to believe he would squeal if he was ever backed into a corner. I'll have more to say about him later.

In the other car was Armon Shannon and his wife from Denver and two other men. Then shortly after we arrived, a third car came, driven by a fellow named Charley. He was supposed to be there but not in the car he was driving, an old English Rolls Royce. He said he'd stolen it in Oklahoma City.

The car was a beautiful piece of machinery, painted brown instead of the usual black; and its fancy trappings almost blinded us, they sparkled so. It was definitely the only one of its kind in that part of the country, and had a strange set of tires which could be tracked anywhere. Charley claimed that he had fallen in love with it the moment he had seen it and just couldn't pass it up.

I flatly told him that he had to get out of there with that car or he'd get all of us in trouble. He could come back after he'd ditched the Rolls Royce, but he had to return in one that wasn't so noticeable.

When he left, I knew he was pretty mad, but I wasn't going to allow that hot car to be responsible for the cops putting the finger on us. All of us were wanted by the police, and that car could put them on our trail. If I'd used my head, we'd have pulled out, because the Rolls' tire tracks could easily be followed on those seldom traveled dirt roads. But I didn't think of that aspect until the next day when things really began popping.

Well, that night we had the radio turned on and heard all about how Charley got his. Someone had spotted the car and the police set up a roadblock at the end of a bridge. Charley saw it too late to stop. When the police started shooting, he got a slug before the heavy car broke through the guard rail and plunged into the water. Charley couldn't work the fancy door handles so he drowned. You can bet your bottom dollar none of those police would get their feet wet to save him. But one thing Charley did was to mess up that fancy car. If the police hadn't been so anxious, they'd have found the Rolls parked on the street all in one piece instead of filled with bullet holes and waterlogged.

Maybe you're thinking if I hadn't sent Charley away, he'd still be around. Well, look at it this way, when you're in charge of an operation, you better be sure no one does something stupid, or he'll ruin everything. What Charley did was downright brainless, and he paid for his mistake. I didn't kill him but I would have if he'd returned with that hot car.

After listening to the radio broadcast I was really on edge. It seemed to tell me that something was going to happen, something bad. I knew that every cop in that part of the country was looking for us because of the Urschel kidnapping, and they knew that Charley was one of my men. I told the others to be prepared for some fireworks.

I had the feeling that the FBI weren't too far away. I began to make plans and to take care of a few things in case they followed us and set up an ambush. I knew an ambush would be pretty hard to pull off because the farmhouse we were in was situated on a little rise or knoll where we had a good view of the landscape in all directions. We could spot them as they came in unless they stole up on us at night.

In order to play it safe, I took Arky's car and drove it down to the back pasture in among some trees, completely out of sight of the road. On the way back to the house I hid my extra machine gun and a drum of ammunition next to a tree stump, then I covered them over with leaves and brush. I wanted to be ready for any action if it came. I still had this strong premonition that something was going to happen.

Early the next morning was to be my first encounter with Melvin Purvis, G-Man, who had become famous for his involvement in gunning down so many gangsters back in the late twenties and early thirties. He had such a loud mouth with a megaphone that you could hear him even after the shooting started. It's what woke me up.

I want to digress here for a moment and tell you about this guy Purvis and explain exactly what I thought of him, then we'll get back to the story. My personal opinion of Purvis at that time was I thought he was the lowest form of a human being. He was only one of two people during those years that I would have liked to torture to death and enjoyed every moment of it. The other person was Arky. Like I said, we called Arky "The Weasel" because he really was a weasel; I always felt uncomfortable in his presence. The first day I met him, I knew I'd have to kill him sooner or later. He forced people to hate him. I guess I'll have to say the only reason I kept him around was he had the reputation of being a good "repairman" — he was handy with a gun and knew how to use it. I was going to keep him alive until after the meet because I figured I'd have use for him. As it turned out, I did.

Stories I'd heard how Purvis directed his G-Men, along with troopers and city police in other ambushes, and how they'd killed some of my associates by completely surprising them by using an ambush, even when some of my friends weren't armed, made me want to kill Purvis. Yes, you'd be right in saying he was a threat to me because of his past success.

I think one of the reasons the FBI was going all out with the ambush strategy was simply a matter of public relations. Such men as Baby Face Nelson, Dillinger, and Verne Miller, along with others were giving the organization a bad time. The FBI's image was sagging around the country which was causing a lot of people to lose faith in its capabilities. Hoover had promised that his department would really benefit the country and rid it of the undesirables. But I think Hoover was seeing what was happening and was out to salvage what little prestige he had left. He made his men go out in brute force and start eliminating as many gangsters as possible. At that time he wasn't interested in sending any of them to prison; he was out to eliminate them and put fear into others who thought of breaking the laws.

I have to say that Hoover was pretty successful; he did get rid of a lot of us. He assigned Melvin Purvis to be his hatchet man in the part of the country where I was operating. Now you see why I developed such a hatred for Purvis.

You see, I was driven into this state and knew for a fact, after I heard news broadcasts about me and reading about myself in the newspapers, that I was wanted dead, not alive. That's what it was all about on my side and theirs. The only way they were ever going to get me was by ambush — dead not alive, civil arrest, or whatever it was called. It still gave the police the license to kill. With Purvis at the helm, I knew that all he wanted to do was to kill me and my men.

Things were a little different in my case. There were only two types of people I'd ever consider killing. First comes those people who don't do their jobs right and cause others to get killed or injured simply because they don't do what they're told to do. Arky fell into this category. He was a good worker, very exact, but he wanted to do things his way whether they were right or wrong. In my operation there can be only one boss, me. Second, anybody who was out to kill me was fair game for me to kill them. It didn't matter if it was another gangster, a policeman or an FBI agent, like Purvis on that particular morning. I looked on the whole thing as a matter of survival because, to me, that was pretty important.

I'm not a vicious man, really and truly, but when I think someone has it coming, I might as well stoop to his level and get it over with. I think Hoover had that attitude about me when he said, "Kelly never fired a shot in anger, only out of frustration." I'm sure he was making a comparison between me and someone else, but I don't know who the other person was.

I guess I've digressed enough about my feelings toward Purvis and my own personal philosophy, so let's get back to the actual facts of this particular ambush when Purvis knew he had us exactly where he wanted us. But he'd never come up against "Machine Gun" Kelly before.

Kathryn and I were upstairs in bed when the shooting started. We'd all slept late, and the one thing I'd failed to do was to assign someone to keep watch. Purvis and his men crept in while it was still dark, but they weren't about to come into the house, knowing that they'd get it from the first one of us they woke up.

Well, he got on that crazy megaphone, introduced himself and said the place was completely surrounded and we didn't have a chance. We were to throw our guns out the windows and doors and step outside with our hands up. I guess he'd managed to catch some second rate operators in the past that way, but the bastard didn't know who he was up against.

Kathryn and I both were fully dressed because I'd suggested it. I came out of that bed and grabbed my machine gun all in one motion. The first thing I did was look out the window and see them all crouched behind some cars they must have pushed into position during the night. I stepped back and blasted out that window, and almost laughed when those guys started hunkering down for more cover.

Then with Kathryn right behind me, we went down those stairs. Every time I'd go by a window, I'd blast some more. We went right on down into the basement where I knew there was a passage way that led to an underground cellar where things were stored in the winter. This cellar had a trap door that locked from the inside, and which could be pushed up and you could walk right out into the yard. Purvis didn't know this.

I told Kathryn to hold the door up for me after I'd unlocked it, and when I looked out at ground level all I could see were over a dozen legs standing behind those cars. I began raking them with machine gun bullets, and those agents started falling down like a row of kingpins, grabbing their legs, rolling in the dirt, and screaming like a lot of stuck hogs.

Later I heard on the radio that I had come out firing two machine guns at the same time, but that wasn't true. I just had the one machine gun, but I was really making use of it. The word was out that I always carried two with me. The FBI probably put out this word on the radio, trying to make themselves look better than they actually were.

Just before I came out of that cellar shooting in every direction, I'd heard Purvis on his megaphone telling his men to stand fast and pick us off if we made a run for it. But my little mowing down operation completely threw those men off balance. When Purvis saw his men falling and heard them screaming, he changed his tune in a hurry. The next time he shouted through that horn he screamed, "Let's get out of here!"

You never saw a bunch of men move so fast. They almost ran over each other getting in cars and heading out. They were no longer worried about cutting us down. The whole battle was over in short order. The two men who had come with Armon Shannon were shot. One of them was named Collins. Bates picked up a flesh wound on his butt. He had a little trouble sitting down for several days.

When Kathryn and I and Arky and some of the others started out across the pasture to the car where I'd parked it, the shooting had stopped and the police had cleared out. When I reached the stump and checked my ammo, it's a good thing I'd hid that other drum; I was just about out of bullets.

We all piled into Arky's car and drove toward the lower pasture gate. There were four cars parked there with two men on guard.

As we approached, I aimed my machine gun and the two guards threw down their guns and raised their hands in the air. One car had been parked about half-way across the road to stop us, but Arky slammed into the front of it with his heavy car, tipping it over as if it were a toy, and we drove right on through. What was supposed to be a roadblock turned out to be a wide open gate.

The ambush episode pulled off by Purvis and his men really put me to thinking. It was responsible for me coining a saying that I still remember and have to smile each time I think of it: "I didn't get away. THEY got away." Don't let anybody else ever tell you otherwise. Purvis came to see us get killed, then cart us off to be buried after he got his name in all the papers. Instead he was lucky that he got away himself, alive. He might have taken us if he'd known about that underground cellar and how it was connected with the basement; but that's the reason I've managed to survive. I always tried to know just a little more than the other fellow. Purvis never dreamed that someone would pop up through that trap door and begin spraying his men with bullets. When he saw them fall as they did, that's when we had him on the run.

I read in the paper the next day the grand total of agents and state troopers who came to the farmhouse in six cars was thirty-nine. That was the largest number ever used in an ambush up to that time. Purvis had to admit that we got away. The paper also said that he had lost four men and it gave me credit for mowing down several others with my raking as I came out of the cellar.

But regardless of what the paper said, I and my men knew there were more than that killed. The papers back in the twenties and thirties never did publish the correct number of lawmen killed by gangsters; it would make them look silly. Take the number released in Chicago back in 1933. I would say at least twenty agents were killed that year, but you didn't read that anywhere. The FBI listed about one-fourth that number. They caused a lot of deaths, too. Let me explain the setup they would use.

There would be at least five or six agents in an ambush. The other fifteen or twenty men would be troopers and city or county police. Out of the deaths there would be many troopers killed unnecessarily because they did what the FBI told them to do; still the FBI got all the glory. Some of their actions were grossly exaggerated. I was surprised how accurate the ambush was in the movie BONNIE AND CLYDE. I guess Warren Beatty insisted that the truth be told. The John Dillinger movie shows him being ambushed. But there was another one about Wilbur Underhill where it showed Purvis putting on a bullet-proof vest, then having a big fat cigar stuck between his teeth. He walks up to the shack, kicks in the door and drags Wilbur out crying and begging for mercy. That was repulsive.

Just a few days after the ambush, I asked Arky to go with me to pick up another car. I knew he had stolen the one he'd been driving in these parts. I had asked him to ditch it but he refused. I found the car I wanted, hot wired it and made sure it ran well, then I climbed in Arky's car as if I was going to give him some instructions. I slid my left arm across the back of the seat, all the time carrying on a conversation.

What Arky didn't know was that I had a .38 in my left hand. I shot him just a little behind the ear and the bullet went out through the top of his head. I left him draped over the steering wheel. I was sick and tired of his constant bickering and just didn't feel that he was needed any more. If we were ever caught, he'd really cross us up, and we sure didn't have any use for that hot car.

"They had me. I wasn't going anywhere unless I got a real good chance. So why cry about it?"

16. G-Men: Government Or Garbage

Following Harvey Bailey's capture at the Shannon home place near Paradise, Texas, he was put into the new escape-proof county jail in Dallas. I was able, through channels, to slip a thousand dollars to a deputy sheriff to help arrange an escape for Bailey. He did escape, even though it was short-lived.

I feel that the main reason I was captured after the Urschel kidnapping was because of my habit of spending one week out of the month with Kathryn. I had been doing this during our three years of association while living with her as my common-law wife. She had gone her way and I had gone mine, and this is what got me in trouble at this time. I was unable to keep an eye on her and didn't know some of the things she was doing. I never knew what her big mouth might spout off when I wasn't around.

I never really loved a woman until I met Cindy, but I was loyal to my women, even to Kathryn. But from the first second after our capture, Kathryn was a sniveling whore.

I went into the kidnapping trial fairly confident and was told it was immaterial who did the kidnapping, they were after a notorious name. What they had put together was hearsay, not evidence. My attorney said that it was a railroad job from start to finish. Kathryn and I were convicted before we ever got to the courtroom.

Mr. Urschel's money was so good that if he didn't want a copy of the trial proceedings there wouldn't be any. I am referring to a copy of the transcript of the court case. He didn't make any statements about me in public, which sure did deflate my ego.

During the several weeks before my capture, Melvin Purvis and J. Edgar Hoover were calling me a dirty little punk. I finally met Purvis in Memphis. I'd heard his stinking voice during the shootout in Oklahoma, and I thought then and still do, that Purvis was the lowest form of a human being. I was already in custody in Memphis; still he took credit for my capture, but had absolutely nothing to do with it.

We were holed up in a house out on Parkway in Memphis, which was a nice residential area. The house was only one story, but it had three bedrooms. Old lady Shannon had rented it for me. She had more guts than any of the rest. There was a rooming house

103

next door, and as a whole, it was a pretty high class neighborhood. I liked it so well that I was in the process of buying the house.

The capture happened well before sunrise on September 26, 1933. I don't recall the exact time, but it could have been around three in the morning.

After hearing what I thought was the milkman, I laid down again and dozed off for about five minutes. They were all in the room when I awoke, having come in through the front door. Kathryn and I were both nude; naked as jaybirds. I had put my machine gun on a table about ten feet from the bed and draped Kathryn's sweater over it. The table was near the window and I think they saw me when I put the gun on the table. If I'd been dressed, I'm sure I'd been killed.

The first thing I saw when I woke up was a man with a shotgun pointing right at me. He said, "You're under arrest. One move and you're dead!" At that very moment they all cocked their guns. I didn't want to be killed, unarmed, and without my clothes on. I was also pretty pissed off that I'd been surprised that way.

I just told the guy, "OK, Goddammit, don't shoot, G-Men; I'm unarmed!"

The capture happened so suddenly that I saw police everywhere I looked. All the streets had been blocked off. I found out later that they had disabled my two cars by cutting the radiator hoses. They didn't let the air out of the tires because they figured that would make too much noise.

Kathryn started screaming like women will do. It was her natural instinct to turn on me. Right out of the blue, she screamed that the reason she was with me was because I'd threatened to kill her if she left. She claimed that she was going to Oklahoma City the very next day and turn herself in so she could help her mother and dad who were on trial there. It was the first trial of the Urschel kidnapping which was already under way while I was still being hunted.

My capture was one of the most famous in FBI history. All of the FBI agents are well drilled and well informed. They may have been told, since that day, that I was the one who started the G-Man slogan. Even though I was given credit for originating the name, the circles I ran in always referred to them as G-Men, government men or most often as garbage men.

There were widespread newspaper reports at the time that Kathryn had tried to talk me into giving myself up to help her parents out. Maybe if I gave myself up, she thought her parents would be released. It wasn't her idea, it was mine. But it just didn't come down that way. I told them I'd give myself up if they would let everyone else go. Kathryn had called two different attorneys at least a dozen times. In their conversations I was asssured that I couldn't be convicted. They just didn't have the evidence on me. I don't think they'd get a conviction today. Urschel led them down a street and made them believe everything he said.

Our trial for the Urschel kidnapping was very rapid. On the first morning a jury was selected; the second day that jury reached a verdict; the verdict was read on the third morning. It was a bombastic, brief trial. The three days I was taken to the courtroom, I was under heavy guard, chained and manacled. I was transported from the jail to the courtroom in an armored car to prevent any possible escape attempts.

Once during the trial proceedings Kathryn was standing near me. There were some guards right by us. Kathryn became flustered and slapped one of them. I stepped in and just as I raised my handcuffed hands above my head I was struck several times. They were afraid it was my first step toward making a break. On the last day of the trial I had a nice big lump on the left side of my forehead, just because I'd raised my hands.

As I've already told you, I always rant and rave when I get frustrated. Things were going wrong. I didn't think everybody would turn on me as they did. Circumstances were going against me; I was full of hostility. I couldn't handle myself when I was in this condition as well as I can now. Age and going through what I have, mellowed me.

People who were involved with me in different ways in the Urschel kidnapping just didn't have it when the chips were down. They could "waller" in the pot but just couldn't take the circumstances which they became involved in later.

I was somewhat amused at the reports circulated about my capture. The papers said that more than a dozen riot guns and machine guns were found in the house on Parkway when Kathryn and I, along with two of my men, were arrested. One of the policemen said that I had more ammunition than the police department. The weapons cache was the greatest array of firearms ever seized in Memphis up to that time.

I had my hair dyed yellow when I was captured. Kathryn had been wearing a red wig. Shortly after our capture Kathryn told the police that I would have cleaned out the whole outfit in Oklahoma

City if I had not been captured. "You got him just in time or George would have killed them all," she said. "That's the way our plans were made. He was going to kill people who put my mother, Harvey Bailey and Alfred Bates on trial."

Sure, I had made numerous threats by phone, telegrams and notes to various individuals who were involved in the trial. I also sent telegrams to the Urschel family. I really sounded like a monster, but I wasn't — in size anyway. Police files at the time listed me as being of medium height and muscular build.

After my capture I maintained an easy going attitude and tried to keep up a good sense of humor. Even after I was locked up I smoked one cigarette after another. I remember when Police Chief Will D. Lee came to my cell in Memphis, as he walked in I snapped at him, "Who the hell are you?"

"I'm Chief Lee."

"Well, give me a light then."

Later during a photo-taking ceremony beside my cell, I was brought out into the passageway and one of my wrists was handcuffed to the bars. I held my hat in my other hand. As the photographer was getting ready to take the picture I turned to a guard standing nearby and said, "Say, can you lend me that machine gun for a few minutes?" I was determined to keep up a nonchalant front regardless what took place. They had me. I wasn't going anywhere unless I got a real good chance. So why cry about it?

At the time of my capture I was wanted for many more things than just the Urschel kidnapping. I was wanted in connection with murders of the three policemen and the FBI agent and gangster Frank Nash who had been gunned down at the Kansas City railroad station; for the robbery of a federal reserve bank messenger and a policeman in St. Paul; and for the killing of Miles Cunningham in Chicago. At the time of my capture, warrants had been issued for my arrest involving murders in three major cities: St. Paul, Chicago, and Kansas City.

I kept up my nonchalant attitude right up until trial time. Yes, it was hard, because I was well aware of what was going on around me. But I have always had the ability to turn off the things which I don't want to bother me. I maintained my composure by doing just that.

My trial had been the occasion for the first federal jury to act under the federal kidnapping "Lindberg Law" which had been passed by Congress in June of 1932. As it would turn out, it was only one of two kidnapping trials actually held under the "Lindberg Law." The second one wouldn't happen until some thirty years later. That was the Frank Sinatra, Jr. case.

In later years stories were put out by J. Edgar Hoover that I was a henpecked, frustrated husband and would jump every time Kathryn would snap her fingers. Bullshit! You didn't see that kind of crap in articles at the time of my capture or when I was on the rampage.

To tell you the truth, I wasn't to be confused with the ordinary criminal. I was smart. I ignored the underworld haunts of the small time racketeers. I associated only with men on the run who liked to be heard and not seen. I changed my appearance often by dying my hair different colors. This is why I could turn up in unexpected places hundreds of miles from where the law was looking for me.

Ballistic experts had already determined, by inspecting the microscopic markings of bullets claimed to have been left by my gun in the body of Miles Cunningham, a Chicago patrolman shot in a mail robbery, that I was responsible for that murder. Other bullets with the same markings were also taken from the bodies in the Kansas City shooting.

My movements for many months really were almost as though I were a phantom. At the time of my capture, federal agents claimed that I'd left one of the bloodiest trails they'd followed in recent months. Actually, for those two months after I let Urschel go, I was a pretty hot item. My name was a household word. Believe you me, the man in the street sure didn't think of me as being henpecked or a pussy foot for some two-bit whore to push around. Hell, I was the subject of one of the most extensive manhunts that had ever been directed in the United States.

While I was running, Bates was arrested in Colorado; the Shannons, R. G., Kathryn's dad; her mother, Ora; and her brother, Armon, were all arrested in Paradise, Texas, along with Bailey.

All the Shannons completely turned on me; my own attorney didn't even have any kind words to say in my behalf during the trial. I carried the load for everybody. The prosecution was willing to let me shoulder everything and let Kathryn go free. Her conviction and life sentence came down because of the testimony of a local stamp collector, who claimed that at least two of the ransom notes had been written by her. But let me tell you again, Kathryn did not write the notes — I wrote them myself. She was framed by the testimony at the trial.

In 1958 Kathryn succeeded in getting an attorney to re-open the case in her behalf. She was twenty-five years into her life sentence, and she demanded that the official FBI files be made public. But if they were, it would be shown that there was definite evidence proving that she did not write the ransom notes.

Kathryn was released in 1958 on an appeal bond after a judge in Oklahoma City ordered that the FBI make public its files in the case — at least the part involving Kathryn.

J. Edgar Hoover was suddenly in one of those damned if he does, damned if he doesn't situations. He couldn't release the files because in them was a statement written by the FBI's fingerprint and handwriting expert. This man had written a report, which he sent to Hoover, saying it was his belief that Kathryn couldn't have been the writer of the ransom notes. This evidence was not brought forth at our trial. Had it been used as testimony, I'm sure Kathryn would not have been convicted, even though the public wanted to hang both of us.

What happened is that Hoover ordered the files not to be opened or released by this reasoning: "Kathryn wants her freedom. We'll let her have it and we'll save face by not releasing the files."

Kathryn — at least as late as July, 1975 — was alive and well and living in a suburb of Oklahoma City. She had been out of prison for seventeen years on an appeal bond; this might be some kind of record.

One of my fondest memories goes back to an incident that happened during my initial interrogation in Memphis right after my capture. As I said before, I had the ability to shut everything which I didn't want to think about completely out of my mind. In this one instance I actually dozed off during an intensive interrogation session. It was a big moment in life to be able to go to sleep while those guys were hammering away. Just as I was starting to wake up, I heard one guy say, "Why, that sonofabitch is snoring!"

Urschel made me Public Enemy Number One. The first time I ever made the Post Office posters was either in late 1932 or early in 1933. I was suspected and accused of several major crimes following the Urschel kidnapping and I drove day and night to get to the West Coast. During this period I only slept the whole night through four or five times. Also during this time I bought more cars than I'd ever bought before; four to be exact. I hit no banks and committed no robberies. I had a suitcase full of money. I didn't want anyone around who knew me. Overnight was the longest I spent in one place until we got back to Memphis.

After the Coors' kidnapping, I knew I was destined to be killed. I felt that I'd never be arrested. It took me three days after I was arrested for the Urschel kidnapping to recover from shock. Honestly, I thought I'd drifted off into another world.

"...That's what I'd call sweet revenge. If a desert wasn't available, I'd lock him in a room for a week; give him no food or drink. I'd cut off his kneecaps, fix him a little soup and later fix him a steak off his own butt."

17. Cockroach Alley

Following my conviction, I was flown in a fifteen-passenger plane to Kansas City. There were eight heavily armed guards keeping me company on the plane. When we reached Kansas City, I was transported by train to Leavenworth. By this time the entourage must have numbered forty or fifty guards. They had enough firepower to start a war. What they were doing was overreacting to a rumor that some of my underworld friends might make an attempt to free me.

Nothing happened.

At Leavenworth I was immediately put into solitary confinement. The officials weren't going to take any chances in letting their big fish get away. I stayed in solitary for almost a year before I was shipped to the new federal prison in San Francisco Bay.

While I was in solitary I had a lot of time for reflecting, thinking of the things I'd done and the things I wanted to do. Many of the thoughts dwelled on Kathryn. I'd been hurt badly because of the way she'd turned on me.

Kathryn! I thought I cared for her, but when I analyzed her whole makeup, I came to the conclusion that I hadn't cared. Everyone she met was just another trick. She was a great actress. She would pretend to have emotion, but she really didn't have any feelings for anyone. Just a two-bit whore.

Sometimes I'd just sit there and get madder 'n hell, recalling one report that called me "Pop Gun" Kelly because I was captured without a shot being fired. Now, let me ask you, just what's so unnoble about not wanting to get killed without my clothes on and without any weapon in hand to defend myself?

"Pop Gun" Kelly — how ridiculous can you get! I was pretty notorious. My record speaks for itself!

There were times when I'd reflect about Brother Bob Beckam. I wondered what my life would 've been like if I'd yielded to the teaching of Brother Beckam, and gotten off the road of crime and turned my life over to the Lord. Those reflections were brief. I fought even thinking about such things. I didn't dream there'd come a day when the Lord would call and I'd listen; that event was forty-one years in the future.

My only consistent friends in solitary were the cooks and the ever-present giant cockroaches that infested the damp underground confinement area.

Back then there were more guys who died in the hole than in the population. I didn't let that faze me. I thought about more pleasant things. They had cockroaches down there big enough to carry a cigarette. This is how we did it. You take your socks and unravel them; that way you can get enough string to fly a kite. The cook in the galley would take a red wrapper and put in a cigarette and a red head—a term we used to describe a match—then he would cover it with mashed potatoes. The cons who did the cooking had prepared it so you'd have a smoke once in a while.

Every few days they would fix mashed potatoes, and in the middle of the potatoes they would plant the cigarette and match. Then I'd use the string from my socks to make a harness to tie on the cockroach. By tying the cigarette and match a certain way they could be hitched onto the cockroach. The knack was to place the weight on the right side if I wanted the cockroach to go in that direction and on the left side if the delivery was to be made in that way. There were seven cells down in the solitary confinement area, and by this method I could send my cockroaches to any one of them I wished.

I reflected a lot on Melvin Purvis. He was in the same class with J. Edgar Hoover. I think both of them were frustrated homosexuals. I never heard or read about Hoover ever being in the company of a female.

But Purvis was the one I really hated. He's a cheat; he's a liar; he's a glory hound. He likes to be glorified. He's one man I could kill and never take a look back. I could have done that without even getting angry. He's one man I'd like to have tortured to death. I've envisioned how I'd like to do it. I'd take him out in the desert, tie his arms with buckskin strings, wet them so they would shrink as they dried, then tie him to a bush so he couldn't get any closer to me than five feet. I'd sit in the shade of a tree with a tall glass of milk partly filled with ice cubes. As the sun got hotter, I'd tinkle the cubes in the glass and make him beg for a drink and laugh at him as he got real thirsty. The buckskin would begin to eat into his arms, cutting off all circulation. I'd keep the animals away at night and watch him die the next day. That's what I'd call sweet revenge.

If a desert wasn't available, I'd lock him in a room for a week; give him no food or drink. I'd cut off his kneecaps, fix him a little soup and later fix him a steak off his own butt.

Now if you were a psychiatrist, you'd make something of these thoughts. You'd say I was showing my animalistic tendencies.

I spent a lot of time daydreaming about how I would carry out revenge on Purvis. There are only two people I ever wanted to do these things to. Purvis was one. I killed the other man. That was Arky, "The Weasel."

My solitude was interrupted very infrequently. Twice I was taken out to be questioned by authorities in regard to other crimes for which I was a suspect. One incident I was questioned about was whether or not I'd been involved in the meat hook episode which had happened two years earlier when Bates and I had killed the two underworld hoods in Colorado and had stuck them up on meat hooks to freeze. I was questioned at least four more times about the incident during my prison career. The last time I was asked about the two men was as late as 1972.

The food in Leavenworth, which was served to the cons in the hole was main line chow the same as the other prisoners got except that everything was ground up and made into a loaf. If a prisoner didn't like carrots, he still got the carrots. You were eating something of everything. After a while it started tasting pretty good.

I went through some periods when I was given my food at irregular intervals. Maybe I'd get the regular food loaf every fourth day, then there would be bread and water in between. That irregular rotation explains to a large degree why us prisoners down there developed ingenious methods in peddling cigarettes and matches by using the cockroaches. If all the solitary cells were full, and there were seven prisoners down in the hole at one time, it might be two or three weeks before all of them had a bowl of mashed potatoes. And there would usually be only one cigarette and one match smuggled down. This would make them anxious to share what they received. If a con acquired a couple of smokes a month from other cells he might have to send one-half of a cigarette and a match to his right by a cockroach and the other half to his left. The second con would have to get his match from another source.

During the course of my stay at Leavenworth, I heard by the prison grapevine that Kathryn had been shipped to the women's prison in Alderson, West Virginia.

FBI agent Doug Hopkins tries in vain to pry information from a thoroughly disgusted and tight-lipped
George "Machine Gun" Kelly following his November
8, 1974 capture in a Phoenix bank. Kelly, going under the name of John H. Webb, had used hair dye to
darken his white hair in an effort to make himself
look younger than his 68 years.

FBI agents Doug Hopkins, left, and Freddie Cain escort George Kelly, alias John H. Webb, to a Phoenix police station. Said Kelly later, "When I climbed out of the police van at the station, a photographer from THE ARIZONA REPUBLIC snapped my picture, then he walked up to me and said, 'Are you the bank robber?' I kinda smiled and answered, 'Well, I thought I was.'"

The photo was taken on November 8, 1974, after Kelly's capture in the 1st National Bank of Arizona at 35th Avenue and Indian School Road in Phoenix.

This is perhaps the most famous photo of George Kelly. Here is the original caption for the photo:

"MACHINE GUN" KELLY ARRESTED IN MEMPHIS George "Machine Gun" Kelly, wanted in Chicago for questioning in the murder of a patrolman in a payroll holdup, and also suspected of being a member of the Urschel kidnap gang, was arrested in Memphis, Tenn., on Sept. 26 (1933). With Kelly at the time of his arrest was his wife, who is the daughter of R.G. (Boss) Shannon, who is one of the gang held for the Urschel kidnapping. This photo was made in the Memphis jail shortly after Kelly's capture.

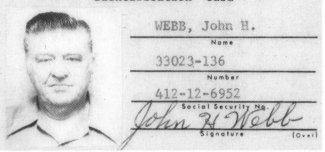

FEDERAL CORRECTIONAL INSTITUTION
FORT WORTH, TEXAS 76119
COMMUNITY WORK AND STUDY RELEASE PROGRAM
Identification Card

WEBB, John H.
Name

33023-136
Number

412-12-6952
Social Security No.

John H Webb
Signature   (Over)

The individual identified on the other side of this card is a resident of the Federal Correctional Institution, Fort Worth, Texas and is authorized under provisions of Public Law 89-176 to participate in a community work/study release program. In case of accident or emergency please telephone 535-2111.

Charles F. Campbell, Warden

Above are the front and back of the identification card that was issued to George Kelly under the name of John H. Webb in 1973. Kelly used the card while working for a Dallas, Texas bailbonding firm. He was an inmate at the Federal Correctional Institution in Fort Worth. Kelly reported to the institution at night while being allowed to work during the day as a participant in the community work and study release program. Kelly robbed two banks in Dallas to make arrangements to secure his bailbonding job.

When it came time for me to be transferred out of Leavenworth to Alcatraz, I was shipped by train from Kansas to California, then by car caravan to Alcatraz. The cars were put on a ferry boat which steamed to the island.

I'd known for months that the super prison, Alcatraz, would be my new home. The word had come down that it was built especially for incorrigibles. In a way I felt honored to be among the first to occupy the completely renovated place which was classed as the new stronghold from which no one could escape. I looked upon the opportunity as a new challenge to try to escape if I ever got the chance.

"There were only two hundred and eighty-six cons there who hated Johnston; that's because that's all the prisoners there were."

18. Welcome To The Rock

It was right near the end of 1934 that I was actually shipped out to Alcatraz. I believe that I was on the third chain of convicts sent out there. I was put in isolation as soon as I arrived.

Their whole ball of wax was to break a con. For the first several months I was there, they tried everything in the book to break me; they couldn't do it. The very first thing they did was to take me before Johnston, the warden. He had a pile of mail on his desk, letters that had actually been sent to me while I was at Leavenworth. Back in those years, convicts in solitary weren't given mail.

Johnston snapped at me, "Out of all this garbage you can have seven of them. Which ones do you want to shit can?"

There must have been at least one hundred and fifty letters piled there. I looked at Johnston, trying to see through the man, but I didn't faze him. He was well known; he was a dog. He got the job because of his reputation. We both had our opinions of each other; that of being tough nuts. He wanted to hard ass me before I could hard ass him. He made an animal out of you; he embittered you. There were only two hundred and eighty-six cons there who hated Johnston; that's because that's all the prisoners there were.

Warden Johnston was of medium build but rather stocky. You would be one hundred per cent correct if you said that everything that has been written about him was false. If everything you said about him was no good, that would be right. All Johnston was is the reason you go to church — to get away from the devil.

One time Johnston called a con before him who had been kneeling to pray. He pounced on the guy and said, "You phony sonofabitch, if I catch you kneeling again I'll put you in the hole!"

During my fifteen years on The Rock, I had no visitors from the outside world, no newspapers or other reading material except what I could smuggle into the prison in the way of contraband.

I just had a Bible. If it hadn't been for some Christian group, I wouldn't have had it. I read that Bible from cover to cover, and when I'd finished I didn't understand a word I'd read, so I started over again. I guess its message of hope never sank in.

Over the years, because of the damp conditions at Alcatraz, and the later years at McNeil Island in Puget Sound in the state of Washington, my health gradually went through a period of deterioration. While I was still at Alcatraz I developed an asthmatic condition. I also developed a bad heart. So much salt air and steel was around that I developed a lung condition along with everything else.

The Rock was strictly a one-horse show. The administration ran everything. No cons had an active part or say in the operation of the place. The administration thought of cons as animals and treated them as such. There was not a power structure. The way you got respect was that you had to be a real con. You couldn't be a sniveling cry baby. Remember, this was back in the thirties.

You could have a visit if you had a written approval from the warden. Of all the years I spent on The Rock, I never had a visit from the outside world. I was in lockup most of the time.

I was sent to Alcatraz for them to keep me, not for me to do slave labor. The only guidelines I was willing to abide by was that the government's duty was to contain me, not make me work at something I didn't want to do. So I didn't work. I never broke during my years at Alcatraz. I figured the only way I'd do that was the warden would have the guards try to kill me.

Nearly every act I performed involved my deep philosophy that everything the system did, I was against it. This is what kept me going. They'd hold something over my head. It would stay there for a year or so. I'd force their hand to drop it. If they didn't, I'd just forget it and go off into one of my daydreams. One of my favorite ones was that some kind of a miracle would destroy the island, and I would float to land and to freedom. Hell, I knew it wouldn't happen, but I never stopped dreaming it.

The cells were six feet by five feet. They were one-man cells. The bunks were on hinges and could be folded up against the wall during the day and let down during the night to sleep on. We would lift them and drop them, and they would make a lot of noise. Sometimes we all got together and did it in unison. This would scare hell out of the guards.

I remember times when the guards would come into the cell blocks and beg us to stop the racket; it was scaring members of their families who lived in houses at one end of the island. If there were only a few guys doing it, the guards would pick them out, take them down into the hole and work them over.

I kept up my interest in fingerprinting. I knew several people who tried to have their prints changed. I had my foundations removed back in '37 or '38. A finger at a time was done every month. The con who worked on them was a doctor who had lost his license in Oklahoma and was sent to prison for some trick he'd pulled. He did my fingers differently than the guy who had done Alvin Karpis' before "Old Creepy" was sent to prison. That guy had tried to peel the flesh back to the bone which made the end of Karpis' fingers look as though they had been put in a pencil sharpener. When Karpis saw the job that had been done on me, he got mad. I think he was jealous. He had my man work on his fingers some more.

Do you know what I used to do with my time? I thought of each holiday throughout the year. There were thirteen in all, and on each national holiday T-bone steaks would be served. When we saw the steaks we knew there was a holiday of some kind. We just learned to pace ourselves and live from holiday to holiday. We would set one holiday to reach, and when it came, we would start latching on to the next holiday. This may not seem like much to an outsider, but to us who were locked up, it was a way to keep on living.

Prisoners had to have a little humorous outlook for their own sanity. For example, one guy would say, "This year I'm giving up sex. Next year I'm giving up alcohol, and the following year I'm going to stop smoking. I've learned that too much of any one of these is injurious to my health." Then the cons would laugh about their promises. What else could we do?

On The Rock the officials would give us what cigarettes we had. Smuggling was almost an unheard of happening because of the tight security. For years I'd smoked cigars, beginning when I was a teen-ager. I thought they made me look like a big shot. When I had my booth back in Ft. Worth, instead of having a beer, I would slowly smoke a cigar. That's what I'd do when we used to have our meets. I'd sit there and smoke a cigar and look like a big shot. I had to quit smoking at Alcatraz. Later I found out that I had a bad pumper and I didn't want to touch it off if I could avoid it. But being the bull-headed individual that I am, I smoked again after I got off The Rock.

You ask how many times I've been in solitary. Let me answer that by asking you a question: How many meals have you eaten?

Every time you would walk crooked, you would be sent to the hole, at least on The Rock. No day was an easy day there; every day was hard.

Toward the middle of the 1930's I was once put in the hole for a total of twenty-seven months and ten days. It was a hell hole. I didn't have a shave or a bath all that time I was down in the shitter. When I came out I had a dark red beard a foot-and-a-half long; my hair was down past my shoulder blades. I was sent down there over a misunderstanding. I understood that I wasn't going to work. They understood I was.

A friend of mine refused to work. He was taken before Warden Johnston and when asked if he would work, he shook his head. "OK," Johnston said, "I'll talk to you next year." They sent the man down into the hole for a year and brought him up again and asked if he would work. He gave up and said that he would. I didn't give up.

During one long stretch that I was in the hole, Archie Hamilton was down in a cell near mine. He had also been put in there for not working. We would yell to each other, because we were separated by another hole. We had no way of seeing each other. The only time a con could see out was through the little slot which the guards used to put your food through. They would also stick other things through there as a form of punishment. This is when they might turn the hose on you or give you no food.

I always ate out of a paper cup and plate. Every chance I got I'd throw a cup of piss on the guard when he opened the slot, so I guess they could justify what they did to me.

One day two or three guards had just spoken to Archie. When they left, I shouted down, "What did they say?"

He hollered back, "They said they were going to do something to us they'd never done before."

I replied, "What in the hell would that be?"

"I guess they're going to fuck us. That's the only thing they haven't done so far."

We had a good laugh. That's the way we kept our sanity.

Part of my punishment, during that long stretch, would be what they called "strip cell status." This happened periodically, a month or two at a time. That's what would break up the monotony. All we had was a blanket and an old mattress pad. There was a hole in the floor just three or four inches across which was our toilet. We would have to squat over the hole the very best we could but invariably we didn't always hit the hole and some would land on the edges. The place stunk awful bad. In fact, it would get to stinking so bad that the guards couldn't take it.

The door was solid steel except the opening which was about six to eight inches high and sixteen to eighteen inches wide. The guards would use the regular old fire hose by pointing the nozzle through the slot. If you tried to get back in the corner, the stream of water would find you. All you could do was curse them. When you have only six feet of space to move around in, it's hard to get away from the water shooting out the end of one of those power hoses.

This was all part of the treatment. They called it therapy. They would say, "That'll teach you to buck Johnston." It only taught me that the system could get me only by killing me. What they really called therapy was a padded cell or wall-to-wall canvas. They would put you in there and try to make you think you were going insane. They argued that they were trying to protect you from yourself. When they would hose you down in the padded cell, it would burn your butt as you skittered across the canvas.

To keep my sanity, every morning I would ask myself a series of questions: Who am I? Where am I? What am I doing here? I would ask these questions just to keep track of what was real and what wasn't. I couldn't believe that one human being could do the things I've mentioned to another human, but they did.

After a few months in the hole, I could still distinguish a holiday meal and that alone renewed my faith in humanity, even though they did slop the food into one big pile.

During the whole twenty-seven months I never saw daylight. It was like going down into a dungeon, all the way down to the bottom. The passage down was a three-foot-wide concrete stairwell, and the cell was six feet long and five feet wide. There was no light. The guards would open the little slot in the door from time to time and shine the light in to take a look at us.

In the padded cell they went to the other extreme. It was bigger. There was a bright light in the corner at each end, and the lights were sunk into the wall so you couldn't get at them. They burned twenty-four hours, and you got so you had no sense of day or night. I preferred the dark in the hole.

There would be periods as long as seven days without food. I got all of this because I refused to work. On The Rock everybody worked. Not working was the cardinal sin. Remember, I spent most of those months in the dark without anything, not even a match.

Finally, I was taken back into the population. I was told not to give them any more static. But I never did do any work on The Rock unless I wanted to. I knew what they were doing; they were trying to break me. I did start helping others in the machine shop if they needed help and if I wanted to do it. Absolutely nobody made me work if I didn't want to.

When I came out of the hole they put me in the hospital. There they put me in a cage as if I were an animal. Bars were on all four sides. This cage was about eight feet by five. They wanted to get me used to the light and also to give me a good checking over. I spent about three weeks to a month there. I was finally clothed, but there was a stripped con right next to me. I was in pretty good physical condition and weighed around one hundred and seventy all the time.

I've seen as high as five legitimate doctors at one time in Alcatraz. Back then the per cent of doctors doing illegal work was much higher than it is now.

Two hundred and eighty-six convicts was about the greatest number of cons on The Rock at any one time. On the chain that went out to The Rock with me were a group of Greeks, a Polack, and a couple of Wops, along with two Blacks. Most of them were out of Chicago. I was the only notorious one on the chain. I'd say that seven out of every ten guys there were either Greek or Polack with a few Wops mixed in. And just about everybody, it seemed, got a dose of the hole. It was nothing to miss someone, who had been sent to the hole, for one, two or three years.

The ferries that ran back and forth from the island to the mainland were old rum running boats which had been confiscated. Later years these ferry boats would be named after different wardens like The Madigan, or The Bennet, after James Bennet who became director of The Bureau of Prisons.

One of the few joys I experienced while at Alcatraz, was when a tornado had ripped through the town of Tupelo, Mississippi, the place where I'd gone to rob a bank and there was no money. In my frustration I shot out all of the windows of the bank. One of the guards remembered the incident and said, "I see by the papers that a tornado just about wiped out your old stomping grounds."

I smiled. "I hope it didn't forget to level that bank."

When I was out of the hole and had a chance to mingle with the other prisoners, on rare occasions they would talk about the lights which they could see across the bay. But I didn't let myself dwell too much on them. I could see the lights of San Francisco. But I knew what I was doing and I could handle it. Some guys would look at them and pretty soon they'd go crazy with the longing to be out. I wasn't going to let myself become a border line case. They weren't putting me in any strait jacket.

Around '39 or '40 I was served with divorce papers. Kathryn had filed for divorce while she was in the female prison at Alderson, West Virginia. According to Texas law, even though we had never really gone before a preacher, we were considered as common-law husband and wife. If either of us ever married again we'd have to have a divorce. Kathryn didn't have the law in mind; she just wanted to get rid of any legal involvement with me. That was her way of doing it. Maybe it was her way of rubbing salt into my wounds.

In 1941 I wrote a letter to Charles Urschel out of frustration. It was an outlet for me to blow off steam. I had a faint hope that Urschel might somehow pull some strings and help me get off The Rock, but Urschel never answered the letter.

One day an official showed me an affadavit which said that I'd been born in Shelby County, Tennessee, in 1911. I chuckled quietly to myself, remembering that was one of the changes I'd made in my records back in 1930, while being held in Leavenworth.

I built up my shoulders, arms and chest area and became very strong during my years at Alcatraz by doing pushups. There's a great little game you play with close associates. If they make a slip in grammar, and you catch them, they pay with pushups. At first I did a lot of pushups, then I started thinking what I was about to say before I opened my mouth. This was one way I got a pretty liberal education. Of course, I've been doing pushups as far back as I can remember just to keep myself in trim.

In '43 I was charged with assault on an inmate. It was the one day I got off The Rock. I had to go to court, and the ride over and back turned out to be one of the greatest experiences I had while at Alcatraz. It gave me a change of scenery and a chance to breathe some free air.

A lot of people on The Rock were queers, but I didn't play the game. I'd let nature take its course. There would be papas and mammas and they would switch around. When I took a shower I'd just wash real fast. A few times in later years on McNeil Island I did get involved in the action by giving some cigarettes for a treat. I found it repulsive so I went back to the shower and my scrubbing.

I lived day by day. There was a grunt here and a grunt there. I could cover the people on one page that I talked to and what I said. Some of the men from out of my past were on The Rock such as

Alfred Bates, Harvey Bailey, John Paul Chase, Archie Hamilton, Doc Barker and Alvin Karpis. They had all tried to buck the laws and the legal systems on the outside just as I had and got caught in their own trap. We didn't have much of a chance to exchange happenings of the past. With all the rules and regulations they had in those early years, it was hard enough just to talk to ourselves. The least infraction was a ticket to the hole.

I actually felt out of place on the Rock. You know you have rules and regulations everywhere you go in a federal penitentiary, but on Alcatraz they were iron clad. They had their do's and don'ts which I thought were ridiculous. The whole system was to make robots out of us. Why? I don't know. At the time when I was doing all my crimes, I didn't have hatred as they seemed to have on The Rock. I was doing the kind of job I had chosen to do and felt that I was darned good at it, but what I did was animalistic to John Q. Public.

One episode comes to mind that happened during an interview with Jim Dobkins. A fly landed on my hand. I jerked my hand and in one quick motion grabbed the fly. I looked at it, dashed it down on the floor and stepped on it.

I dislike flies; they're always around to bother you. Maybe I'm kin to them. Maybe that's the reason I'm here. I bothered a lot of people.

"Then I went for the third one. I was still cutting on him when the guards arrived and jerked me away."

19. Baby-Sitting Can Be Hazardous To Your Health

Even in the airtight confines of Alcatraz, with its purported incorruptible guards and staff, I was able to arrange things. One of the things I arranged was the smuggling in of contraband. I did it through the connections that I made: a kitchen steward here, a guard there.

Before World War II broke out and a few months after my longest sojourn in the hole, I was holding some powerful contraband. Three other prisoners confronted me in the machine shop. They wanted what I had, the contraband which I was holding for someone else. I was baby-sitting; that's what they call it on Alcatraz. In this case it was narcotics, a cache of heroin.

Of course, on Alcatraz anything that was good was considered as illegal. I'm not saying that narcotics is good, but most anything other than the food they gave you and the clothes you wore was contraband.

I was in the machine shop looking for something when the three cons came in. One of them put a shank to me. He stuck it up against my ribs. Then he and the other cons pushed me against the work bench. They demanded that I tell them where the heroin was.

I refused.

On top of the work bench where they had pushed me was a hammer. After making several threats, one of the cons picked up the hammer and knocked me down by hitting me in the back of the head a couple of times.

I didn't realize at the time that those two blows would leave a couple of mighty bad dents in the back of my skull. As I started to pick myself up off the floor, I was seeing double. It was all I could do to get back on my feet. When I stood up once more they grabbed me and put my left hand in the vise which was on one end of the work bench. They began to screw the vise shut, and it became tight enough to make me want to scream.

I did scream as loud as I could and yanked on my hand at the same time and managed to get it out of the vise before they had it tight enough to flatten all my fingers. As it was, I had to have surgery later to repair my wrist, and I'll carry scars on my fingers which the vise caused for the rest of my life.

I guess when I screamed and pulled my hand free, I caught the three cons momentarily off guard. The one who hit me with the hammer had laid it back down on the work bench. I managed to get hold of its handle with my right hand and began swinging. The one who had held the shank on me got the first blow. I struck him up on the side of the head and heard something crack. He dropped the shank on the work bench. I grabbed it and ripped the second con's guts open, practically disemboweling him. Then I went for the third one. I was still cutting on him when the guards arrived and jerked me away.

That little episode greatly increased my reputation as being a dangerous man, especially when provoked. I gained instant respect from other cons who had never even bothered to look at me before.

My wrist, as I said, required surgery. When I jerked my fingers out of the vise, I pulled something loose. It was six months before I could use it again. They also had to put some steel strips in the back of my head where that hammer did its dirty work.

I'm sorry to say that all three of the cons survived, but each one had a long vacation in the hospital before he was able to get up and around.

I'll say again: I never had a fight that I didn't plan on having. When they hit me with that hammer, I made my plan right then that it was either them or me. I wasn't ready to die. I looked on the whole thing as a matter of survival; they would live or I would. My reaction was to save myself. There wasn't time to talk things over.

You ask how the heroin was smuggled in. Well, it came in by someone who was on my payroll. I had made arrangements through a guard to bring it in. You see, I've never underestimated anyone. The minute I saw that guard, I knew he could be bought off.

Yes, those cons would have got the upper hand that day if I hadn't continued my home work over the years of doing pushups. My arms and hands had become so strong that when I got hold of that hammer I was as big as all three of those cons put together.

"Of course, what I should have done was to swallow two or three pages of newspapers and then a pair of glasses. I could read the paper in a nice quiet way and nobody could see what I was reading."

20. Of Buttons, Spoons And Toilet Paper

Many men tried to escape from Alcatraz during my years on The Rock. None succeeded. I saw the remains of two fellows who'd gotten to the water but were defeated by the cold and the crabs; their faces had been eaten off and their chest cavities had been eaten out. But even seeing such sights did not deter me from making my own escape plans.

I don't believe anybody ever made a successful escape from Alcatraz. They didn't have any death row on The Rock. The whole island was a death row. I'd say that nearly all the prisoners thought deeply at different times, trying to figure out ways to escape. Not many of them actually tried though, and were most certainly not successful, at least during the years I was there.

Some escape atempts which I became aware of never did materialize. Other cons, like myself, just dreamed of escape. It proved to be another way of spending time and exercising the brain.

One time I had a connection through a hospital employee and a kitchen steward. Those were the associations I used at the time when I went on deadlock. I had my fingers operated on and had the foundations removed from my finger tips which would alter my fingerprints. They had plenty of time to heal because I was on deadlock. I had money which helped me arrange to take care of the work. We called the doctor "Burnie" or just simply "Doc." Money to pay him was channeled through one of those staff members.

Through these same arrangements I managed to get the devices with morphine called jabbers. They were used while the doc was butchering my fingers. The jabbers cost a nice sum of money over a period of months. I'd had money put in boxes at a bus station and at a railroad station. There were people on the outside who were anxious to help me; they helped with projects such as these.

The money would be put in one of those places and my contact on The Rock would be told where to pick it up. It was all part of a plan which never materialized. I wanted to bust off The Rock, but I didn't want to bust off like Nash did, the time we got him at the Union Station. The people who were helping me were there primarily to really give aid when I got off The Rock. And of course my end, to get off The Rock, was the hardest part of all.

I figured out that my best chance was to become deathly ill, to come up with a type of illness which couldn't be treated there on The Rock. They would have to send me to a public hospital or at least some place on the mainland. This would give me a chance to escape.

My first step was I ate a whole roll of shit paper, trying to get sick. I had a hell of a physical constitution. I got it all down. The funny thing was it started tasting good. I was afraid I'd get hooked on toilet paper. Somebody had told me that eating paper was a cinch. It would cause blockage and I'd have to have surgery. After I'd consumed the paper, I realized that I'd eaten my two weeks' supply. We were only given one roll every two weeks.

Well, my action got me in trouble; I had to start wiping Japanese fashion by using my fingers. I also have to add that I've never found any two tissues with the same flavor. Of course, what I should have done was to swallow two or three pages of newspapers and then a pair of glasses. I could read the paper in a nice quiet way and nobody could see what I was reading.

One con smuggled in a large metal spoon out of the kitchen area. He swallowed it — he told me ahead of time what he was going to do. When he was in the exercise yard, he held his head back like a sword swallower and pushed the spoon, which he had greased from the fat of a piece of meat, down his throat until it slid into his stomach. All they did was take him to the prison hospital, operate on him by cutting him open, and removed the spoon. He was back in the population ten days later. I never heard of his swallowing anything else. After I had seen what happened to him, I made up my mind right then that I didn't want to swallow anything big.

One time in desperation, I swallowed twenty-five buttons I'd collected. All that happened was I gained a pound-and-a-half and nobody knew the difference. Someone did say there were some buttons missing. Another con ate a spoonful of lye. They cut him open, did some scraping, then stitched him up and he, too, was back in the population in less than a week. This incident made me more careful than ever what I put in my mouth. But as careful as I became, I managed to get food poisoning and had to get my stomach pumped out. This time I wasn't even trying to get sick.

As my influence grew while I was on The Rock, I could have things done that had to be done. But I never tried to get a gun. I knew it wouldn't have done me a bit of good. What finally got me off The Rock was graft, pure and simple.

"Two of the men, who were put in strip cells after the riot, decapitated themselves. Yes, the story was they had cut their heads right off. But what really happened..."

21. An Identity Crisis

Through the development of two "great white fathers" in the United States Justice Department, plus official concern that I might be killed by some convict status seeker, gears started turning in 1945 for a possible change of location and identity for me. This was the beginning of a new life. Let me elaborate.

The identity change was supposed to be permanent. It was never to be brought to anyone's attention. Law enforcement officers were not to know about it. It was not to be detrimental; it was to be for my benefit.

Of course, I planned on abiding by the rules that were set up for me to follow. I could look ahead now that they were taking steps which would bring about my release in four or five years; but this was an assumption on my part. The way everything was being handled, I thought I would be released in that time limit, which would still be in the 1940's. This would give me a chance to start life all over again with another identity, aside from "Machine Gun" Kelly.

I honestly felt that the government was going to use me, when I was approached for the identity change, for some kind of cancer research. This was just another way that they could build up an excuse if something drastic happened during the experiment. Since I was a con, if something did happen, nothing would ever have to be explained to the public or to my family, who wouldn't give a damn anyway.

But thanks to the riot, the identity change procedure was tabled, but not until the records had been prepared indicating my death. It was those records which prompted Richard Hammer, in a 1973 series of crime articles which appeared in PLAYBOY MAGAZINE, to write that I died in 1946 while in Alcatraz.

Someone came out from the Bureau of Prisons. I think it was early in 1946. They talked to a group, two or three of us, and started laying the groundwork for our identity change. We were a little leery of the situation because we'd heard some talk through the grapevine about some kind of drug experimentation program. You'd never guess what our big interest was — extra smokes for us. That was the attitude we had when we went before the representative from the Bureau.

He explained to us about an identity change. He claimed that we as convicts would be changed completely, that all efforts would be taken to cover up our past. Eventually we'd have a good chance of being phased back into society in such a manner that it wouldn't endanger our lives.

I was doubtful if the plan would work because it hadn't been too many years when my life wasn't worth a plugged nickle. If certain people found me, they wouldn't hesitate to gain revenge. All I could do was wait and see what would happen. At least it was a chance to get off The Rock.

My "great white fathers" were earning their keep. Of course, I knew their plan — they wanted to make a rakeoff. They had looked after me since they were youngsters. I had known them in the 1930's. I've always had someone to look out for me, even now. Yes, I have one at the present time, the fourth one I've had in the last almost forty years. He doesn't work directly under the Bureau of Prisons; he works in a special office of the Justice Department. I don't know the official name of the office.

Two of them were working in my corner before 1945 and right up until the riot happened. I've given them my word that I will never reveal their real names to anybody.

Convicts coming out of the war were a younger bunch of guys, a different breed from the old cons. If they didn't like you they would ease up behind, stab you and vanish. Once you get a shank stuck in your kidney, you can't defend yourself very well. In a way they were responsible for the riot of 1946. When it started I didn't get out in front, but the fact that I was on The Rock made me a participant.

The officials ordered five thousand combat marines to come to the island. When things really got under way and some heads were being cracked, I went back to my house and listened to the noise from there.

There were eleven or twelve inmates killed during the fracas. When it was over we were all put in the lockup; there were no work crews for a while, which caused the loudest protest of the whole riot. That night everyone raised bunks and let them slam down which made a tremendous racket. This was the time that some of the guards came in and pleaded with us to be quiet because the noise was scaring the daylights out of their wives and children who were living in the guards' quarters on the island.

In the aftermath of the riot they only tried six cons after bringing indictments against twenty-nine. The first six they put the snatch on were convicted. It didn't make any difference which six. Most of these cons already had nine hundred years or so. One had three life terms plus nine hundred years to serve. He was either a Polack or a Greek out of Chicago. He couldn't care less how much additional time he got.

Two of the men, who were put in strip cells after the riot, decapitated themselves. Yes, the story was they had cut their heads right off. But what really happened, two guards had been killed during the early part of the riot, so some guards singled out these two cons and cut their heads off. Records were prepared indicating that these two inmates had committed suicide. The whole thing is mighty strange. Can you imagine anyone living long enough to cut his head completely off?

Old Man Stroud, who later became known as "The Bird Man of Alcatraz," was one con you didn't fool around with. He was a degenerate queer. He was what we called "released to death." He is the only con I knew who had cigarettes all the time. His cell was double size, and there was a storage room next to his cell, and he was allowed to use it. He'd take cigarettes wrapped in a towel down to the shower and come back giggling and say, "I got two today!" He was a dirty old homosexual and was also psychotic.

Well, during the riot Old Stroud sure had a ball! He went around disemboweling bodies of the dead cons and laughed as if he were at a wild party. I never did like the old son of a bitch, but when I heard this I hated him more than ever. Any time after that he'd come up and try to rap with me, I'd walk away. I didn't want to associate with him. After all, I did have a certain amount of principle that he never had. Yet, the book and movie entitled THE BIRD MAN OF ALCATRAZ made a hero out of him. He was absolutely the scum of the earth.

"Because President Eisenhower was responsible for getting Meatball sent back to Japan, I could never stomach Ike after that."

22. A Hanging For Meatball

Tomoya Kawakita was a Japanese fellow born in El Centro, California. Not long before World War II broke out hot and heavy on the Pacific front, he went to Japan to study at Meijii University. He stayed there after the fireworks started, building up quite a reputation as a foreman at the Oeyama Prisoner of War Camp on Honshu. He was an evil man. His trademark was kicking fallen GI's in the face and then having them rolled into a cesspool. He came back to the States after the war; was nabbed in 1948, then was given the death sentence which President Eisenhower would later commute to life. He eventually was sent to Alcatraz.

We called him Meatball.

The word was that he was responsible for killing thirty-five hundred American GI's. That made him the scum of the earth. He sure had his nerve just up and coming back to California when the war was over.

But the guy couldn't stay anonymous.

One day he was seen by a GI who'd done time at Oeyama, where Meatball was the big cheese. He went to the authorities and told them about many of the terrible things Meatball had done and that he allowed to be done at his orders. Meatball was arrested and later went to trial. He was convicted.

My association with Meatball was brief.

At Alcatraz, Meatball spent his time mopping floors and living in the hospital facility. Putting him with the regular prison population likely would have meant certain death. I and another prisoner, a big Polack named Trianoski, had our own plans for Meatball. Ski, the nickname given Trianoski, and I had adjoining cages in the hospital. We had just been brought out from a tour of duty in the hole at the same time which caused us to be neighbors in the hospital.

The episode happened early in the 1950's shortly after I'd been returned to Alcatraz from Leavenworth for a punitive measure. Ski had taken his towel and torn it into thin strips and then tied them together. He and I lured Meatball close enough to our cages while he was in the process of buffing the floors, and grabbed him.

The guards rushed in and rescued him before we could do a good job of hanging the son of a bitch.

But that didn't stop us. Two days later we grabbed Meatball again. This time Ski tried to pull hard enough on Meatball's legs while I held his head and shoulders still. We already had the towel pieces around his neck and were doing a fine job of stretching it. Once more the guards rushed in and saved the bastard.

Meatball really was dumb. He allowed Ski to lure him back two days later after we'd tried to kill him. He just couldn't resist Ski's Polish charm. He'd say, "My gosh, Meatball buddy, I'm sorry things turned out the way they did. To show there's no hard feelings, here's a cigarette for you." And two days later we had him hanging again, but, like I said, the guards rescued him.

Neither one of us was mad in our determination to kill Meatball. We'd do anything to get off The Rock so we'd be shipped to Springfield or to some other facility where we'd have a better chance to escape. I've used so many maneuvers to get my way. When I'd act insane, the authorities knew that I was playing a game with them. But I always had visions of being put in a state institution where I'd have a realistic hope of making an escape.

I don't know if it was true or not, but years later, I heard that Meatball was found decapitated in an alley only a month after he was deported back to Japan. All of the safety precautions that were taken at Alcatraz, having him live in the hospital area twenty-four hours a day, did not prevent him from getting what was coming to him. The officials weren't taking any chances of a possible international incident of having him killed by an inmate in the population.

Because President Eisenhower was responsible for getting Meatball sent back to Japan, I could never stomach Ike after that. I hated him so much that I even started thinking of ways to kidnap either David Eisenhower or the Nixon girls, Julie or Tricia. This would have been my way of getting even with Ike. Tricia would have been my pick. She was dumb but she had a good body.

"Dr. Tensil believed me, but not the head doctor. As soon as my doctor went on vacation, I was on the first train to McNeil Island."

23. The Drain Pipe Is A Stadium

An unusual escape attempt materialized when Ski and I wound up with "P" numbers, the "P" standing for psychiatric. This happened at the same time when we were in the federal prison hospital at Springfield, Missouri. Ski had been assigned the job of being a butcher in the kitchen and he found out about the drain pipe beneath the freight elevator. Ski, myself and two other prisoners planned an escape through the drain pipe out into a dry lake bed.

There was an elevator in the dining room and underneath the elevator was where we went into the drain pipe. Ski planned the whole thing. It was my idea to be the last man out so the other three could get a good start. I crawled in behind them, and when they reached the other end of the drain pipe some guards were waiting. Of course, they caught me, too.

Immediately I started putting on one of the best acts I've ever pulled in prison. I told them I was just watching a baseball game in a stadium. I was quite convincing. My doctor, Dr. Tensil, a Harvard graduate, was naive. He was totally convinced that I, as his patient, had simply followed the other three inmates, thinking that they were watching the same baseball game that I was going to. Dr. Tensil believed me, but not the head doctor. As soon as my doctor went on vacation, I was on the first train to McNeil Island.

I was informed later that Ski had been taken out of the butcher shop and was transferred to the hobby shop, which was underground.

Ski was a big, easy-going Polack, but he was a man, and he was mean. I couldn't want a better friend; he was loyal. He'd gotten a fifty-year sentence for bank robbery. He'd been framed because they wanted him. They knew he was guilty of a lot of stuff they couldn't get him on so they set him up in this bank robbery frame. The last I'd heard of him, he had put in nearly thirty years and was going to be released on probation.

"I had already been deceased, buried and the whole thing when I was informed of my passing."

24. Premature Burial

My "official" death took place at Leavenworth on July 17, 1954. It was arranged on the prison movement sheet, showing me checking into the hospital late one night. I'd been sitting by the handball court earlier that day and they arranged it so it would look like I had a heart attack and died during the night.

Actually what happened, I went to get my medication in the hospital. They made it appear that I'd checked in. During the middle of the night they put me in the hole. Six days later I found out what really happened.

I had already been deceased, buried and the whole thing when I was informed of my passing. All different kinds of thoughts ran through my mind, because that first night, when they took me down into the hole, they didn't tell me anything. They just locked me up. I wondered then if they had found some kind of contraband; money I'd hidden or a knife I'd stashed away. I always had contraband.

I didn't know what was happening. I'd already agreed to the identity change which the "great white fathers" and the Justice Department would eventually arrange, but after the riot several years earlier on Alcatraz, I never thought that would come about. Although I must admit my hopes flared sky high for a while in 1948 when I was transferred from The Rock to Leavenworth.

Then when they finally came, six days later, and talked to me, imagine my surprise when I was told that I'd been buried out on Pissant Hill, which was a "no name" cemetery at Leavenworth. Hear me right. They claimed that George "Machine Gun" Kelly was dead and buried.

Well, I know one thing for sure, the guy wasn't me.

On the same night that I was taken down into the hole, extraordinary arrangements were effected for the benefit of the other inmates and the public. Earlier that day an old con had been stabbed to death. He was put in a simple wooden box and was given my name. This body was taken out, and all who saw the box were told that the cadaver inside was George "Machine Gun" Kelly, who had died during the night from a heart attack.

Later I found out that the wooden casket was shipped to the

133

Christian Brothers Funeral Home in Decatur, Wise County, Texas. R. G. Shannon made the funeral arrangements. The funeral was an afternoon affair on July 25, and the mysterious cadaver was lowered into a six-foot hole later that day at the Cottondale Cemetery.

Meanwhile, the Bureau of Prisons had released a news story listing me as having been born on July 17, 1895 and kicking the bucket on my fifty-ninth birthday, July 17, 1954. I really and truly have no idea where the 1895 year of birth originated. I do think that the choice of the cemetery was a nice touch. It's just a few miles from the old Shannon farm where I held Charles Urschel captive twenty-one years earlier.

On the night when they came into the hole to tell me that I'd already been buried, they told me I was being shipped out to Kansas City. I hated like hell to be taken to another jail because I'd come to look on Leavenworth as home, if I had to be locked up. But they said this was my first step toward the new identity change. I didn't have any choice but to go along with their plans.

I say Leavenworth had been good to me. Let me elaborate. In 1950 three of my children visited me there: Doug, Wayne and Gail. It was the first time I'd ever seen any of them. They each had different mothers and they were now about sixteen or seventeen. From then on they visited me from time to time over a period of years.

At Leavenworth I learned to slow down the pace of my heart. I became a slow walker and a slow mover. Yes, I learned to relax and to rest. I would often sit in what was called the handball circle and watch handball games. Sometimes my old friend, Harvey Bailey, would be there with me. Other times I'd visit with Doug Hardy, who was around quite often. I also worked in the library and figured out methods to improve their old archaic filing system.

But bad pumper and all, I wasn't able to keep out of trouble. I was charged as being a ringleader and starting a riot in the mess hall. Another time I was caught with a supply of contraband milk. I was put in the hole and pounded on by four screws. Big Mitch, a three-hundred-and-seventy-pound guard, later evened the score for me by personally working over the instigating guard at a place outside the prison complex. Those guards took turns beating on me. I worked back the best I could, but I was pretty badly outnumbered. The hole was the only place they could fight you and not get into trouble. Oh, they did it in other places, but the hole was pretty secluded.

When Big Mitch saw me all beat up he made me tell him what had happened. He was something else. If you wanted to fight him, he'd fight you fair and square, all three-hundred-seventy pounds of him. He was only about five feet ten and most of him was muscle. He'd knock you down every time you got to your feet and started toward him. Then he'd laugh and say, "Now come on, man, you can do better than that. You wanted to fight. I'm standing here waiting for you to begin and you're laying around on your tail like you're all worn out. Don't keep me waiting. I've got things to do."

Anyway, while the Bureau of Prisons had assigned me an 1895 birth date, the new Kelly, John H. Webb, had birth dates ranging between 1911 and 1922. Various files had Webb being born in 1911, 1915, 1916 and 1922. Who says certain prison and Justice Department people can't be funny?

Not very many guys can be born during that many different years. Probably before I die, I'll also be killed that many times. Hell, nobody's going to kill me. You just wait and see. I'll die because my old pumper stopped working, not by anybody's bullet.

"That morning I experienced a new kind of thrill, real excitement, as I watched that door swing out. I had that chair leg raised high over my head and almost wanted to throw back my head and laugh, thinking what I was about to do."

25. 10-B For Torture

Like I said, I'd spent six days in the hole at Leavenworth when a visitor told me I'd died on the night of July 17, 1954, of "coronary thrombosis." I was to be smuggled out and would start on a long series of trips which were all supposed to be connected with my identity change.

I was no longer George Kelly but a John Doe. I was taken out of the hole in the middle of the night and rushed away to Kansas City where they kept me for two months. Next, I was taken to Oklahoma City, where I stayed for almost six months. Then I was sent to Dallas County Jail where I was kept in isolation.

It was in Dallas that I was given a choice of names. The first one was Merle Hydeman; the second was John H. Webb. The H. stood for Harvey. How they came up with John Harvey was because it was part of my old pal's name, John Harvey Bailey. I had told them about him when we were talking about possible names. I recalled how he and I used to trade names when we would send a telegram to each other. We wanted to confuse anyone who was sending them.

For the next few years I was traveling. I'd spend a few months in one place while they were waiting for a U.S. marshal to come along. Then I would be a body for that marshal to take to another place. They wouldn't fingerprint me or book me. I was just John Webb, on hold.

At first I figured that it wouldn't be too long before I'd be released back into civilization with my new identity. But after a number of months, when there was no further contact with representatives from the Justice Department, I figured the only way I'd ever get out would be for me to use my own initiative. I would wait for a chance to present itself, and I decided to take advantage of every opportunity. From then on until I was released, I would attempt eleven escapes.

Behind the scenes, my "great white fathers," who worked in the Justice Department, were putting into effect a TX number for me. A TX number is not commonly known to the public. The numbers are assigned by the Justice Department to certain individuals for various reasons to have their identities changed. There is a master file in the Department which lists these TX numbers given to persons throughout the United States.

After the TX number had been assigned to me, I was given a completely new identity: prison records, rap sheets, etc. A woman in Memphis, Tennessee, had been contacted to pose as my real mother should the need for such a person arise. She had been a friend of mine back in my youth and had helped me in various ways at different times since then, such as handling some business arrangements after my crime sprees.

She was ten years older than I was but looked more than that. She had always been someone I could turn to when I needed help. I can truthfully say that she was really more of a mother to me than my own, and I'll always be thankful that she protected me as she did.

I've already told you that we were not allowed to write letters at Alcatraz, but when I was at Leavenworth I wrote to her and she would write to me. It was back in 1949, right after the first big heart attack I'd had at Leavenworth, when I started writing to her regularly. I had a whole string of other attacks which popped up like popcorn. She sure was a big help getting me through this period. Even when I would write and inform her of the trouble I was having with my pumper, and that I knew that one of those attacks would do me in, she would write back and cheer me up. I'll always be in debt to her.

I experienced my worst solitary confinement in the Los Angeles County Jail. Naturally, the second time I was going to be put in there, I began to plan an escape. Shortly before we were to arrive I started telling the marshals that I had to go to the bathroom right then or I'd be forced to go in my pants. They stopped at a filling station and one of the marshals escorted me to the toilet. After I'd finished and was going back to the car, I saw a T-Bird pull into the station and watched the driver jump out and go into the building.

He left the engine running. Even though I was handcuffed and had chains around my ankles, I saw that the marshal guarding me was still in the rest room so I quickly hopped over to the T-Bird, dumped myself into the seat, got it rolling and raced away at full speed. Taking an evasive turn into what I thought was a road leading off the main highway, I ended up right in the middle of a highway patrol maintenance yard.

After that, when anyone asked me if I considered myself an

escape artist, I would crack a faint smile: "Yeah, about five minutes worth."

My attempts have never really paid off. I've jumped out of cars and tried to run. I knew I didn't have a chance, but there's always that possibility that the cuffs and leg irons might fall off. You've got to keep hoping. I wouldn't let myself believe that I'd never get out.

I guess my determination mounted after spending time in each place where I was locked up. I remember once while I was in transit, they dropped me off again at the Los Angeles County Jail. I was put in the small confinement area which couldn't have been over seven feet deep by six feet wide. It had a commode and one little sink. There must have been fifteen prisoners in there, blacks, whites, browns — all in one big heap. When we stretched out to sleep we had a real problem. When one of us turned over, all of us had to turn over. I raised hell with the marshals when they came to pick me up. All they did was say, "Well, we'll look into it."

Finally, they put me in Springfield, the federal prison hospital in Missouri. During my stay there I was able to eat more than the normal food portion because of a crazy con named Snyder. He was a big guy. I always made it a point to walk behind him in the chow line and he got so he liked me. As we went down the line he would say, "Three for me and three for my friend." He was so vicious looking that the fellows on the line never gave him an argument.

During my several visits at Springfield — I spent about seventeen months there — I never slept in dormitories. They always put me in a single room. As far as I was concerned, Springfield was just one large nut house.

I do remember a woman psychiatrist there whose name was Rose. She had studied my jacket and learned that I was a violent man. I guess this was responsible for her being afraid of me. She would never allow me to get close to her. One day when we were together, I volunteered to go on a simple errand for her. She needed something in a hurry and was willing to send me for it. I made the trip in record breaking time. When I returned she thanked me, then we sat down and talked. She admitted that she had been afraid of me and had judged me wrongly. She should have discussed my problems with me before forming an opinion.

After that we became good friends. She would allow me to do many things for her such as pouring hot coffee, running errands, and so forth. I was kind of sad when they yanked me out of the facility and put me on the road again. Frankly, I think Rose was sorry to see me go. I tried to argue with the officials that she was really helping me, but I was just another con to them, another body to shuffle around. I didn't mean any more to them than a bag of potatoes.

I was taken to the Rocky Butte Jail in Portland, Oregon, then to a jail in Medford, Oregon, and finally back to the Los Angeles County Jail where I spent eight months in that stinking place. It was really a drag as a jail. An earthquake had damaged it since I was there the last time, which made it worse than ever.

I grew more bitter and decided that I was going to try every means to escape whether an opportunity presented itself or not. I anxiously waited to be transferred again so I could put a few of my ideas into practice.

After they had staged my funeral in my behalf earlier, I figured it wouldn't be too long before I'd be released. Quite a number of months had now passed since I'd had any contact with the Justice Department. I wondered what had gone wrong.

The year 1958 was one of varied events for me. That was the year my sons, Doug and Wayne, legally changed their last names from Wilson and Rhodes to Webb. That was also the year Kathryn got out of prison on an appeal bond when the FBI refused to make public its files on her. Those files could exonerate her for her alleged part in writing the ransom notes. I heard that after she was released she went to the Cottondale Cemetery and walked across my grave. She'll be madder 'n an old wet hen when she finds out I'm not buried there.

Also during 1958, J. Edgar Hoover remarked in a speech, "Kelly, that punk, is still safely behind bars." It was a slip on Hoover's part.

It was also the year I heard about Melvin Purvis committing suicide. I regretted that I'd been unable to fulfill my dream of using my own special means of torturing him to death. That rotten scum Purvis was so bad and such a liar that he couldn't live with himself any longer. He had to put himself out of his misery.

Finally I made the circle. I was returned to Springfield. Immediately I was subjected to what they called "punitive treatment." It was torture. For six consecutive weeks I was taken to Ten B, one of the major buildings. Each building at Springfield is numbered or lettered. Ten B was the psychiatric building.

Ten B therapy was brutal and illegal. It consisted of placing me in a strait jacket, then they put me in a large metal tub which had a few inches of water in the bottom. Next they stuck my head through a canvas cover stretched over the top of the tub, and brought out my arms, then they made the canvas secure just under my armpits. When everything was ready, someone flipped the switch. A couple of buzzes knocked fire out of my ass and the skin off the bottom of my feet. I actually felt that I was burned to a cinder. I don't know the voltage they used; it would take an electrician to figure that out. All I know is if it took an electrician to rob banks, I'd be the best electrician.

This kind of treatment made me take great joy in fighting the guys in the goon squad. They'd come and get me on Wednesday morning and I'd be waiting for them. As luck would have it, I'd managed to break the leg off a maple chair and smuggled it into my room. This was after the third treatment. I'm not exaggerating when I say I'd kill every one of those guys if I got the chance, and now it looked like I had a chance to at least mess them up. I sure didn't want any more of those treatments.

They came and knocked on the door to my room. One of them said, "OK, Webb, come out right now."

"I'll come out in thirty minutes."

The goon leader shouted, "Get your ass out here or we're coming in after you!"

"Why, come on in, fellows," I said. "I haven't had any company since you were here the last time."

I didn't budge. I had taken up a position against the wall where they would have to come inside the room to see me. I knew they'd try to rush me. I had to get my licks in fast and hard. They knew better than to come in my room casually. Usually I'd get some good licks in with my fists before they overpowered me with blows and kicks.

That morning I experienced a new kind of thrill, real excitement, as I watched that door swing out. I had that chair leg raised high over my head and almost wanted to throw back my head and laugh, thinking what I was about to do. Two of them crowded in at the same time. I got both of them with one swat. Before they hit the floor, I slammed the chair leg into their faces and was delighted when I heard the cracking of noses and cheek bones. My arm was just going up for another swing when two other goons rushed in and grabbed me. We all went down to wallow in the blood and gore spurting from the first two.

The head guard's name was Callahan. He was one of the two to come into the room first. He and his friend were out of circulation for almost three months, and the word I got was concussion, broken noses and face bones. You see, they never did pull any punches, and I didn't see any reason why I should. Of course, I got some additional shock treatments, but the punishment didn't bother me nearly as much as my treatment bothered those two goons.

You get so you'd rather they would treat you mean physically; this gives you a chance to react. Beating those two guys up wasn't the real reason their friends gave me additional shock treatments. They just had to show me that I wasn't so tough. It was the sum total of everything they didn't like about me. You see, they couldn't make me conform. They knew I'd swing on anyone and everything, even the wall. They didn't feel I was off my rocker. They felt that I was a rebel and they were out to break me. Of course, they never did.

Next to the last time they put me in the tub, they came inside the room after me. I was flailing them with my fists for all I was worth. They got me out in the hall while I was still fighting. I got one arm free and brought it around in a good roundhouse swing and made a blind connection. One of them had his arm around my head. When I managed to get my head free I saw Rose, the psychiatrist, laying on the floor. She had passed by right at the instant I'd made that swing. I had connected on the end of her chin. I really felt like a heel.

Later she told me that she didn't hold my actions against me. She knew that it had been an accident; I wasn't trying to clobber her. She was sympathetic to my situation and what they were doing to me. Right after that the shock treatments stopped. I'm sure she was responsible in bringing them to an end.

I shortly left Springfield and did not return until four years later, in 1962.

"When the gagging started, I'd lean as far forward as my chains would let me, and as the vomit would come up I'd spray the backs of the marshals' necks and shoulders."

26. Mush And Cigarette Butts

My eleventh escape attempt proved to be my most crude, yet most successful. It happened in 1962. Two United States marshals were transporting me and another prisoner called Pappy from Springfield to McNeil Island. The escape took place in New Mexico, a short distance from Albuquerque, in the early evening.

I'd been urping for three days in the car, which one of the marshals had told us belonged to his wife and he wanted us to help him take care of it. That was my invitation to go into action.

At night when they'd leave us in a county jail, Pappy and I would plan our strategy. Just before we'd start riding the next morning, I'd eat a couple of "roll your own" cigarettes, paper and all, which I'd have rolled up in my shirt sleeve. They were handy. I could grab them with my teeth without either of the marshals being the wiser. The usual breakfast menu consisted of oatmeal, and I'm here to tell you that oatmeal mixed with swallowed tobacco makes quite a rotten vomit.

I'd wait until we'd get out of town, then start pumping up a lot of spit and swallowing it. It's a repulsive taste when that mixture begins bubbling around in your stomach, but once I got to barfing, I'd barf for hours with little assistance from anything else. And when I got to gagging, those two marshals would start ducking. Pappy and I knew that sooner or later one or both of them would get careless.

When the gagging started, I'd lean as far forward as my chains would let me, and as the vomit would come up I'd spray the backs of the marshals' necks and shoulders. They sure didn't like that and would cuss a blue streak. Of course, I remained as innocent as Mary's little lamb. I claimed car sickness. At the next stop they would have to take time out to clean up so they could stand themselves. They'd get a hose and give the inside of the car a good going over.

Well, they finally got careless late in the afternoon of the third day we were on the road. We were driving along south of Albuquerque. It was about five in the afternoon. I knew we'd soon be stopping for the night, and I was anxious to be on my own, not in some county jail. I started to gag and just then there was a sign that said there was a rest stop just up the road.

The one driving turned around and said, "Hold it, Webb. I don't want any more of your damned vomit. We'll pull in and you can throw up your liver for all I care."

I looked over at Pappy and gave him a big wink.

The car we were riding in was a two-door. Of course, me and Pappy were all shackled and handcuffed in the back seat. Even before the car had stopped, the marshal who wasn't driving, had turned around and was unlocking the leg irons so I could walk to the rest room. When the car stopped, Pappy and I jumped out and the marshal undid the waist chains on me. "Since you're about to puke, just walk ahead of me toward the toilet."

I knew that very instant I had him, and Pappy knew it, too. I'd already pegged this marshal as being the more lax of the two. I'd been studying him ever since we left Springfield. All I had to do was catch him off guard. In the past, the other marshal always went into the toilet first to look things over. He had never loosened the chains that bound me and Pappy together. This time both of them had let down their guard just because they didn't want me to spray them.

When I stepped through that rest room door, he was right behind me. I gave him a backhand right across the bridge of the nose with my handcuffed wrist, and as he was falling I place kicked him in the groin and smiled when I heard him grunt. He had no more than hit the floor of that large wash room when I had his revolver. I knew exactly where he kept his key to the handcuffs and it didn't take me but a minute to get it and set myself free.

I picked him up and set him on his feet and pushed him out the door in front of me with the barrel of the .38 pointing at the side of his head. We had taken a few steps before the other marshal turned to look at us. When he saw what had happened, it was too late for him to reach for his gun.

Pappy went into an Indian war dance after I made the second marshal free him. We went around in back of the men's room and started walking out of the clearing until we reached some scattered scrub oak. Pappy was carrying the chains and handcuffs we had removed. I ordered the marshals to take off their clothes, down to their underwear, and made them stretch out on the ground. Pappy handcuffed them to each other, then used the shackles to spread-eagle their legs to two bushes. I then tore my shirt into strips and gagged them.

After inspecting our work very carefully I said, "Sure hope you guys sleep well tonight. I saw some big red ants but they probably won't find you until tomorrow. If you manage to get those gags off, don't start yelling for another thirty minutes or we'll come back here and blow your brains out."

Pappy and I dressed in their uniforms. Mine fit a little tight, but it would serve the purpose until I could get to Albuquerque and buy some clothes. Together, the marshals were carrying around four hundred dollars which would give us plenty of spending money.

I found out later that a woman walking her dog came across those marshals and notified the police.

We took their car and drove in style until we reached Albuquerque where we parked it on the street. After we went shopping we picked up another car and drove it all the way to Barstow, California, where we changed again. We drove the third car to Victorville.

As we drove we discussed the two marshals and decided that they were just doing their job. They weren't such bad guys. But cons are funny. We try to escape from somebody we don't like or have it in for. In our case, it wasn't that we didn't like the marshals, we just found one of them lax and knew this would be the opportunity to make good an escape. One thing I haven't done since then is to eat oatmeal and use cigarettes as a chaser.

Even back then, when marshals were hauling me all over the country, I never failed to catalog every bank we passed in my mind for future reference. I must have put a hundred of them in the recesses of my mind and it was only natural to plan on going back to doing my favorite job.

I talked it over with Pappy. He was ready and willing. He had never robbed one before and was all ears when I explained to him exactly what he had to do while I was busy getting the money. After he understood everything he smiled, "This is going to be a picnic. Hell, I'm in for twenty years. I'll be up in my seventies if I'd waited for them to turn me loose. Might as well enjoy myself now."

He and I got thirty thousand on our first and last job. We split. I was sorry that he didn't want to stick around, but he claimed that his fifteen thousand would last him for a hell of a long time, and there were some places he wanted to see. He didn't want any part of Los Angeles. I heard that he was out for six years before he was caught.

144

After I'd eaten all the good food I could hold, seen a few shows and got plenty of rest, I began to look around for a woman. I wanted a real companion who would give me the attention I needed, after being away from them for so long.

The first one I found was in her early twenties. Her name was Burns. She was perfectly willing to set up light housekeeping. I rented an apartment and we moved in. There was something I didn't like about her from the very beginning, so I ran her off at the end of two weeks.

My new freedom made me have the desire to walk and look around, especially in the parks where there were trees and singing birds. Shortly after I'd ditched the Burns girl, I was going by a hospital. Across the street was a little park where there were benches. Sitting on one of these was a very attractive young woman reading a book. I thought maybe she was someone who had come out of the hospital for some fresh air. It was worth a try.

I crossed the street and sat down beside her on the bench. She looked at me and smiled. "It's so lovely here, I couldn't pass up this place."

I agreed with her and we continued our conversation. I invited her to lunch and she accepted. She told me that she lived in an apartment close to a city college not too far from Hollywood, that she was fed up with the routine of married life and taking care of a young son. I invited her to move in with me. I could most certainly break the routine. She agreed.

Two days later she left her husband, whose name was Clem, and her small son. Her name was Gloria. She claimed to be related to Lawrence Welk.

I would say that Gloria was around twenty-two, with dark hair and beautiful. She was well stacked and knew how to wear her clothes to the best advantage. Right off I knew she was starved for sex. She told me that Clem was a once-a-week shot, and she needed it almost every night. Well, I kept up with her for a while until I ran out of steam, then even I had to taper off. This was a whole new ball game and I had to get back in practice.

I often went on walks by myself. Not too long after Gloria moved in with me, I returned from one of my walks and Clem was there. He started giving me some static about stealing his wife. I punched him in the mouth and he decided to leave and not come back.

Gloria knew I was different. I didn't tell her any stories about my past. She knew me as John Webb and that I always seemed to have plenty of money to spend, so she didn't ask any questions. I've often wondered how she would have responded if she had known that I was Geroge "Machine Gun" Kelly and that I'd robbed banks, kidnapped and killed a number of people. She was really a good person, and I'm sure she would have been a good wife to Clem if he could get rid of some of his crazy ideas and settle down to the business of taking care of his wife.

Gloria and I probably would have stayed together much longer than we did, but she didn't play our little game lightly. She had to let herself become too attached. She began telling me and showing me that she was really gone on me, head over heels in love. This I couldn't take because I might get picked up any time, then where would she be?

She also told me that she had become pregnant while we'd been together. I needed to be saddled with a pregnant woman like I needed a hole in the head. I gave her some money and told her to go back to her husband, that my vacation was over and I had to go back to work. I really wasn't exaggerating there. My cash was getting pretty low.

Being the kind of woman Gloria was, I'm sure she really raised a storm when she saw my picture in the Los Angeles papers and read that I actually was a bank robber. I've wondered a hundred times how she and Clem made out and if she really did give birth to my child. The last time I heard about her they were living in North Dakota.

In the summer of 1962 I was fifty-seven years old. Through contacts, associations in prisons, especially on McNeil Island, I'd managed to keep pace with new innovations introduced over the years in the bank security systems. I knew how to detect alarm areas, alarm positions. I knew where the trigger money was in the bank drawers, and knew that I always had to warn the cashier not to touch it, because it would set off a silent alarm.

Although the bank that me and Pappy robbed was the first I'd done in twenty-nine years, I still kept my mind active and up to date with the times. I also knew that I always had to have proper identification, birth certificates and even car licenses and a driver's license. I'd been told of a place in Los Angeles that could fix me up with all of these for the sum of three hundred dollars. That was where I met Larry Stahl.

Larry and I formed a bank robbing partnership. He was one of the coolest operators I've ever known beside myself. He listened to my coaching, then we carried out the job without a hitch. I only wish Pappy had stuck around. The three of us could have taken any bank in the Los Angeles area.

Larry and I robbed three of them in pretty short order and got about one hundred thousand for our efforts. We then decided to lay low. I had a sneaky feeling that I should leave Los Angeles. In the past I usually listened to these kinds of feelings, but I didn't this time. Hell, I thought I would never be caught again. Los Angeles was just too big a place to be spotted. I lived in a respectable neighborhood and stayed away from the business districts as much as possible. I was too smart to make a wrong move. But what I didn't know, I was already under surveillance.

About ten-thirty one morning I was driving down the street in a new car I'd just bought. I approached a light that was yellow and barreled right on through. I hadn't gone over a block when a red light was dancing in my rear-view mirrow. I thought, what the hell, he'll just give me a ticket so I pulled over. The police car parked behind me and I started reaching for my wallet. Before I knew what was happening there were four unmarked cars hemming me in and plain clothes cops all over with drawn pistols. I didn't have a chance.

I was charged with robbing three banks. This was later thrown out when they found I already had a ton of years hanging over me. Stahl had been picked up earlier that same morning. I'd been free for a total of eighty-seven days and had lived every one of them as if I were royalty.

"I liked to crochet at night and do my tatting during the day. Tatting makes an off-beat noise which could be heard five tiers up. Some of the cons objected to having their sleep disturbed."

27. McNeil Island And The Porno King

My new cell at McNeil Island was pink. At most federal prisons the cells are pea green in color. We used a colored cement on textured walls to get the shade we desired. This is the way we'd get it done: An order would come through when certain bosses were not around. There would be an order for a paint crew to paint the cell and we'd switch the paint. The crew didn't give a damn. All they were there for was to do the job. Then a year or so later someone would come around and say, "How in the hell did this cell get painted this color?" Then they'd send the order out to have all the cells painted back to pea green. Another six months would go by and many of the cells would be different colors again.

Prison administration referred to our actions as manipulation. The cons would refer to it as improvising. Of course, painting cells was pretty much of an impossibility on The Rock. It didn't happen at Alcatraz. We were under lock and key there.

It was during my years at McNeil that my asthma really got bad. And toward the late sixties and early seventies, I began to develop emphysema. All during the fifteen years I spent there, including a few departures to Springfield for various reasons, my health gradually deteriorated.

What I'm about to tell you now is an ability I hadn't intended for Dobkins to find out about. One time he went down to Florence to visit me, and my wife, Cindy, rode down with him. When they got there, Jim took off a sweater he had worn on the trip. It was a knit sweater which his wife, Marty, had made for him several years previous. Before Jim and Cindy went into the Federal Detention Center, he took off the sweater and locked it in the trunk of his car. As he laid the sweater down carefully, Cindy made the remark, "George can make things like that."

Of course, Jim with that snoopy nose of his, sort of lit up like a Christmas decoration. "Oh, really?"

And Cindy, who is too snoopy most of the time for my comfort, just naturally said, "Why sure. He can knit and crochet."

When they got inside, Jim confronted me with his new found information. He really caught me by surprise. I snapped, "How

148

did you find that out?"

He just smiled and said, "Cindy told me."

Well, the cat was out of the bag, so I figured I might as well tell about this talent. Who'd ever dream that "Machine Gun" Kelly could crochet? I made my own hooks from toothbrushes. They wouldn't let you crochet in Alcatraz. They would only let you breathe, and they were jealous of that. But in the mid-fifties, somewhere in that time period, I learned how to crochet on McNeil Island. Everybody was crocheting. It was a challenge which didn't belittle us. We were always wanting things, sweaters and such, to pass on as gifts to our children or grandchildren. I'd crochet anything, from sweaters to women's suits, even topcoats. To make a suit you figure you tie 45,000 knots. I also made a few ponchos.

I once knitted a fancy complicated suit for my daughter, Gail. She promptly went out and sold it for several hundred dollars. When I found out, I had her taken off my visiting list for a while. I felt that my daughter, in the act of selling my piece of work, which I'd made especially for her, was releasing the anger she harbored for me. She was almost grown up when she found out about me kidnapping her mother and getting her pregnant. I don't think Gail has ever forgiven me for that.

At McNeil, the tier I was on had fifteen two-man cells on one side and fourteen two-man cells on the other side. A shower was at the end. This place wasn't for sissies. Thirteen out of the fifteen cells on my side were filled with cons who crocheted. Nine out of those in the fourteen cells were lifers or better. By better, I mean they were in for long terms, thirty and forty-year terms. No, none of them were sissies!

I liked to crochet at night and do my tatting during the day. Tatting makes an off-beat noise which could be heard five tiers up. Some of the cons objected to having their sleep disturbed. Everybody around had fancy sweaters; every sweater you made, you made it custom. I hated knitting when I got out on the street. I've had to show Cindy where she made mistakes in her work. With me, crocheting or tatting is like robbing banks or doing any other type of work. I'm a perfectionist. It should be done just the right way or not at all.

Although I became an expert at crocheting, even to the point of originating my own designs and making my own hooks out of toothbrush handles, I continued to be a feared and violent man. Sometimes the violence had its own brand of humor. Like the time

I managed to incite a riot while umpiring a baseball game.

I was umpiring the game between these two prison teams and one of the players didn't like my call. He was getting ready to take a swing at me, so I had to defend myself. I hit him in the face with my umpire's mask. The first thing I knew, there were baseball bats cracking heads all over the island. A couple of us, who helped to stir up the trouble, managed to get out of there real fast. We hurried to the barber shop and got ourselves locked in for a few hours for our own protection. There was a certain satisfaction watching tempers cool down.

The doctors at McNeil Island were amazed how my heart seemed to repair itself. Over a period of time I had taught myself to slow down, to move almost in slow motion. Undoubtedly this caused the heart tissue to regenerate itself and accomplish a repair job which baffled the doctors. After that I didn't have too much heart trouble for a period of years.

A garden snake incident proved to be interesting. There was a ten-man cell right above me on the second tier where somebody had put a garden snake. There were seven blacks and three whites there. One of the whites, Lee MaSaur, found the snake in his bunk and actually became paranoid. After that he thought something terrible was going to happen to him, like being eaten alive by a snake. He stayed in his cell and didn't participate in most of the activities. He became so upset that he tried to commit suicide by cutting himself with a razor blade. The cuts were so bad that it took two hundred and fifty stitches to sew them up. He hardly recovered from this when he began whittling on himself again. This time it took over three hundred stitches to sew him back together. He lived in the hospital for about a year, refusing to go back into the general population. Because of his refusal the officials put him in the hole where he hanged himself.

This is a method the prison officials used to make everybody conform, and their way was death. They had every indication that Lee would commit suicide, yet they didn't do a thing to help him to get his head on straight. They knew what he wanted to do, so they put him in the hole to make it easy for him to do that very thing. See how the hate and violence technique is manipulated?

There was another inmate from Hawaii whose name was Earl Kim, who was involved with drugs. He wanted to kill seven people, which he did. Afterwards, he went to a lot of trouble to get arrested on a drug rap which would keep him out of circulation only one or two years and give him an alibi he thought would throw the hounds off the real scent. He would up going to a lot of trouble just to get to sit in the electric chair.

Even though I was imprisoned under the name of John Webb, I had a lot of influence on McNeil Island. My control and direct tap into the prison grapevine were reliable and exact. A guard at McNeil Island fell prey to one of my schemes. I wanted to get the guard fired. As usual, I handled the situation cleverly.

I told the guard for several months that he was going to get fired if he didn't watch his activities more closely. I said, "They suspect that you're bringing in narcotics in your shoe polish."

You see, I planted the idea in his mind. Sure enough, in a shakedown check they dug into his shoe polish, found narcotics, and he was fired. As I've told you before, just because I was locked up didn't turn off my mind. I knew the guard had a weak streak so I did the state a favor.

I read a lot about dogs. I checked every book out of the library they had on the subject. The librarian even sent away for more books. My desire was to learn how to breed a dog that would eat policemen every day, you know, like the one-a-day vitamins. The dog I finally decided on was the mastiff. It grows to be very, very large and is strong. I studied dogs for around five years and became well informed; but I never got the chance to carry out my plan.

Always one to keep my hands in the available action, I operated like a one-man business conglomerate for over a decade on McNeil Island. I ran a continuing low-ball poker game, paying off winners with cartons of cigarettes; and operated a pornography rental service with the help of a friendly guard. I also became the local loan shark, then devised an ingenious method to keep a pill racket going. Hell, I even went into partnership with another prisoner bootlegging.

At one point I had over eight hundred cartons of cigarettes stowed away in different cells when I was finally caught. I argued that a series of killings might erupt if I lost my capacity to pay off low-ball house debts. The guard captain conceded, and I kept my cigarettes.

Whole sides of beef would mysteriously disappear from the prison freezer. I had a deal worked out where I could get my hands on some choice cuts of beef, then I'd smuggle them into my cell. By rolling the lids off tobacco tins or sardine cans, which I'd smuggled, I'd have a cooking utensil. I'd also use tinfoil from cigarette packages for still another cooking container. Combining two tins or two pieces of tinfoil, I could cook pretty large steaks. My stove was the hot water radiator in the ten-man cell I was now in.

I would trade cooked steaks to other cons for cigarettes. Of course, if they wanted to pay cash, I wouldn't turn them down. Now and then I would use a choice steak for the winner in my low-ball operation. There were those who preferred having steaks instead of taking their winnings in cigarettes.

You just can't imagine the different things that cons can improvise. How many people in the outside world would ever think of cooking steaks on tinfoil gotten from tobacco pouches?

I and other prisoners went to trial in Tacoma on the charge of conspiring to murder another con known as Snake Arnold. The trial concluded on an unusual note. The jury's summation read, "Although the defendants admit their guilt, we find them not guilty." Those accused of being involved in the conspiracy won because the jury figured that since all of us had so much time remaining to serve, any additional time wouldn't make any difference.

Sure, I thought about escaping from McNeil Island. I even tried twice, but you're handicapped there. There's a lot of water between you and the mainland. It's cold. I wasn't really interested in taking such a chance because I had a good thing going on the island.

Did you know I used to be the pornography king? Well, I was. I developed a very close friendship with a certain guard who used to buy a pornographic book for around five dollars. He'd bring the book to me and I'd pay him ten dollars for it. Then I'd rent the book out to various cells, getting money or cigarettes in return. My guard friend brought me several books and I made a lot of money. Some of the other inmates got to calling me the Porno King.

Through the years I also became the chief loan shark. I'd loan a con two dollars and get back three. Sometimes I did my business with cigarettes, loaning two packs and getting three. Once in a while I'd catch a fellow in a bind who needed money in a hurry — I'd loan him five dollars and get back ten. The repayment would be a week, sometimes longer, according to who was getting the money. In deals such as these, I found the cons pretty reliable. After all, if the guy welches on his deal, where is he going to hide?

During a time when hospital guards were instructed to shake down the inmates, I was suspected as being one of the kingpins in smuggling money. Money was not supposed to be in anyone's possession; it was contraband. I was collared while walking down a corridor. Immediately I got a "strip shake." A strip shake is when they take you on the spot without warning. They make you remove all your clothes, turn all the pockets inside out; even the seams and the cuffs are checked. The collars of the shirts are fingered. They see if you've anything stuffed up your rectum or between your false teeth and gums or under your tongue.

As it happened, I was carrying a pack of Winstons and a pack of Pall Mall cigarettes. There was a lot of money in each of the packs, close to a hundred dollars in tens, twenties and fives. Each pack was full of cigarette stubs. The money was stuffed underneath the stubs and also hidden between the two layers of paper on the sides of the pack.

I was casual as they started to strip me down. The lieutenant supervising the shakedown, stood right in front of me. I simply took the packs out of my pocket, handed them to him and he held them during the whole procedure. When they were finished with me the guards shook their heads because they didn't find anything. They knew I'd tricked them, but how? When I was dressed the lieutenant handed me back my two packs and gave me a warning about taking any chances of getting into trouble. As they went on to the next unlucky con, the guards were still shaking their heads and glancing back at me.

I forgot to tell you that the money in the two cigarette packs was loot I'd collected from a "pill" racket which I'd been running for several years. I'd go on sick call every once in a while. A fellow working in the infirmary was also working for me. When I would get up to him in the line, he would look at my throat and say, "You'd better come back and let me spray that." We'd walk into another room and he'd give me some pill bags in little brown envelopes. I'd slip him a match book with a bill folded up inside.

Indians loved the pills. They were my main market. One Indian, whose name was Yo-Kash, was a regular client of mine. He always wanted some stumblers. I usually delivered these in a cellophane wrapper. One time I delivered to Yo-Kash enough stumblers for him and four of his friends.

He had just taken his stumblers when a team of guards suddenly appeared to search him. Before they could get their hands on him, he popped the rest of the pills into his mouth and swallowed. He couldn't stand up for a week, he was so knocked out. They even had to carry him into the prison court. What the court consisted of at McNeil was three or four staff members acting as a panel of judges. They would dish out the punishment in small cases.

One time I went in on a bootlegging venture with "Chester," a con who had a limp. For one gallon of booze he'd get about eight cartons of cigarettes. When he got busted he had eighty gallons of booze. Making the booze was a two-day process. We did it all in a ten-man cell by using plastic Purex jugs for containers. I had the connections to get the ingredients; "Chester" was the boss of the work. I was about the only con who could get credit from the commissary. They knew I could pay for anything I ordered.

I know it's on your mind. Yes, there were a number of cons who knew who I was. One was my old buddy, Alvin "Creepy" Karpis. He was released around 1968. As I understand it, he was given his choice of lifetime parole in the United States or no parole if he left the country. I heard that he went first to Canada and then to Spain. He's several years younger than me; he wasn't born until around 1911, so he's probably got several good years left in him.

Sometimes one of the younger cons would come up with some smart remark about how tough I thought I was. I had an answer for them. I'd say, "You look at the money figure, then think why I'm here." Normally they'd cut a wide path after that. A little asking around on their part would reveal that I was for real. Most of them were in for some two-bit job like stealing a bag of mail or some other government rap. When they found out that I'd had two hundred thousand dollars in my hand at one time for kidnapping, in addition to other things I'd been mixed up in, they gave me an even wider path — especially after they'd heard about the time I wiped out three guys with a hammer.

One of the inmates was Sam Bowers, the grand Wizard of the Klu Klux Klan; another was a doctor we called Dr. Frankenstein. He was the doctor who used to give drugs to the actor Boris Karloff.

As at all prisons, McNeil Island was not without its share of violence. One time I saw a con cooked in a pressure cooker. The meat just fell off his bones in hunks. Another body turned up in a lettuce bin. It was discovered about half way down in the bin. Nobody else would fix salads that day.

One time I was looking down from my cell and saw a con executed in the prison yard by two other cons who drove a spike through his heart, pinning him right to the concrete bench where he had been sitting. Sometimes it's pretty hard to stomach the vicious things the cons would do to each other. That's a man doing something to another human, but a lot of the cons were nothing more than monsters. You couldn't call them animals. Most animals wouldn't do the things they did. But when you get to thinking about it, when you take a man's freedom away from him, his hope goes, too.

One time I saw three young punks cut out a man's heart. The only reason they did it was to impress the other cons. Then to add further insult, they took turns defecating in the chest cavity. When you think about it, that kind of action is pretty sickening.

In the late sixties, while still on McNeil, I took a lot of IQ tests. I tested out on the sixteenth grade level and was pretty proud because I'd never finished grade school. Like I told you before, I've always felt that I was much smarter than the average guy.

Once more I got to go to Tacoma, this time to take part in a perjury hearing. The prosecution asked me about some statements I'd made at the murder trial. When I was asked my name, I replied, "George Kelly."

The man looked confused, and he snapped, "According to the records, you're supposed to be John Webb!"

I smiled and said, "Oh, that's right."

I always tried to be honest in situations like that. They thought I was being cute with them; what they didn't know, I was telling the truth.

"I had to find a way to get out; that house needed a couple of occupants, and one of them was not going to be Betty's mother."

28. A Stewardess Named Betty

Even while shackled by the limitations of McNeil Island, I struck up a continuing, maturing relationship with a woman that had all the potential of developing into marriage. Betty was a TWA stewardess who had been introduced to me by my daughter, Gail.

Gail only visited me once or twice a year, and Betty just happened to accompany her on one of these visits. We seemed to be drawn together from the very beginning. She made a weekly round-trip flight from Seattle-Tacoma International Airport to Vietnam, and would visit me on the weekends.

Her name was Betty Fowler; she had worked as hostess for TWA for several years. Gail had met her either in Honolulu or L.A. Like I said, we hit it off from the start, and when I got out our plan was to get married. Each time she would land at Sea-Tac, she'd come and see me. This was back in '68 and '69, right after Gail and I had our falling out over the suit I'd crocheted for her.

Betty was medium build and weighed about one hundred and five pounds. She was blonde but I think it came out of a bottle. She was in her early thirties, a quiet, conservative type. She liked to drink and was honest about it. She wore pretty clothes with a real style about her. I told her where I had some money stashed away from the bank robberies I pulled in L.A. She got it and together we began to plan a house we'd build. It was her job to see that the plans were carried out so the place would be ready when I was released.

The house was ready to move into in early 1970, but I was still behind bars. Betty leased it out for a year. Maybe you think it didn't gall me to know that we had a fifty thousand dollar home just waiting for us in North Hollywood. Of course, Betty put her mother's name on the deed in case anything happened to her. I had to find a way to get out; that house needed a couple of occupants, and one of them was not going to be Betty's mother.

Back in the early sixties, Gail had helped create interest in getting signatures for a clemency petition on my behalf. When Betty became a weekly part of my life, she put a lot of energy into helping Gail. During a period of months, over seventy thousand signatures were acquired; naturally, the name on the petitions was John Webb.

There was a program comprised of different religious groups on the island which turned out to be a training program for chaplains. One of them, who was still serving as a student chaplain, became interested in my case. He discussed my situation with the other chaplains and they, too, became interested. When they went back to their home areas in different states they took petitions with them which played a vital part in raising the biggest part of the seventy thousand signatures.

Bob Hessie had been a bank robber and worked as a chaplain's clerk on the island. He played a part in encouraging these men to come to my aid. After he got out of prison, he began to work as a teacher and counselor at the Ft. Worth Correctional Institute.

The matter of clemency became an obsession with me. It became apparent that the only way I was ever going to get out of prison would be by my own initiative. I began filing clemency petitions. I filed the first one as far back as 1955 from the county jail in Los Angeles, but it was immediately denied.

It works this way: Ten thousand petition requests get denied and only one gets granted. To file a clemency petition is nothing; to have one be effective is a miracle.

There is a clemency board made up of a panel of lawyers from different parts of the country. The board meets periodically to go over all the petitions and requests which have been submitted. When this board passes favorably on a petition it is then turned over to a legal board to decide eligibility; then there is more filtering. If it does pass the legal board, there is a good chance that clemency will be granted.

A little saying which you learn quickly if you're in prison for any length of time goes like this: "Exhaust all remedies in line." Believe me, I exhausted every avenue possible to get my freedom. I only had one desire — to get released so I could be with Betty.

You can imagine my shock when I was told that Betty had died. I had never experienced such a loss. I'm here to say that I didn't love her; I liked her better than anyone I'd ever known.

I was stunned at her going the way she did, as quick as she did. I'm not sure if I would have married her. I don't know why I told her that I would. It was a case of my needing help. I was clutching, grasping for a straw, any straw that could get me out of prison. Betty had been my mainstay in this program. Suddenly she was gone and with her my hope.

She had been a woman of the world; she had been around. She had been through the wringer and knew what life was all about. I had just begun to have a pretty good understanding what she wanted out of life. She used to tell me, "It's gotten so that every time I leave the ground on one of my flights, I have a hangup; I almost go crazy."

After twelve years of flying, Betty wanted a change, and I, John Webb, was to play a vital part in that change. We had discussed the matter of the house, which was to become our home, for a year or two. She was as sold on the idea as I was. She had never married, but for the first time in her life she was ready to settle. Ours was a case of helping each other. The situation was such that we were leaning on each other's shoulders. I don't know for sure, but I think Betty was an alcoholic. She needed me badly. We were really an odd couple.

She was visiting me, almost weekly, every chance she could, making the trip over on the ferry sometimes both Saturday and Sunday. We had been meeting this way for almost four years. Suddenly the lid blew off. I was told that Betty was dead, strickened with spinal meningitis, and three days later she was gone!

Something went out of me that day, a strange emptiness occurred. There was a great big hole in my life and I didn't know how to fill it.

"Snotty got fed up with my self-pity routine, all that feeling sorry for myself. He came up with a psychological ploy that worked miracles."

29. The Guard Who Cared

I was stricken with a stroke which left me partially paralyzed in my left side, especially my left hand and leg, and frustrated in my mind.

It happened right after Betty died. It wasn't from worry of her. I was sick one day and began staggering in the tunnel that led from the main hospital area to a corridor. I felt a tremendous pain that began in my chest and went to the back of my head. I collapsed.

The next thing I remember they'd just taken by blood pressure, and I heard the doctor say that my pressure was 158 over 156, and that I couldn't stand having pressure that high much longer. Something had to be done very quickly. Apparently, the attack had been caused by a blood clot, probably stemming from the old head injury when the three goons attacked me with the hammer at Alcatraz.

They put me in the hospital and I stayed there for several months. A guard by the unlikely name of Snotty had taken a liking to me. I was about sixty-four years old, and what he saw in me I'll never know. There was another guard whose name was Sparlin who would come to see me with Snotty. The two of them would stay an extra hour visiting after their work day had ended when they could be catching the early ferry to the mainland.

Being cooped up in a hospital for so long was something new for me. Although I'd had several hospital stays during the preceding twenty to twenty-five years because of heart flare-ups, this was my worst experience. In the past my heart had done a pretty good job of healing itself because I'd learned to slow down, doing things generally in a modified slow motion manner. This new attack on my physical condition caused me to become so depressed that I thought I was going to die. Actually, it was worse than that. I'd reached the point where I knew I was going to die. I wasn't afraid of death; I've never been afraid of it.

There have only been two times in my life when I felt sure I was going to kick off: in 1970 when I had the stroke, and again right here in Florence this last December (1974). I was in between an asthma and emphysema condition; the emphysema caused me to have problems breathing in, and the asthmatic condition made it difficult to breathe out. When I'd have a severe attack, my face would turn blue and I'd have a hell of a time breathing. This one night around three, the attack hit me. I did something I hadn't done in a long time, I prayed real hard. I told God that if He would just let me keep breathing for another hour, I'd make it. If He couldn't give me an hour, just give me a few minutes. You know, after I had prayed, a few minutes later I went to sleep. The next morning I woke up, breathing normal again.

Snotty got fed up with my self-pity routine, all that feeling sorry for myself. He came up with a psychological ploy that worked miracles.

Right after work one day, Snotty came storming into the hospital wing where I was. He didn't say a word of greeting. I was just sitting in my wheelchair feeling depressed. He grabbed that wheelchair, spun me around and wheeled me out of the hospital wing to a pickup he had parked at the entrance. He took me to the passenger's side, jerked open the door and ordered me to reach up and grab something so I could pull myself out of that chair and get into the seat. I did. He slammed the door shut and walked to the driver's side and climbed in.

I thought we were just going for a ride. McNeil Island is around seven miles in length and five miles at its widest part, and it sits in Puget Sound. There are roads to all parts of the island, and I thought Snotty wanted me to have a change of scenery. But there was something wrong with his attitude that I couldn't figure out. Suddenly he began landing into me about my present state of mind. "All you do is sit around, feeling sorry for yourself — that is a hell of a way to spend your time. If you stop thinking of yourself all the time, you'll start getting better."

He drove the pickup out about half a mile from the sally port gate. He stopped on a little rise, threw open his door and came around that truck in a big huff. He yanked open my door and practically jerked me out of my seat and propped me up against the truck so I wouldn't fall over. All the time he was chewing me out.

Suddenly he pointed to the grave markers and looked at me. In a very sarcastic way he demanded, "Pick out a spot where you want me to put your old carcass, cause you're going to die pretty soon, the way you're going. After I help bury you, I'm coming out here every day and piss on your grave."

All I could see was the little red light that comes on when I get good and mad. I made up my mind right then that he wasn't going to tinkle on my grave! If I'd been physically able, I'd killed him right there. In my fit of rage I committed myself that I was going to do whatever was necessary for me to regain the use of my left side; then I was going to square matters with Snotty. I'd killed men for threatening to do less.

Snotty ordered me to get myself back into the seat of the pickup, then he slammed the door. This time he walked around the truck slowly as if he had forever to get in. I followed him with my eyes, swearing that I'd get even with him. He also took his time driving back to the sally port gate, as if he knew I was mad and he was going to let me stew in my own juice. He didn't say a word.

I was so mad, all worked up in my rage, that I didn't see the logic behind what Snotty was doing. I wouldn't realize that for some time to come. But his psychological approach began to work. I started showing improvement immediately. It wasn't long before they took me out of the hospital wing and put me in an eight-man cell.

I was determined to stick to the promise I'd made to myself, that I was going to do everything possible to recover and get back the use of my whole body, the way it was before the stroke. I got one of the other cons to move my bed so that I had to lay on my right side. I began forcing myself to use my left hand. Somebody got me a handball out of the gym. I'd sleep with that darned thing, forcing myself to hold it in my left hand and squeeze it for long periods of time. At first I had to concentrate on squeezing, to make my fingers work. I'd look at those fingers and say, "Fingers, close on that ball." I'd stare at those fingers, demanding that they move, that they squeeze and prove they had strength.

I'd have one of the cons wheel me down to the gym where I'd stay for a few hours each day. There, I'd strap a small dumbbell to my left foot. At first it wouldn't move, but I started talking to that foot just as I did to my fingers. It took almost six months before it heard me, before I could get it to react. Then one day there was just a quiver of movement; and from then on I knew that foot had heard me. It was going to answer my bidding.

As the weeks and months went by, I could almost squeeze that handball flat; that left leg started moving higher and higher. Only then did I know what Snotty had been trying to tell me. All the rage and madness I'd felt toward him went out of me. I sent for him. When he came up to me, I stuck out my hand and said only one word, "Thanks."

161

It wasn't too much longer before I was walking around with the aid of a cane he gave me.

There was another con, a guy by the name of James Mitchell, who was living in the eight-man cell I occupied. He was about six-foot-three and wore about a size fourteen shoe. The thing I remember about Mitch were his movements. They were those of a sixteen-year-old girl. Everybody called him Betty; that's just the name they called him. Betty made up my bed for nearly two years. He took care of my laundry because we were close friends, and he felt sorry for me because of my stroke. Whenever he had a lover's quarrel, he would come and cry on my shoulder.

Betty was more sensitive than I realized. He confided in me about the surgery he wanted done. One time when he was telling this I said, "What are you going to do with those size fourteen shoes? You'd look like a plow hop." He cried for two days. Finally, when Betty was in a happy mood and hadn't had a lover's quarrel for a couple of weeks, he confided in me again. "When I have the operation to change me into a woman, I'm going to climb a tree and sit out on a limb where there will be a lot of men walking by. I'll pull up my skirt to my waist and call down to the men and say, 'Look what I've got!'"

I don't know whether that ambition was ever satisfied, but Betty had a real sense of humor. He cheered me up when I felt I really needed someone to help me get my head on straight. He made it easier for me to overcome the odds that seemed to be stacked against me after the stroke.

"When she handed me that seventy-five dollars, I was convinced that she thought she'd been with a real man. I'd made her feel all woman. She didn't do it because she felt sorry for me being a con; she did it because I'd satisfied her needs."

30. What Became Of Valachi?

The year 1971 was still on the calendar when I was transferred to Latuna Prison in El Paso, Texas. I renewed an acquaintance with a con I'd known at Leavenworth. Johnson was a MTA which stood for medical technical assistant. I liked him because he seemed to understand my asthma problem better than the doctors and went out of his way to help me. Although he never admitted it, I'm sure he knew what was happening in regard to changing my identity.

The last time he saw me I was George "Machine Gun" Kelly; now I was John Webb. He told me an interesting story about Valachi, the famous Mafia squealer. Here's pretty much what Johnson told me:

"I was told about a certain prison official who had been assigned to stay with Valachi, and was put in his custody each time he was transferred. They were gone for about four years before they returned to Latuna. This official's name was Gookins. I recognized him when I saw him, but we never became really acquainted.

"Shortly after they returned to Latuna, Valachi was declared dead. One day before this happened and for two days following, all of us were locked up and no normal movement was allowed by the prisoners. Before this, during the visiting time, Valachi's family members came regularly. They'd bring groceries and special things for him to eat.

"They didn't come the day he was supposed to have died. The next day a body was displayed on a slab in a hallway in the hospital area. They'd put a sheet over it and a tag on the toe of the cadaver, which read Valachi. All I was able to see was the top of the cadaver's head and his feet. I knew they were making this display to satisfy the curiosity seekers.

"An ambulance from the veterans hospital, located about twenty miles away, removed the body. This was absolutely unheard of. Something was terribly fishy. What they'd done was to bring another body in the ambulance to display as Valachi for two or

163

three days. This was no problem because there were twenty-five hundred patients at the hospital and they were dying all the time.

"I'm sure Valachi was slipped into that ambulance and hauled away right under the noses of the officials with only one or two knowing about it. This was nothing more than an elaborate ruse. Hell, I had a pretty good hold on the prison grapevine and didn't miss anything. The officials might think we're pretty dumb, but they don't fool us very often.

"If you were able to go to the grave that was supposed to be Valachi's, I'll bet you wouldn't even find a body in the box. They were just doing some first class staging and creating an illusion to fool everybody.

"Why didn't the Valachi family come to claim the body? They simply stopped coming and completely disappeared. My guess is that Valachi was smuggled out of the country to keep the Mafia from finding him, because if they did, they'd kill him on the spot. From a practical standpoint, this move sure saved the government a lot of money. It would have taken a lot of money to protect Valachi and his family for the rest of his life."

I don't know from personal first-hand information exactly what became of Valachi. All I know is, if Johnson said there was something fishy going on, it'd be a mighty safe bet to believe him.

Now let me tell you about an incident I considered very unfair.

It's sometimes hard to kill a human. This one guy at Latuna was hit with a rusty, dirt-filled pipe which was around four feet long. The blow laid the back of his head wide open. I was in the hospital when they brought him in. It was during one of my asthma attacks. I actually saw the brain throbbing where the hole was in the back of his skull. I lay there and watched them pick splinters of bone out of the wound.

Six weeks later the guy had recovered and was back in the prison population, but he got five years for possession of a deadly weapon. When they found him, he had a knife taped to his leg. He never got to use the knife against the guys who tried to kill him. Still he got socked another five years for having the knife; the cons who tried to do him in didn't get anything.

Latuna was afraid of me. They didn't know what to think. A lieutenant there, who I knew on The Rock many years before, couldn't figure what was happening. I heard him tell one of the prison captains: "That Webb's just been here a short time and he's already got a foothold." This remark delighted me. It sent my ego soaring. I hadn't made any attempt to organize anything, but just having them thinking I was made me feel like a big shot.

While I was at Latuna a hunger strike was staged. A number of us prisoners got together and declared the food was terrible; we refused to eat anything for three days. One of my "great white fathers" from the Justice Department was sent from Washington to check into the situation. He requested to see me privately. When we were alone he studied me for a few minutes and said, "Are you the ringleader?"

Without batting an eye I asked, "How much extra are you able to rake off on one of these trips, seventy-five or eighty dollars a day? Next you're going to tell me that this is just a routine check." The "great white father" dropped the subject. He knew better than to get into a discussion with me because I probably knew more about the rake-offs than the man knew himself. It was just another way to pad the inspector's income.

One of my activities at Latuna was to coach a baseball team which turned out to be the team to beat in the prison league. The players were Mexicans and they called themselves The Bandido Misfits. Believe me, they knew every trick that could win a game.

I had a favorite gimmick to get better food. What I did was pose as a Jew. I knew when the Jewish cons attended the services with the rabbi, they were given special treats, so every Saturday morning I attended Rabbi Schur's service.

I wasn't at Latuna very long. By 1972 I'd already been transferred to the Ft. Worth Correctional Institute. This was a minimum security facility which gave emphasis on convict drug problems. They tried to dry out the addicts and help them recover from their drug habits.

An incident took place in 1973 which made me madder 'n hell. It was in the spring. I'd been feeling real good. But one day I got to feeling under the weather and went on sick call. After a quick examination, they put me in isolation without explaining a thing. I stayed there for three days. I got to demanding what was wrong. They said they'd found something that had to be checked out. The way they went about saying it, I was scared half to death. I got to thinking that I had some kind of cancer and they wanted to isolate me from everybody else.

But what burned me up, they didn't give me any tests or shots all the time they kept me in isolation. This caused me to grow suspicious. Something was up. Somebody was playing a dirty trick on me, and I was going to find out what it was. They were keeping me out of someone's hair. Pretty soon I got to calling everybody bad names and swore that I'd get to the bottom of the whole mess. Experience had taught me that prison officials frequently work in strange ways.

Right in the middle of my isolation period was the weekend. I didn't think of this until I was released. Then I learned by the grapevine that I'd had a visitor who the prison officials didn't want me to see. He was Walter Maxted, a con I'd known on McNeil Island, who had wanted to write my life story. Now living in Arizona, he had driven all the way to Ft. Worth to see me. He'd been busted for dope. The feds were watching him very closely to see that he didn't go back to the first offense — being a pusher. They figured that he was going to try to smuggle some dope into the prison with my help.

You have to give the feds credit; when they get on an ex-con's trail, they are like a bunch of bloodhounds. They don't stop at anything. They sure were trailing Walter.

When I first came in contact with Walter at McNeil Island, he already was known as "The Robot." While waiting for a verdict to be announced at a trial in the Federal Building in San Diego, Walter was planning an escape from the third-floor holding tank. He and another guy decided they'd jump from a window to the sidewalk below. Walter went first. The poor guy shattered both of his ankles, busted his back, fractured his neck, just a mess. The other guy saw what happened and decided not to jump. It took a ton of bolts, screws and steel pins to put Walter back together. The jerky, methodical motion Walter had after that just naturally led to him being called "The Robot."

I had kind of been a father to Walter at McNeil. Because he went to the island with a snitch jacket for having been an informer, his life wasn't worth a plug nickel. I befriended him when nobody else would even get near him. In his case, I really didn't feel he deserved all the cold shoulder treatment he was getting. He was one of my cellmates for a while.

Walter worked as a MTA in the hospital. He had seen my medical records, and he'd noticed the manner in which I and Karpis held conversations. He began to put two and two together and came up with the notion that I must be someone other than a con named John Webb.

But there was one act I never really could forgive Walter for committing — like I said back in Chapter 13 — which was keeping me from putting Blackie Audett out of his misery when I had the chance to smother him with the pillow at McNeil Island. After

Walter had pulled me away from Blackie, he put the old rat-fink fart on a rescuscitator and revived the scoundrel. The old guy must be at least eight or nine years older than I am. I got quite a chuckle during the spring of 1975 while I was still at Florence, when I heard about Blackie and one of his elderly cronies getting nabbed for pulling a bank job in Seattle. I gotta give the guy credit. He never gave up. I understand that the way he and his partner pulled off the heist, they should go down in history as the "Geriatric Duo." They were counting the money in their apartment when the law came a-tapping.

Anyway, at Ft. Worth, the urge to get back in the free world began to eat away at me. I decided that my days were numbered; I wasn't going to do anything to jeopardize my release. I was positive that strings were being pulled to make me a free man, so I was going to make sure I maintained a perfect conduct record. In fact, my record was so good that I and another prisoner were given a furlough to fly to Florida where we appeared on a TV documentary which dealt with the makeup of convicts who had served long prison terms. Of course, we were accompanied by prison officials. One of these officials arranged to have me spend the night with a woman, a member of the June Taylor Dancers, who were appearing at the same studio where the documentary was being made. The official approached me after we arrived in Florida and asked, "Say, Webb, what do you desire most in a woman?"

I snapped, "What kind of a woman do I like? All my life I've thought that a woman's most pleasing factor was that she's a female."

That night the dancer came into the room where I was all alone, a tall shapely woman in her middle twenties. The first thing I noticed about her was the delightful perfume she was wearing. She told me the name of it — Rapture from Avon. We had one hell of a night together! She seemed to be hungry for sex like I was. Just before the guard let her out the next morning, she handed me three bills — a fifty, a twenty and a five. "Get the guard to go buy you a nice pair of slacks, a shirt and tie. I want you to look good on TV. You've made me one happy woman."

About a year after that I saw this dancer on TV when the June Taylor chorus was appearing in a commercial, advertising panty hose put out by Sears. When she handed me that seventy-five dollars, I was convinced that she thought she'd been with a real man. I'd made her feel all woman. She didn't do it because she felt sorry for me being a con; she did it because I satisfied her needs.

"I must admit that it was through a strange chain of events that I qualified for the work release program as a bail bondsman in Dallas."

31. Clemency From Nixon

President Kennedy's assassination had happened just weeks before a possible clemency was to be signed to free me which would coincide with Christmas of 1963. President Johnson had also been approached about setting up clemency. Johnson was too busy stealing to give my clemency bid even the time of day.

My clemency petitions were filed under the name of Webb, so the people behind the scenes would know. I had filed four times after the middle fifties. Each time I would state that I was completely rehabilitated and that I had spent enough time in prison.

Eisenhower had signed clemency for Jesse Flores, a fighter, and this gave me hope that mine would be approved. I felt that my two "great white fathers" were doing what they could to help me.

Every couple of years a reference was made to the petitions which contained the 70,000 signatures that my daughter Gail, my girl friend Betty and the chaplains had collected on my behalf. Still nothing came of these petitions. I learned that sometimes it takes as long as two years to get back an answer concerning one's clemency. So far, mine had all been negative; I'd start all over again.

It got to the point where I went out of my way to serve in responsible positions so I could prove that I was ready to return to society. I was even an instructor for government prison officials from a ten state area. It was my job to brief them of all the things I'd learned that went on behind prison walls in regard to the way the cons lived from day to day; how they acted; what they did, both good and bad. I told them and showed them with clear cut examples just how cons could run the prison from the inside and defeat guards physically, verbally and with contraband.

They asked some stupid questions and half of them didn't believe a word I said, but if and when they become involved, they'll find that just because a man is behind bars, he doesn't stop thinking. All of that thinking goes toward beating the System. I could have told them the following story how I and some other cons got rid of a guard we didn't like:

While at Leavenworth I and two other cons framed a guard and got him fired. This guard's name was Jack. He had been giving us a hard time and we wanted to get rid of him. We figured out a scheme where we could use an orange ballpoint pen and some heroin. One of the cons in on the deal was a trusty. He went to Lieutenant Watson and told him how the heroin was getting into the prison. It had to be a guard bringing it in and he had learned by the grapevine that it was a guard who owned an orange ballpoint pen.

Lieutenant Watson assigned the trusty to help him watch for the guard with the orange ballpoint. The third man in our group, another trusty, stationed himself out near the fence to watch for Jack, the guard. When he saw him, he waited until Jack was on the inside, then started walking toward him. When he got alongside him he bumped Jack hard, and while helping him regain his balance and apologizing for being so clumsy, he stuck the orange pen in his shirt pocket. The inside of the pen was filled with one-half ounce of heroin.

The funny part of it was that Jack even apologized to the trusty for not watching more closely where he was going and went on his way. As he approached my trusty friend and Lieutenant Watson, the former pointed him out by saying, "There's the guard now with an orange pen in his pocket."

Lieutenant Watson, a folksy, middle-aged man, looked at the guard and smiled. "Why that's my brother-in-law, Jack. He wouldn't smuggle even a kitten into the prison."

The trusty insisted that Jack be searched since that had been the only orange ballpoint pen they had seen so far. Lieutenant Watson called, "Hey, Jack, I'd like to see you for a minute. Come over here; I've got to check something." When Jack walked up to them, Watson said, "Give me that orange ballpoint pen there in your shirt pocket."

Jack said, "Why, I don't have any orange ballpoint pen." Then he looked down and saw it there in his pocket. "That's not mine! I never saw it before! It's been planted on me!"

The lieutenant's face turned red. "Don't give me that stuff, Jack. It's in your pocket. You put it there and I'm checking it."

He grabbed the pen, unscrewed it and found the heroin wrapped up in a piece of wax paper. He took Jack to the warden and he was suspended for being a pusher. There was a trial and he was given five years in a work camp. I never met the fellow after that. I've often thought that he was such a stinker; it couldn't happen to a nicer guard.

It was during my stay at the Ft. Worth Correctional Institute when prospects for clemency suddenly brightened. But before I could be released after President Nixon had approved my clemency, I had to prove that I could exist as a productive member of society; this was necessary before an actual release date could be set. However, they went ahead and agreed on November 15, 1973 as the tentative date. Action was taken to prepare my records which would include a driver's license, and a birth certificate under the name of John H. Webb.

I knew I'd be able to participate in the work release program. It had taken thirty-four months to get the actual release effected from the filing date, and another nine months after Nixon had signed the clemency. I'm sure he was not informed who I really was.

Sure enough, I was set at liberty November 15, 1973, on what is called a CR, meaning a conditional release. There was a six-year string attached; this was a paper that they could hold over me in case I got out of line. They did this because of the escapes in my record.

All told, during my prison years, I'd had four six-year sentences added to my life sentence. Two were for assaults, two for escapes. Later, when I was captured in Phoenix for bank robbery, the papers stated that I was a parole violator. This statement was made because of the six-year hold they had on me, and they didn't have to say who I really was, even if they had known.

I must admit that it was through a strange chain of events that I qualified for the work release program as a bail bondsman in Dallas. I was free to work and socialize from eight in the morning until midnight, when I had to be back in my prison room. These hours were in effect from Monday through Friday. I worked for Rocky Lane, a black man. His office was located at 1928 Main Street, between the City Hall and the Dallas County Jail.

Some money had to exchange hands in appropriate places for me to get the bail bondsman job; substantial amounts of money. I raised the money myself by pulling two bank jobs in the Dallas area. And I did both heists while I was a resident at the Correctional Institute. Anything is possible when you have the right connections and proper transportation; on those occasions, I had benefit of both. Hell, I even knocked off one of those banks minutes after a seven a.m. grand opening ceremony. I was back at the Institute in time for everybody to see me leave at my usual eight a.m. departure time.

I don't think it would be right for me to say anything more about how I raised this money, because the statute of limitations hasn't elapsed on those crimes.

Rocky Lane and I got along well together. I was left in the office alone for short periods of time. I could talk and relate to those people who came out of jail. They understood me. I was given duties which would necessitate me being in the courthouse or in the jail. My rapport was excellent. I was all business from the start. I quickly gained a reputation as a fair and honest bondsman who would go to bat for my clients. In fact, I went to bat in one case with a county sheriff that almost got me in trouble.

The parents of this teen-age kid came to Rocky Lane's Bail-bonding. They wanted to make bail for their son. The bail was only five hundred dollars. Their boy was being held in jail in the next county.

I fixed up the necessary papers and gave them to the boy's parents, telling them to present the documents to the sheriff of that county and their boy would be released. The sheriff happened to be an old southern, country type who acted like he was king and lord of the territory. He must have had it in for the kid; and when the parents arrived, he gave them a long line of bull that it was too late that day for him to release their son. They would have to come back the next day. It didn't make any difference to him if they had to travel a long distance.

Well, the boy's parents drove back to Dallas to see me. I got on the phone and talked to the sheriff and he told me to mind my own business. He was running the jail, not me. I told him that the parents would be there the next morning and hung up.

They started back to the jail early the next day and only a couple of blocks away both of them were killed in a car crash.

When I heard the news of the wreck, I got on the phone and really chewed the sheriff out. He told me that I'd better never cross his county. If I did and he caught me, he'd throw me in his jail and I'd rot before I got out. He refused to believe that he was in any way whatsoever responsible for the death of those people. I hope that he looks over his shoulder for the rest of his life, expecting that boy to be gunning for him.

"The next Sunday when I was baptized, I cried like a baby. My crying wasn't from sadness; it was for sheer joy that I had at last found peace. I had the feeling that I had been forgiven for all the sins I'd committed."

32. Cindy, George's Woman

The woman who was to make the greatest impact on my life and who later was to become my wife, was a heavy-set, strong-willed woman, twenty-three years of age, from a small town in Texas. We met in Rocky Lane's Bailbonding office. Here I was old enough to be her grandfather and I fell head over heels in love with her at first sight.

Cindy came to our office to arrange a bond for her boss, who'd gotten himself into a heap of trouble. I asked her to have dinner with me that evening. I got no positive response. But, you know me, I'm determined when I set a goal. I called her at work several times. She finally said she would meet me for dinner.

Well, when I got there, Cindy wasn't around. She stood me up. I guess she'd never done that to anybody before because she called me the next day and apologized.

That evening we went to a steakhouse about a block from where I worked. I got right to the point. I looked right through her eyes into her mind. I told her, "Cindy, from this time on you are going to be my woman."

Fire lit up her eyes. "Man, you're insane, totally insane!"

Well, before the evening was over Cindy had agreed to quit her job and go to work for me. We began spending all our time together, right up until I had to be back at the Institute at midnight. She knew I was a con, but she had absolutely no idea as to my real identity. She also had no idea how old I really was. My weight was down to a reasonable poundage and my hair was quite dark from using Grecian Formula 16. The gray had all but disappeared. Every time she'd ask my age, I'd smile and give her a different answer. It drove her crazy because she's one of these people who thrive on knowing precise answers to direct questions.

All she really knew about me was that I was good at my work and had lived some thirty-nine years or so behind bars. I think what really got her hooked on me at first was her curiosity. She wanted to know for herself what it's like being with a man who's supposed to be vicious and violent. My advisor at the Institute told her it would be in her best interest to steer clear of me; that I had a violent past I could never live down. Naturally, that sealed the matter right then and there. All the encouragement Cindy needs to do something is to be told not to do it. She has to run off and experience the forbidden fruit.

I must admit it wasn't long before Cindy got a sampling of my violent side. One morning we were in the courthouse elevator. A tall Mexican man breezed in and accidentally stepped on my foot. I had no choice but to take a stand. I looked up at him and said, "Where I come from when you walk over somebody, you apologize or get ready to fight."

The Chicano just laughed down at me and made some silly remark that I should keep my feet in my pocket. He was a big man, a whole head taller than me. Well, he just shouldn't have said that. I could feel my face burn and I could see that red light flash on, like it did that time when Snotty told me what he was going to do on my grave. I braced myself against the wall of the elevator, doubled up my fists and hit that fellow in the stomach three times before he fell to the floor. I stopped the elevator at the next floor, drug him out, then stepped back in and we went on about our business.

When I was released from the Institute on November 15, 1973, as scheduled, I asked Cindy if I could move in with her. What I was asking her to do was against everything she'd been taught to believe; but by this time we were both deeply in love. In a way, we were each other's security blanket. Without her, the outside world would get me in serious trouble.

To be truthful with you, I was sort of like an animal just freed and not knowing which way to turn. But Cindy was amazing. She really understood what I was going through. All those years I was in prison, society was changing. TV, new kinds of cars, airplanes, ships, and yes, even people. It was a whole new world for me.

Cindy would sometimes catch me shaking my head in disbelief, especially at the way people dressed—the men with long hair; the women wearing mini skirts. Most people had already been taking such things for granted, but I hadn't reached that point. You just go ahead, go out there and spend forty years in prison and just pop out and expect everything to be smooth sailing.

Cindy arranged for me to meet her folks. It went great until she told her mom that I had a prison record. That did it. Her mom all but disowned her on the spot. But Cindy, my sweet Texas Lamb Chop, held her ground and told her mom that she loved me and was not going to dump me just because I'd been behind bars. That was my one and only visit with her folks.

I started writing love notes to Cindy. I'd stick them all over the apartment; on the bathroom mirror, under the edge of the toaster in the kitchen, by the phone, anywhere the mood hit me to stick a note. At first she thought I was crazy, but soon she got where she looked forward to finding them. It was just another way I used to tell her how much she meant to me. I never stopped hiding those love notes until I was arrested the last time.

Cindy kept after me, wanting to know my real age. And she wanted to know who George was. I'd called her George a couple times in a teasing manner, "Now, George, you shouldn't do that." I told her that if she knew all of my secrets, I'd no longer be a mystery to her.

My sleeping habits drove her crazy. I'd sleep for an hour, then stay awake for five or six. I still had the habit of sleeping on my left side with my left foot dangling off the edge of the bed. She questioned me about this and I told her that there'd been a time in my life when getting out of bed in a hurry and grabbing a gun meant the difference between living or dying.

Because I had a knack for talking and answering questions in my sleep, Cindy found out about my harem. She confronted me one morning, wanting to know who Dorothy, Frances and Sally were. I knew she was a good detective, but not that good! Finally she said I'd told her these names while I was sleeping. Believe me, I tried to program my thoughts more carefully after that when I went to bed.

The one thing Cindy absolutely didn't like about me was my singing voice. It's like a fog horn and is completely off key. I'd get wound up in the shower; she'd pound on the door and threaten to call the police if I didn't shut up.

Cindy encouraged me to grow a mustache because she thought it would make me look distinguished. I must admit that it did.

I was always buying little gifts of perfumes and things for her; but I think what she enjoyed most was my habit of getting up early in the morning and fixing her breakfast in bed. I guess I spoiled my Texas Lamb Chop from here to Chicago.

Cindy was pregnant. It wasn't my baby; however, I told her I hoped it turned out a red head just like her. Personally, I just didn't want to be responsible for bringing any more into the world. My oldest son, Doug, had turned out bad. He was known as the "Mad Dog" killer during the sixties. He was crazy. I was afraid he got that way because he was my son; it must have had something to do with heredity. He finally was caught and put in prison after being convicted of killing Abe Swartz, an underworld figure in Nevada.

As far as I know for sure, I have four children: Doug, Wayne, Gail, and a son who married into a prominent family in Colorado. Wayne and Gail, for the most part, have turned out to be good citizens. As I said, I think Doug is insane. And my other son, well, from what I hear he's power and prestige hungry. We never had anything to do with each other. The family he married into is so prominent that if word ever got out that I'm his father, his social status would crumble. Anyway, I have absolutely no desire whatsoever to go to Colorado. That'd be like signing my own death warrant. There's folks there who don't care much for me.

I may have another child or two, but I have no way of knowing for sure. I understand that Gloria has a teen-age daughter who is the right age to be mine, as a result of our living together back in 1962. But I have my doubts.

Cindy's pregnancy ended when she slipped on a loose carpet and fell down a flight of stairs, causing a miscarriage.

After a few bad weeks, including me having a falling out with Rocky Lane, I determined it would be best for us to set out for California. Cindy was all for the idea of taking up roots somewhere else.

It was during the bus ride to Los Angeles that Cindy found out my true identity. Up until that time in January, 1974, whenever she'd ask me about my past I'd kid her along and leave it at that. Frankly, I thought she'd leave me if she knew some of the actual facts. I just didn't want that to happen. I had the feeling that my whole life would have been different if I'd met Cindy forty years earlier. She never made demands of me, yet she made me feel that I didn't have to prove myself to anybody. I never loved a woman for herself until I met Cindy, even though I was always loyal to my women. She made me come out of my shell, and I never went back in. No longer was I withdrawn.

The first night we were on the bus, I started out just kidding around, asking her if she really wanted to know who I was. She tried to throw cold water on me by saying it didn't make a lot of difference to her but she'd play my game.

I told her that I went by a nickname that had been pretty famous in the late twenties and early thirties.

"I know you're not Scar Face Al Capone," she said. "I've seen pictures of him and you're not Italian. You're not tall enough to be Pretty Boy Floyd. Anyway, I know he was killed. John Dillinger was also shot down when he came out of that movie house. So who are you? I give up."

"Think of a main part of a car."

Cindy became irritated. "I can name a hundred parts of a car and probably wouldn't get the right one."

"Well, I'll give you a clue. The last word is gun."

"You're telling me that your nickname was 'Machine Gun'?"

"That's right!"

I was sorry I'd started the conversation dealing with my past. I should have let well enough alone, but I knew she would find out sooner or later. It was best that I told her. She made me understand that it really wasn't too important what I had done — it was significant what I did with my life from now on since I was free of prisons. I should cut all links with my past.

Right then I made a silent vow that I'd never do anything to make her ashamed of me. I'd failed to keep such promises in the past; but now I had someone to live for. Life had taken on a new meaning for me. I'd had my fill of stinking county jails, city jails, and penitentiaries.

Cindy said that James Newth, my attorney in Dallas, told her that I was a man of my own convictions. When I set out to do something, I'd do it in spite of all odds. Well, here was my chance to make an honest man out of Newth and also myself.

I've been pretty bull headed in the past, but while riding that bus into California, I realized that I had to change for Cindy as well as for my own good. If I didn't, I'd be right back behind bars where I'd already spent most of my life. I had to forget who I'd been. If the word got out that "Machine Gun" Kelly was still around, some punk who wanted to build up his reputation would be taking pot shots at me.

Soon after we arrived in Los Angeles, Cindy and I worked with Larry and Liz Erickson cleaning and renovating apartments. Larry told us we wouldn't get rich, but the work would pay a good living wage and if we put forth the effort it required, the money was there.

Larry and Liz also encouraged us to attend their church. In fact, the very first Sunday after we arrived in L.A., they talked us into going to church with them. I wasn't too keen about going because I'd always felt uncomfortable in churches the few times I'd gone. Of course, while I was in prison, I'd go sometimes just to do something different. But once there I'd close my mind to what was being said.

Cindy kept at me to go since our friends had already done so much for us. So when Sunday morning came, we went to the Bethany Foursquare Church in North Hollywood. The pastor's name was Reverend Hal Rapp. Well, it seemed that very first Sunday he was preaching right at me. I respected him from the beginning. He was the only preacher I'd ever heard who made me sit up and take notice. He related God's message in a way that I understood what it was all about. When the Ericksons introduced me and Cindy and I shook hands with Brother Rapp as we walked out the door, I felt that he was genuinely interested in me. We set up a time when I could go see him and just sit down and talk. He was for real; he didn't want a thing from me other than that I give myself to the Lord.

Cindy and I went together one evening, and the three of us really had a talk. When we told him that we were not legally married, he suggested making it legal on his and his wife's wedding anniversary, which was only a few weeks away. The next Sunday we joined his church, but I told him that I wanted to wait at least a week before being baptized. I still had some more things to tell him about myself. I knew that I was in need of some psychological and spiritual help. It seemed that the Lord was working directly through Brother Rapp in satisfying those needs.

When Cindy and I walked down the aisle, I felt something actually pulling me toward the altar; it was like a great magnet. After Brother Rapp introduced us to his congregation and remarked that I would be baptized later, I felt better than I'd ever felt before in my life. Cindy was thrilled over the change I was going through. She had been a good Christian all her life until she met me; now both of us were experiencing a new birth.

We had another session with Brother Rapp; that's when I got a lot of things off my chest. Cindy sat spellbound, too, because I'd never mentioned most of these things out of my past to her. I told them that I just couldn't go into that water and be baptized until I revealed that I hadn't lived the best of lives, but I'd always led my own life, even to robbing banks and killing people. That I'd never done anything I disliked doing. I didn't see any reason to beat around the bush; I told the truth right down the line.

I told them that I was good in what I had done, and I even doubted my ability to rob another bank since I'd served so much time in prison. But when I did rob those two banks the year before in

Dallas, I realized then that I was still the best bank robber in the business.

Brother Rapp wanted to know what my present feelings were. It wouldn't do me much good to be baptized if I still had my old beliefs. Would I go right on committing my old crimes all over again? I told him that the way I felt right then, I'd never go back into crime. From then on I was going to be a child of God and follow Christ's teachings.

The next Sunday when I was baptized, I cried like a baby. My crying wasn't from sadness; it was for sheer joy that I had at last found peace. I had the feeling that I had been forgiven for all the sins I'd committed. From that day forward I was going to be a good man, a man to be respected and looked up to. In one of Brother Rapp's sermons he had said that God would not tolerate a liar. At that point in my life I was never going to do anything again that God would not tolerate.

Cindy and I were legally married by Brother Rapp in his church in June, 1974. We went through the whole ceremony in front of witnesses. Everything was complete but the marriage license. I argued that we were already legally common-law husband and wife in the state of Texas, so why go to the trouble of just getting a slip of paper to tie everything up in California. Cindy gave me some static, but she finally saw it my way.

My singing annoyed Cindy, especially in church, but the spirit of the Lord was in it. I was giving praises to Him regardless how off key I sang. The song that became my favorite and the one that really worked me up emotionally was "It's No Secret What God Can Do."

The five months that Cindy and I attended Brother Rapp's church and associated with the members of his congregation were the happiest months of my life. Cindy and I could communicate with each other without saying a word; we really understood each other.

I think the reason everything turned out so well was because the church was small. We got to know everyone. No longer was the Bible just a bunch of words that I had read while I was locked up; now those words had real meaning for me. I made up my mind I was going to live by them.

I found that all you have to do is open up to God and He'll step right in. I came to know this more than ever after I was baptized. I used to get up early in the morning while Cindy was sleeping and go down by Brother Rapp's church so I could pray and be by myself. During this time it was just me and God. I had a direct pipeline to Him. Everything was Great!

"A man would be a fool to pull the job I had in mind without knowing the lay of the land. The police station was almost right across the street."

33. A Bank Robbery Trilogy

No. 61

The worst mistake I ever made in my life was leaving Los Angeles and relocating in Mesa, Arizona during early summer, 1974. You see, getting away from Brother Rapp's church made it easy for me to put "Machine Gun" Kelly in control of my life and put the Lord on the sidelines. I still had a big problem with my ego, and that problem wound up getting me and some other people in trouble.

We'd rationalized we could find plenty of the same kind of work we'd been doing. But house cleaning jobs in Mesa were few and far between, and we watched what little money we had dwindle away.

Walter Maxted was living in Mesa. He vouched for me and Cindy so we could move into an apartment.

Every day I'd go out and look for work but there just weren't any jobs available that I could do. We'd lived in the apartment for about a week when Walter dropped by to check on us. After listening to my story of dejection he said, "Come on, let's you and me take a ride. I've got something to show you."

I guess you could say that ride was responsible for destroying all the wonderful faith Brother Rapp had built up in me, because in an hour's time I made up my mind the only way Cindy and I were going to stay off poverty row was to do what I could do best.

When Walter let me out of his car at the curb, my mind was made up. While walking to the front door of the apartment I'd figured out the words I was going to tell Cindy.

"Well, what did you see?" she asked as soon as I stepped inside.

"A little bank that's just begging to be robbed."

"Oh sure, you told me that story before."

She had heard me make such statements but nothing had ever come of them. I stood there looking at her, thinking how neat she was. If she'd just lose about forty pounds, she'd be a real good looker. She had such a pleasing, well-modulated voice. And I was always amused at the little gesture she had of pushing her rimless glasses back in place when they would slip down on her nose. She could easily pass for a secretary or young business woman, most certainly not as the gun moll I had in mind turning her into.

The following Sunday afternoon Walter and his wife dropped by the apartment for a visit. After we'd sat around and talked, Walter asked us if we'd like to go for a ride and see some of the sights. Finally we ended up on Mill Avenue in Tempe, and I told Walter to pull into the parking lot in the shopping center, just before we started back around the curve in front of the Arizona State University campus.

"What are we stopping here for?" Cindy asked.

"Oh, I want to show you my little toy bank."

We all piled out and slowly walked around the small structure that was built of heavy native stone, but the walls only reached to a height of four feet; then there was dark tinted glass which completed the remainder of the walls which seemed to disappear into a wide expanse of aluminum roof. The flat roof sloped gently to its middle, which gave the top part of the building the appearance of a seagull in flight.

I noticed that the east and west sides of the roof flared out from the main building for at least six feet to shelter cars whose drivers preferred window service. The entire building was literally anchored to earth by four steel girders, towering above the roof. These were bridged by two heavy cross beams which formed a ninety degree angle in the sky.

I judged that the motor bank — a branch of First National Bank — was twenty feet from the sidewalk which ran along Mill, the main thoroughfare of Tempe. Three-fourths of a block north was University, the busy east and west artery. Tempe Center was the shopping area, and across a wide expanse of parking lot was a string of six stores, built parallel to Mill, the largest being a T & G Market. One block wast of the stores was the sprawling campus of Arizona State University. Walt told me that over thirty thousand students went there.

Cindy and Walter's wife were walking ahead, talking up a storm, not paying any attention to the bank, but I was studying every detail, taking a mental picture of those details and filing them away for future use. A man would be a fool to pull the job I had in mind without knowing the lay of the land. The police station was almost right across the street.

"You're sure you want to rob it?" Walter asked.

He sounded skeptical. I looked at him and smiled. "It'll be a breeze," I boasted. "Let's look for some possible getaway routes." Walt called to the girls and told them to go look through the stores, we'd be back in a few minutes to pick them up. We climbed in his car and drove up and down the Tempe streets and I studied every possible avenue of escape. When I had things pretty well figured out, we drove back to the apartment and completely mapped out the strategy I'd use.

Walter continued to question my plans. "You sure you want to go through with this? That's a mighty busy place. I know. I cash my pay checks there."

"Stop worrying," I said. "You're as nervous as a bitch dog in heat. I'm glad it's busy. No one will be expecting me."

I didn't like a whiner, especially one who tried to tell me not to pull a job I'd already made up my mind to pull. A few months later I'd live to regret thinking that Walter was a man I thought I could trust. Things had been different when we were at McNeil, but on the outside, especially in a job such as bank robbing, there had to be teamwork, a faith in each other's ability.

Before we went back after the girls I made it clear to Walter that I had to acquire an old car which ran well and I'd need Fred Wilson's camper for Cindy to use to pick me up after I'd ditched the drop car. He promised me that he'd take care of getting both cars. He and Fred worked as carpenters at the Anchorage Alaskan restaurant and he could borrow the camper with no problem.

On Monday after work Walter dropped by the apartment and said a man had sold him a light gray, two-door Ford sedan for $300. No names or identities were discussed in making the deal. Walter had parked it on the street only a couple of blocks from my little bank. As he handed me the keys he asked, "When will you do the job?"

"Not until I feel that everything's just right. What about the camper?"

"Fred said you could get it in the morning and use it while he's at work."

"Fine. You drop by for Cindy," I told him as I followed him out to his car.

When Cindy returned with the cab-over camper the next morning I looked it over before she took me to where the old car was parked. I started its engine, listened to it run for a few minutes, then told her to follow me. We drove by the bank, turned west on University and stopped well back on the south side of University

Square shopping center located three blocks from the little bank. Checker Auto Parts, Sir Speedy Printing, Michael's Apple Pie and Snide's House of Pizza were the stores on the south edge of the parking lot.

"Wait for me here," I told Cindy. "I don't know how long I'll be."

She nodded and checked her watch. "It's nine-thirty," she said. "I'm going to get me a paperback or magazine to read. You're crazy if you think I'm going to sit here and look into space."

I patted her on her big fat knee and smiled, "That's my girl. Just be here when I need you because things could get pretty sticky if you're not around." I started to walk away, then remembered something. "You should start the engine about every hour to make sure it'll run when we need it." She nodded in agreement and I left.

Well, she read a pretty thick paperback that day and another one the next day because I just wasn't satisfied yet how things were stacking up. A funny thing happened around one o'clock the second day. She tried to start the camper on the hour as I'd told her to do and the damned engine wouldn't cooperate. A man, who had parked next to her, saw she was in trouble and offered to help.

"I'm waiting for my husband," she told him. "He'll be here pretty soon, and if he thinks I've damaged his truck, he'll probably shoot me." The man proceeded to pull out a screw driver from his tool box and soon had the engine running. Cindy was afraid to turn off the ignition so she let the engine idle for two hours.

That afternoon I parked the drop car on the street again and walked over to the camper and told Cindy that I'd been sitting in front of the T & G Market all day, pretending to read a newspaper. I hadn't missed a single bit of action that had taken place in my little bank and told her that I thought tomorrow was the time to make the heist. I asked her why she had the engine runing. That's when she told me the story about how the man had helped her get it started. "Don't worry about it," I said. "We'll take it by Fred's and get him to check it out. He's a pretty good mechanic."

The third morning I drove the drop car into the parking lot and took a slot only twelve spaces away from the bank. Soon after I turned off the ignition, burglar alarms began to ring on all the stores to the east of the bank. Man, I didn't know what to think!

Within minutes at least twelve police cars raced into the parking area. I watched the coppers jump out of their cars, some with pistols drawn, and run into the stores. Someone finally discovered that a street crew, doing road repairs, had dug into the shopping center's alarm system. Then I noticed a police car parked across the street. I climbed out of the old Ford to get a closer look. Two policemen were inside a store dusting an ice-making machine for fingerprints. I asked a few questions and was told that the place had been robbed the night before. I smiled to myself, thinking how things would be after I left the little bank.

When all my questions had been answered I walked over to my position in front of the T & G Market and was surprised to see still another policeman sitting on a motorcycle directly across from the bank. He seemed to be looking right at me, watching every move I made. I'll let you know I did some quick thinking. Had someone read my mind and those cops were waiting for me to make a move?

Hell, I'd sit it out. I bought an ARIZONA REPUBLIC from a paper vending machine, scanned the headlines before I took my seat. I was ready for another long day if necessary.

At eleven-thirty I found a pop vending machine and bought a coke. Everything was back to normal. I took my time drinking the coke and savoring its coolness. About an hour later I carefully folded my newspaper, tucked it under my arm and walked casually back to the old Ford.

I unlocked the car on the driver's side, tossed the newspaper onto the front seat, then removed a light brown coat I'd draped over the steering wheel to keep it from getting so hot. I felt in the right pocket of the coat and brought out a blue steel .38 pistol, pushed it under the waistband of my trousers on my left side with its handle pointing to my right. I pulled on the coat and climbed in under the steering wheel. After starting the car I backed it out of the slot, drove ahead about thirty feet and stopped so that I was directly in line with the front door of the bank. It was just too hot to walk very far.

I checked my watch. It was one-ten.

When I stepped out of that car, my movements were deliberate and purposeful. I walked straight to the glass door, pushed it open with my left shoulder. The three tellers in the room were talking and laughing among themselves. The one at the east drive-in window was busy on a calculating machine; the one at the west window was perched on a high stool gazing out at the passing traffic. Both of her shoes were off and her panty hose-clad legs dangled carelessly. The third teller was leaning against the back wall, apparently idle at the moment.

As the door closed behind me I spoke in a casual way, "Is it hot enough for you ladies?"

The girl on the high stool turned to smile at me. "This is the kind of day I'd like to jump in the old swimming pool."

"So would I."

My eyes centered on the woman who was leaning against the wall. She was five steps away from me.

"What can I do for you?" she asked with her professional smile.

"Well, I hope you ladies don't get nervous or anything, because I'm here to get your money." With two quick movements my right hand reached underneath my coat and produced the .38 caliber pistol. With my left hand I brought out a folded brown paper bag from my hip pocket. "Do as I say and no one will get hurt. I just want the money, not you." I motioned to all three of them. "Back up against that wall and put your little old hands up where I can see them."

They quickly did as I'd told them. When they were in positions that satisfied me, I spoke one word, "Freeze!" Their eyes glued to the pistol that I pointed at them. For one brief moment I wondered how they would react if I told them that I was George "Machine Gun" Kelly and I was about to rob my sixty-first bank at the tender age of sixty-eight.

I walked behind the counter and pulled open the teller's tray and began to fill the brown paper bag. As I worked I carried on a conversation with the three women. When I asked them a question, they answered politely with a "yes, sir" or "no, sir."

I heard a car drive up to the teller's window on the west, my blind side. Picking up the pistol which I'd placed on the counter, I turned toward the sound of the car. I saw two men; the driver was looking directly at me. Over the intercom system I heard the driver say, "Why, that sonofabitch is robbing the bank. Let's get our ass out of here!"

Very methodically I removed the last bills from the tray and put them into the paper sack. I considered going to the tray at the drive-in window but got to thinking how the two men had burned rubber as they drove away. They were probably looking for a phone to call the police. I faced the three women. "I've got all the money I need. You've been very cooperative. Better lie down on the floor for a while."

I opened the glass door again, using my shoulder, and left. I hadn't been in the bank over four minutes and hadn't touched anything but money.

I drove through the parking lot to University where I got behind a police car which I followed for two blocks to Ash. Then I made a left turn and drove to the back of the stores, pulling up close to the wall of the second one. As soon as I stopped I began wiping down the ignition key, the steering wheel, the door handle and the seat with a large handkerchief. I always carried three of them with me when I went on a job so that I could erase any fingerprints. Usually I start this procedure as soon as I get the car moving, but the policeman in the patrol car ahead of me that afternoon made me take it easy. He just might look in his rear-view mirror and become suspicious.

When I was satisfied I'd done a good rubdown I jammed the handkerchief into my front pocket, picked up the newspaper and the paper bag, got out of the car, then pushed the door shut with my knee.

Cindy had the engine of the camper running as I climbed into the back and wedged myself into the space under the bed. She told me later that before she'd gone two blocks a couple of police cars passed her in a great big hurry, on their way to the bank. It took her twenty-two mintues to drive to 408 East Third Street in Mesa.

The first thing I said to Cindy after she'd stopped the camper in front of our apartment and I'd climbed out was, "Go to the Colonel's and buy some Kentucky Fried Chicken." I fished in the paper sack and handed her a ten dollar bill.

"Can't that wait?" she asked, surprised.

"No, it can't wait. Aren't you hungry after doing a day's work?"

She looked at me as if I were a damned fool, dropped the ten spot in her lap, then smiled. "I guess you want the large barrel with all the trimmings?"

"Sure. Don't you? We haven't eaten much for the last three days. It's time to put on the feed bag."

When she returned to the apartment I was still counting the money. Finally I finished. The tally was a little over four thousand dollars. I looked up at her and said, "After we eat and rest for a while we'd better drive over to Walter's and give him and Fred their cuts."

"Well, you be darned sure you keep our cut. We'll be flat broke without it."

I counted out four hundred dollars and handed it to her. "Go pay the rent for a couple of months in advance."

"What about money to live on?"

"We'll take care of that later."

It had to be later, because within a few hours we were flat broke. I'd turned over all the money except the four hundred we'd used

for the rent, to Walter Maxted.
Cindy was mad as hell.
Don't ask me why. I don't know the answer. I never could hang
on to money.

"We walked into the bedroom and I dumped the money on the bed. Then I did a strange thing. I stretched out on top of all those greenbacks and literally wallowed in them."

No. 62

I guess you think I'm pretty crazy giving all that money away, but that's the way I've lived. Sure, I got static from Cindy, but she probably talked Walter's wife out of a few dollars because we had groceries.

Anyway, a few days after the little bank robbery I was totally relaxed in a big vinyl-covered lounge chair, with only a pair of shorts on. My feet were propped up on an ottoman, and I was working on a heaping bowl of vanilla ice cream watching a John Wayne movie on TV, when there were four sharp knocks at the front door.

"Come in, the door's open," I shouted, not even bothering to take my eyes off the TV. It was only ten o'clock in the morning. I thought it might be one of the neighbors wanting to borrow something. I heard the door open and close, but old John Wayne was doing his thing in the movie so I kept right on watching.

A moment later Dean Warren and Walter Maxted were standing in front of me, blocking my view. I started to chew into them, but I'd seen the movie three times before and knew how everything turned out. "What's on your mind?" I asked.

"Man, you've got it made!" Dean said. "Flat broke and you sit around on your throne without a worry in the world."

I switched off the TV and motioned toward the couch. "You guys have seats while I eat the rest of my ice cream. Start talking and I'll listen."

"Well, as Dean said, you've got it made," Walter smiled. "I took the day off so we could talk business. You need some more money, don't you?"

"When I do, I know how to get it," I told him.

"But do you know where to get it?" Walter interrupted.

"Not right at the moment. I'll leave that up to you two. Find me a bank and we'll start making plans."

Dean started looking around the room, and I knew what he was going to ask before he said anything, but I thought I'd let him ask it. "Aren't you about ready to move out of this place?"

I never did like for people to pick and choose for me. "Oh, I don't know. Cindy and I like it here." I scooped another heaping spoonful of ice cream into my mouth.

"You sure seem to like that stuff. If I ate it this early in the morning I'd puke."

"Well, let's put it this way," I said, "next to Kentucky Fried Chicken, ice cream's my favorite. I can eat two quarts while watching a good movie, and I haven't puked yet."

Dean laughed. "Yeah, I guess you can; it's showing big around your middle. You need to get on the end of a shovel."

"Never found one to fit my hand."

"Well, you sure look like you've done something to develop those arms, shoulders and chest. From the waist up you're built like a weight lifter."

"That's from all those pushups on The Rock."

I've always been kinda ashamed of my legs because they're so short and spindly, but they've always got me where I wanted to go so I never worried too much about them.

I studied the men after I'd taken my last bite of ice cream. "As I said a while ago, if you've got another bank that's begging to be robbed, point it out to me and we'll make plans."

I knew them well enough to know that all I had to say was, "Find me a bank." They'd hound dog a good prospect.

Dean was only twenty-eight but was quite a physical specimen. He was six-four and weighed around two-twenty. His strapping body was crowned with sun-bleached blond hair which he wore long. He was crude and vulgar, yet he appealed to women, that is, until he opened his mouth. Then he showed a quick temper; when drinking, a mean streak surfaced and he became vicious. He had to prove his masculinity by beating on women, especially his wife, Mary Sue. She was around twenty-five and some seventeen inches shorter and one hundred and thirty pounds lighter than her husband.

Walter told me a story about Dean that had only happened a short time back. It seems he and one of his friends got in a fight. Dean knocked the man down and kicked him in the face, blinding him permanently in one eye. Another time Dean and his mother had words. He got so mad at his old lady, after she had ordered him out of her bar she owned in San Diego, that he broke a beer bottle and went after her, cutting her several times.

Frankly, I thought the man was a coward and loved to brag of his exploits to cover up what he really was. But I'd been around his freaky type most of my life and knew how to handle them, especially if they got out of line. I'd leave them alone as long as they stayed out of my hair, but if they got to pushing me, I'd let them have it.

I already told you that Walter was a carpenter, just like Dean was. They often worked together on construction jobs. Walter was good at layout work and cabinet making — one of the best; but he was arrogant, which had probably been intensified by drugs he'd taken. He claimed they were necessary to fight the pain from his old injuries when he'd smashed himself up on the sidewalk.

I must admit that Walter was very good in helping plan a robbery; but he was the kind of person who didn't want any of the physical risks or dangers in the actual robbery.

As soon as those guys left, I snapped on the TV again. I wanted to see the stampede in the John Wayne movie. If you ever saw RED RIVER you'll never forget that stampede and how Wayne took care of the cowboy who had caused it. Remember, that guy was always stealing sugar. Well, this one night it was stormy and the longhorns were restless as all hell. The cowboy turned over some pans, making a hell of a racket and set the cattle to running. But before I could watch the ending of the movie I had to get me another bowl of ice cream.

Dean and Walter were back within a few hours. They said they'd found a branch of the Great Western Bank, located out around 67th Avenue and Indian School Road in west Phoenix, that looked like a sure thing.

I said, "Sure, I know where it is. It's tacked on to the east end of the A. J. Bayless Market. As soon as the girls get back, if Ginger's not too tired, she and I will go over and case the place. Nobody will pay any attention to an old man leading his granddaughter around."

Ginger was Dean's little girl. She was crazy about me and always wanted us to go somewhere together. Of course, the reason was I bought her ice cream cones and we'd walk around eating them.

I didn't tell those two guys that I'd already done some investigating about that particular bank. There was just something about the slogan of the Bayless store — "Your Hometown Grocer" — which made me feel comfortable that the bank next door was probably real friendly.

This particular bank branch was in a large sprawling red brick building which faced Indian School Road, and was bordered on the east by Sixty-fourth Drive. An L-shaped parking area was in the front, which needed to be resurfaced.

The moment the girls returned, Ginger ran to me and jumped in my lap. "Let's go get some ice cream," she begged.

"Well, go ask your mom if it's all right, and if we can use her car. Tell her we won't be gone too long."

Ginger went off on her errand while I disappeared into the bedroom to dress. As soon as I came out the door Ginger grabbed my hand and popped in the car keys. "Come on, let's go!" she said. She almost pulled my hand off before I could get out of the apartment.

I led her out the door and helped her into the car. We drove to a place where they sold several different flavors of ice cream, and I let her choose the color she wanted. Then we drove to the Bayless market. I wanted to freshen my memory of the place. As we climbed out of the car I told Ginger that in a few minutes I'd show her something real pretty, but first she had to eat most of her ice cream cone.

I began to study the building as we slowly walked up and down the sidewalk, both of us munching on multi-colored cones. I saw that the middle panel that separated the bank branch from the market was a glass wall. The entire surface of the wall was covered with gray-brown, mesh, draw drapes which hung from a track about twelve feet high. The same type of curtains covered the glass panels in front of the bank as well as those on the east wall.

There was a drive-in window recessed in at the northeast corner of the building, and long cement markers guided motorists to the window teller. At the front of the bank, the high double entrance doors were made of wood covered with sheet steel and painted a dark blue color. Each door had chrome covered pull handles which looped out for easy grabbing. Underneath the handle, on the right door, was an embedded lock. Three strong, swivel-type hinges supported each door; no screws were visible. Those doors were about the only thing on the outside of the bank that looked strong.

I took the last bite of my cone, wiped my fingers on a handkerchief, then leaned over to examine Ginger's face. For a three-year-old, I must admit she did a good job of getting the ice cream in her mouth and not on her dress. I put the handkerchief back in my hip pocket, took hold of her hand and led her toward the two big double blue doors. "Come on, baby, let's go inside this bank and look at the pretty silver things they have to show us." I'd seen the silver display case through the window and had watched customers stop to examine it.

As we walked in, three customers were looking at the display. None of them noticed me, a stocky old man, and a little girl who was still munching on her ice cream cone. I wanted to give the impression that I was studying the silver display, but you can bet your last dollar my eyes didn't miss a single movement behind the counters which separated the tellers and other employees from the customers.

After a few minutes Ginger grew restless. She tugged on my trousers and looked up at me and said, "Uncle Kelly, let's go home."

"Sure, baby, I think we've seen everything we came to see." She had finished her cone and I had finished casing the next bank I was going to rob.

The next morning I pulled into the parking area in front of the bank, so I could watch customers walk in and out. Finally I got out of the car and walked once again past the plate glass windows. I didn't go inside; I didn't have to; I had the right feeling. This job was right.

The following day I contacted Fred Wilson. I asked him to buy a drop car we would use on a new job. I'd known Fred for about two months now but had grown to like and trust him, even if he was a strange one. I'd judge he was around forty — had red hair and possibly weighed one sixty-five, which fit well on his five-nine frame. He wore a neatly clipped beard he said attracted women to him.

The one thing I didn't like about Fred was he admitted to being married to at least three women, all at the same time. Even this didn't stop him from being a woman chaser. He especially liked them young, between sixteen and twenty-three or four. One thing I will say about him, he treated his women royally, at least up until the time he got tired of them, then he'd disappear and was clever enough to cover up his trail. "Is your phone on a party line?" I said.

"Man, are you crazy? I'm unlisted, non-pub, private as Ma Bell will let me. I don't want my women calling here all the time — day and night — disturbing my sleep, telling me their hard luck stories."

I looked Fred in the eyes. "Your job is going to be to block the space at the drive-in window. When you buy that car, get a light colored Ford or Chevy; they're not to conspicuous. Stay with the mid-sixty models; make sure it runs good."

"No problem. I already got a bead on a 1965 Ford sedan, light tan."

I'd no sooner got back from seeing Fred when Mary Sue and Ginger drove in our driveway. Once more the little girl hopped out of the car and made a beeline for me. She wanted to know when we were going to see the pretty silver display again. I told her we'd take care of that in a few days.

Mary Sue winked at me and picked Ginger up in her arms. There was almost a blank look on the woman's face. I couldn't talk to her very long without feeling that she was an extreme introvert. I knew she feared her husband because of the way he treated her. Being poorly educated and not too bright, she was unable to take care of herself and Ginger without Dean's help. She would gladly do whatever Dean requested in order to prevent one of his tantrums. She was exactly the opposite of Cindy, who is outgoing, friendly and speaks with authority on almost any subject.

Though Cindy is forty or fifty pounds overweight, she has a pleasing personality, is likeable, and has a sense of humor. Even if I did talk her into driving the getaway car in the little bank robbery she could get almost any kind of job where it's required to meet the public. There's sure nothing wrong with her mind. Mary Sue couldn't do anything but keep house, yet the two women seemed to enjoy each other's company and palled around together.

When Mary Sue said something about wanting Cindy to go grocery shopping with her, I interrupted and said that Cindy and I had something important to talk about; she could drop by again soon. As soon as she and Ginger left, I began to discuss the second bank job with Cindy.

I wanted her to lengthen the front pocket on the right side in my favorite pair of trousers. She wanted to know why and I said, "So I can shove my .38 into it, button my coat and no part of the pistol will show."

She looked at the pants and the pockets. "That won't be hard to do," she said, "but I can't understand why you have to wear these pants."

I smiled at her. "Baby, these are my lucky pants."

"You're nothing but a superstitious old fool."

"Some day remind me and I'll tell you about my superstitions." All kinds of things began flowing into my mind.

She said, "Well, why not right now; we've got plenty of time."

"OK. First I always like to wear a hat when I do a job. I

especially like my little fedora with a small brim that I can tilt any way I want. This is my gangster hat. I used to tilt my hat down and to the left. Then one day back in the early thirties in Oklahoma, when the law was hot on my tail, they were really shooting at me, so I had to commandeer a car and get out of there fast. It just so happened that an elderly woman was driving by. She was not aware of what was going on. I jumped on the runnng board of her car, holding on to my machine gun. The lead was really flying so I climbed inside. My head hit the ridge above the door, knocking my hat back off my forehead. Everything went smooth right after that. Not another shot was fired and I got away OK. To me, that was a good omen. From then on every job I did, I cocked my hat back on my head. I'd even go look in the mirror to see if it was at the right angle."

On Wednesday, September 18, 1974 Cindy left the duplex in a borrowed camper. She parked in Andy's parking area in back of the Golden Mirror Cocktail Lounge on Grand Avenue in Phoenix. But I figured this was not to be the day of the robbery. There were too many people going in and out of the bank which prevented me and my helpers from getting a clear shot at it.

On Thursday we all went to our assigned locations, but Cindy came to me and called it off. She had moved her position to a spot on Clarendon and Sixty-fourth Drive which was only two blocks away from the bank on a one hundred and fifty foot long paved strip of Clarendon that ended at the property line of the houses on Sixty-fourth Drive. A wide expanse of plowed field reached clear to Sixty-seventh Avenue on the west. By driving to the end of this paved strip she could get a clear view of the bank, and was directly in line with the drive-in window.

Cindy told me she had no sooner parked and reached into her handbag to take out her crocheting when she glanced down Clarendon and saw a parked police car. The officer was watching children crossing at a busy intersection on their way to school. She just didn't feel secure having me meet her there. Then, a few minutes later Walter drove up and parked next to her. He wanted to know if she had seen a suspicious looking car around the corner.

"Sure, I've seen it. I've been watching it," Cindy told him.

"Well, there's a couple of FBI agents inside," Walter said.

"You're crazy. They're a couple of high school kids sitting there smoking grass," she laughed at him.

"How do you know?" Walter insisted.

"Because I saw them walk out of that house that has the fence around it; they were smoking then."

I guess old Walter drove away in a huff, which didn't seem too cool to Cindy. Five minutes later she had a right to be worried. Hearing a helicopter flying overhead, she stuck her head out the window to see it, and read one word, POLICE, written in large black letters on its bottom. When it started circling around over the camper, she knew she had to get to me and tell me that everything was off — too many things were piling up against us.

She arrived just as Dean and me were getting ready to walk inside. I'll never forget how she drove into that parking lot: skidding her tires and honking the horn, all at the same time. When she told me what was happening, we all went back to the duplex. I told Cindy that we'd go out later and find a new parking place for her. The job was postponed until Friday.

Cindy's new parking place was at the Elim Baptist Church which was located at Sixty-third Avenue and Clarendon, five blocks south and a little east of the bank. A big white sign in front of the church said that Elim was a Bible believing Christ centered church. The parking area was on the south side and to the rear of the classroom building, but I told Cindy not to stop there, to go all the way to the back of the building. The church itself was built of light brown cement blocks with a hip roof. The white spire topped by a cross drew my glance upward. I was hoping that God wasn't watching me.

Friday morning, five minutes to ten, we all left in separate vehicles. I told Cindy to pull into her pre-arranged parking place and assume the posture of waiting for someone to come out of the church. As it turned out, she only had to wait for eighteen minutes before we needed her.

At 10:05 Dean and I stepped to the sidewalk outside that branch of the Great Western Bank. I counted four customers as they entered through the big blue doors. I already knew that four tellers and three other employees, besides the manager, worked there.

I walked into the bank, closely followed by Dean. He drew his .38. In a firm voice I called for everyone to keep calm and to move to the far wall. Dean followed his instructions to take charge of the people and to watch for any newcomers who might come into the bank.

Tucked under my right arm was a canvas bird bag, the kind hunters use to store game while hunting. I walked behind the counter and over to the man I knew was the manager. He looked up from his desk; the usual professional smile creased his face. "What can I do for you?" he asked. Unbelievable! He hadn't even caught on yet that his bank had been taken over. But believe me, his smile vanished when he looked into the muzzle of my .38.

"All you need to do is stand up, walk toward the vault and keep quiet," I told him.

When he saw all the other people bunched together he said, "Stay cool, he won't hurt anybody."

"I told you to shut up," I repeated. The man continued to show his concern about the others, telling them not to be afraid, nobody was going to get hurt.

"You just keep quiet; I'll give the instructions," I reminded him for the third time.

We walked the rest of the way in silence.

I knew the key box inside the vault had to be opened by using special keys. The manager had one key, the assistant manager had the other, and I was sure the slender dark-haried woman, responsible for new accounts and safety deposit boxes, had the third. I'd already collected this information.

After the three keys had been put to use, I took the manager and his assistant into the vault with me and started loading the olive drab canvas bag, taking everything that was green in color. I ignored the "trigger money", which I knew would set off an alarm.

As I loaded the bag, I thought how smoothly everything was going. My plan was working to perfection, except for the babbling bank manager. After I'd filled the canvas bag I walked over and pushed the button on the drive-in window microphone. "Sir," I said, "someone will be with you in just a moment."

This was the signal that told Fred he could leave. The job was complete. Before I walked to the front door, I glanced once more around the bank to be absolutely certain nothing was overlooked.

When we got back on the sidewalk, we hurried to the corner of the building. Fred turned to look at us. I motioned for him to leave. He got so excited that he stepped down hard on the gas pedal; his car bumped into and bounded right on over the six-inch high cement markers. I wanted to watch him leave to be sure that no one followed him. If they had, I'd have shot out their tires.

Dean and I quickly stepped to the first row of cars in front of the bank where we'd left the drop car. I tossed the canvas bag into the back seat, then climbed in under the wheel and drove away. Dean still had his .38 in his hand and was keeping a sharp lookout for anyone leaving the bank. It was already planned that if we were followed, we'd go to a designated spot and get in with Fred. I sure as hell would never lead anyone to Cindy.

Three minues later I guided the car into the south parking lot of the Elim Baptist Church, then continued around to the back. We got out, wiped down the car carefully with the handkerchiefs I'd brought for the occasion. Only then did we climb into the back end of the waiting camper. While Cindy waited at Indian School Road for a break in traffic, I heard two police cars going by with their alarms screaming. We followed the speed limit back to the duplex.

Now the big job faced us — counting the haul. Dean began laughing, letting off the steam that had built up inside him. We walked into the bedroom and I dumped the money on the bed. Then I did a strange thing. I stretched out on top of all those greenbacks and literally wallowed in them. When I stood up once more everyone was watching and smiling. "That's one thing I've always wanted to do. May never get another chance. I'm not crazy, just letting off steam my own way. Now, everything would be complete if we just had a big barrel of Kentucky Fried Chicken, but I guess that can wait. Let's split the money."

I remember studying that cluttered bed for a long moment and then saying, "Looks like pretty good pay for five minutes work."

We all pitched in and began to count the money. After we'd added it all together, we found that the take was a little over thrity-five thousand dollars. I gave Walter five thousand for locating the place; Fred was given four thousand for sitting in his car at the drive-in window; Dean got thirteen thousand, five hundred; I took what was left, over thirteen thousand.

Cindy and Mary Sue had stood by and watched the action. Later, Cindy told me she had noticed Mary Sue make a quick movement, then watched her leave the room. Cindy couldn't figure out what had taken place. Later she found out — Dean had handed his wife a stack of twenty-dollar bills amounting to fifteen hundred dollars. Mary Sue had left to put the bills in her underwear. We all laughed about it — but it was the one great mistake Dean should have never made. I wouldn't go out of my way to make vengeance on anyone, but cheating was something else. I should have received the message that afternoon that Dean couldn't be trusted. A few weeks later this same man was my downfall.

I'm here to tell you the next twenty-four hours caused all of us who had been involved in the bank robbery to do some strange and unusual things. Walter put his cut in a paper sack before he left the duplex, then he tied the sack together so it couldn't possibly come apart. I followed him out to his truck and watched him raise up a stack of inner tubes, which he was carrying in the bed, and stick that sack under them. He redistributed the tubes to make them look like he and his kids were going to ride down the Verde River.

Dean went to his car, deflated his spare tire, pried loose a section of it from the rim, and inserted his brown paper bag inside. Then he got a hand pump and pumped away until he'd filled that tire; then he went to a hardware store, bought a piece of chain and a heavy padlock, and chained that tire to his pickup. After he'd finished the job he said he and his family were on the way to Oklahoma where Mary Sue's parents lived. The next night he called us and said that they were at a motel and he'd taken that spare tire into their bedroom with them. Didn't see them again for several weeks. When they returned to Phoenix, Dean was driving a new Regency Buick. He told us they'd bought a house in Oklahoma.

Walter and his wife were the only ones who stayed with us.

They helped us eat a barrel of Kentucky Fried Chicken. That night Cindy and Walter's wife packaged four thousand dollars and put it in the bottom of a large trunk, then Walter laid two shot guns on top of the money and covered them with blankets and other items. After the trunk was filled, Walter installed two heavy hasps, then secured the lid with two Yale locks. We helped them load the trunk into the camper and then we took it to the Greyhound Bus Depot and shipped it to San Diego.

The next morning all of us headed for Las Vegas. Before the week had passed, I'd lost five thousand dollars at the game tables. The rest of the money was spent on a tractor which had a skip loader. We also bought some other equipment. Walter and I decided to go into the construction business in and around Mesa.

At the time it seemed a lot safer than robbing banks. We had to let things cool off again before we made another move.

"When I climbed out of the police van at the station, a photographer from THE ARIZONA REPUBLIC newspaper snapped my picture, then he walked up to me and said, 'Are you the bank robber?' I kinda smiled and answered matter of factly, 'Well, I thought I was.'"

No. 63

For bank robbery No. 63, I picked the First National Bank near the corner of Indian School Road and Grand Avenue. It was in the middle of an industrial complex which offered many avenues of escape.

Before I mentioned my intentions to any one, I studied the layout off and on during a two-week period. I was in no big hurry until Dean Warren returned to Phoenix on his way to California. I told you that he'd left for Oklahoma right after we'd knocked off the Great Western Bank on September 20th. It was decided than that he should stay away for six months. His sudden appearance triggered me into action. I wanted this bank within the next two days, but Dean reasoned with me.

"Man, it's not like you to dive right in without a lot of preparation."

"Preparation!" I stormed. "I've got it all figured out. All my plans are right here." I pointed to the side of my head.

"But you're a sick man, coughing and spitting like you're ready for the TB ward. You better get yourself straightened out or you'll die when we make our strike, right inside the bank."

"It's just a flare-up of my asthma and emphysema," I argued. "I've been taking treatments." I paused to scratch the side of my nose. "OK, you go on to California for a week; I'll go back into the hospital and get my lungs pumped out. By the time you get back, we'll be ready for business."

When Dean returned, we cased the bank, but I was still a sick man. I'd been in and out of Mesa General Hospital and had to go to emergency twice. The next time I was admitted, the doctor wanted to keep me there until my trouble was completely cleared up.

The night before the robbery was to take place, Cindy visited me and I convinced her that she must talk Dr. Barnett into releasing me on an overnight pass, using the excuse that some urgent business in my construction firm had to be taken care of.

It took a lot of urging from Cindy, but Dr. Barnett finally agreed. He cautioned her to bring me back the next morning because I was still a very sick man.

The doctor was right. When I was ready to leave I had to lean on Cindy just to walk out of the hospital and get in the car. On the way to the duplex, Cindy told me if I wasn't careful I wouldn't live another two years. She said it was a disgrace the way I was treating my body. I tried to accept her statement graciously but inside of me I was really suffering. You see, I'd developed a fear of dying during this time period when I'd gotten so far away from God.

At home that night I began to feel better and started asking Cindy about my dark blue stretch pants and the hat I'd worn in the last robbery. She said she'd destroyed both of them to cover up my identity just in case the law came snooping around. She said Bill Stone had cut up the pants and then she had burned them. They were determined to completely cover up my trail.

Then Cindy began to tease me about my superstitions. "Remember Tempe? You wore a yellow cloth hat with a plaid band. You lost it when we were tubing down the Verde River. Well, you didn't get caught in the second robbery when you didn't wear that hat."

"Well, I would have worn it if I'd found it," I told her.

"Your second hat was the yellow straw with a little red feather in the band. If they'd found it, you'd been in trouble. People remember those things even if they don't remember too much about your looks." She put that teasing smile on her face. "What are you going to wear this time?"

"Not any; I'm going bareheaded. That's the reason I've got this feeling that something's going to happen. You kid me about my superstitions, but I've always believed in using things that work for me."

Cindy put on that teasing smile again. "I'm sure glad I don't have those kinds of hangups. Nothing's got me all tied up in knots."

"Oh, yeah!" I blasted, "explain that cigar I caught you smoking the other night. How long you been tied up with them?"

She looked like a rat cornered by two cats. "Oh, I forgot about the cigars. I've been sneaking puffs on them maybe four or five years. Some girls dared me to try one when I started complaining that I didn't like cigarettes any more. One of the girls handed me a Cherry Swisher Sweet. After I took a few drags, I was hooked.

But I didn't want you to catch me."

"OK, let me have my superstitions and I'll go along with your crazy cigar habit."

Then Cindy suddenly noticed that I was practically dancing around the apartment. "What's happening? A few hours ago you acted like you were on your deathbed."

"What do you mean, what's happening? I always get sky high before a job. Just thinking about what I'm going to do tomorrow is great medicine. Just think back; I was floating around like a feather before the last two jobs. You didn't notice it so much because I wasn't real sick those times. Now you see me getting thirty years younger under your nose and it comes across as being dramatic. Well, it is dramatic. Remember that time last March in Los Angeles? That day I was so sick and I asked you to drive me to the nearest bank. You almost had to carry me into the place."

Cindy said, "How could I forget; I sat you there about a half-hour. Then, just like that, you jumped up and said you'd had enough. You took the keys and dragged me back to the car!"

The next morning when the robbery was to come off, I canceled it. I thought everyone was too jumpy; a getaway car had not been bought yet. Fred Wilson had to wait too long to get in the drive-in window line; too many people were going in and out of the bank. All of these reasons made me cautious. I also wanted to dye my hair a dark brown, and I needed to buy a wide elastic belt which I could wear around my waist to hold my belly in and make me look thinner and younger.

That afternoon Cindy took her friend Suzie Diamond with her to look for a drop car. Suzie was not clued in on any of the details. She was under the impression I needed the car for my business. They found one in a residential district with a "for sale" sign on it. When they stopped to look at it, an elderly man came out into the yard and began to elaborate on the car's good qualities. He claimed he hadn't been able to do much driving since he'd been forced to turn in his license because of poor eyes. He'd just put on four new tires and had the engine tuned. Cindy drove it and was pleased how quietly the engine ran. She asked his price.

"Well, since I'm never going to drive anymore, you can have it for $150."

Cindy paid him the money out of the cash Dean Warren had given her that morning. The old man didn't even suggest getting the papers notarized or to close the transaction in a business-like manner. He merely signed where he was supposed to and pocketed the money. In less than a week's time he would have to forfeit the money over to the police.

Cindy drove the car to a bar where she picked up Fred Wilson and also Dean and Mary Sue. After she took the Warrens to their apartment, Fred drove Cindy home and told her that he would park the car on the street until the following day. I never saw the car until the morning of the bank robbery.

On Friday, November 8, 1974, Cindy borrowed the same camper she'd been using. We got up at six that morning and went to a restaurant to enjoy a good breakfast, the last one I'd really relish for a long time. No sooner had we sat down when a man known as New York Mike joined us. He had been brought into the picture by Fred and Dean. They told me that he wanted to be an interested bystander, watching exactly how a job could be pulled off. Then Dean began conning me to let Mike take part in the action.

I studied the six-foot-two Italian-looking guy carefully. I judged that he was around thirty, a pretty clean cut man. Something kept telling me to say no, but Dean was so insistent. He claimed that Mike was an old hand and was just passing through Phoenix and wanted some action. Finally I said OK. I'll never forget the look Cindy gave me. When Mike and Dean left a few minutes later, she really let me have it.

"Dean's wife told me that guy's served time for dope smuggling and every underhanded thing you can mention. That stuff they've been giving you in the hospital's really got to you. I wouldn't trust that Mike to walk me across the street. I'll bet you'll be sorry you listened to Dean before the day's over."

Now, I wished I'd listened to Cindy, because things turned out just like she'd said.

We finished our breakfast and went to meet the others. When Cindy kissed me good-by, she seemed to hang on to me for dear life, as if it was the last time she'd see me as George Kelly, a free man. I should have gotten her message. The next time we met was under entirely different circumstances. My name went back to being John Webb and would remain John Webb.

It had been planned that when we had crawled into the camper after the robbery, there would be a second dropoff point. Cindy would let Dean and Mike out of the truck where Mary Sue would be waiting at 59th Avenue and Bethany Home Road. They would get their share of the money while traveling between those two points. Dean and Mike would climb out of the camper and leave with Mary Sue. Cindy and I would then drive to Bill Stone's place. Bill was Suzie Diamond's boy friend.

At ten-fifteen that morning Fred Wilson drove up to the drive-in window and stopped his car. Dean, Mike and I walked into the bank. Dean and Mike took places just inside the door so they could take care of all customers who were already inside and also those who entered the bank during the robbery. I was to handle the nine employees, herd them to the vault, fill the canvas bag and a briefcase we'd brought along. Walter had picked the accordion-style briefcase up for $2.85 at a park and swap. Our plans were to be out of the bank in less than five minutes.

I went to the drinking fountain next to the west wall, took three swallows, turned and studied the whole layout. I suddenly noticed a man in a business suit who had just turned away from the teller's window. A big bulge was underneath his coat. My educated guess was he was an FBI agent. I walked up behind him and brought my .38 from my front pocket. "Put your hands on your head and lock your fingers together," I ordered.

I motioned to Dean and Mike to take out their pistols and to move the customers to the far side of the lobby. I reached under the man's coat and pulled out a .38 Cobra, the standard weapon used by the FBI, and jabbed it into the man's back.

"Walk straight ahead and go behind that counter," I said in a way there wouldn't be any misundersanding.

The man turned to look at me. "I'm an FBI agent. Here's my ID."

"Don't worry about your ID," I said. "I've got you where I want you. Shut up and keep walking. If you try to reach for a pocket again, I'll open up your back."

As soon as we were behind the counter, I took three quick steps to a PBX machine and pulled its electrical plug. There sure as hell wouldn't be any messages going over it now.

For one brief instant I thought of sending Dean or Mike into the vault for the big money while I held everybody at bay. But on second thought I wasn't sure that either one of them knew how to operate back there. Later, I wished I'd followed my hunch. Being sick and under pressure I knew I was thinking crazy. Neither one of them had given any reason to doubt them, that they were not doing their jobs. Again, I should have followed my hunch.

In the old days I was the one who worked the front. The machine gun I carried made people wilt or they froze so stiff they were like

203

wooden Indians. I read many articles in the papers after one of my jobs how the people felt when they looked into the muzzle of "Machine Gun" Kelly's popper. That machine gun was my trademark. I wished I had one right now. That Thompson Model 21 was something else.

I told the surprised assistant manager to make all his employees line up against the wall next to the vault. Then he was to go to the vault and work his part of the combination. "After your part, tell your boss to use his numbers and complete the opening."

While the bank manager was down on his knees and turning the dials, I saw that his hand was shaking as if he had palsy. After the vault was opened, I herded all the employees and the FBI agent inside, then instructed the manager to open the bottom safe first. I put the briefcase on the floor next to the tray, flipped it open and pulled out the olive green canvas bird bag. Reaching into the tray I lifted out three bundles of one dollar bills and shoved them into the briefcase. I saw that the second tray also had only one dollar bills. I turned to the manager. "Where the hell's the big money?"

"That's all we've got. We've had a bad day."

"What in the hell are you talking about? Open that other drawer before I change the shape of your face."

He got busy in a hurry. When he pulled open the drawer, I looked in and saw stacks of ten, twenty, fifty and hundred dollar bills. There were several stacks of hundreds. I'd already stuffed the briefcase three-fourths full of the ones so I quickly filled the rest of the space with tens, twenties and fifties. Snapping the bulging case closed, I then very methodically filled the canvas bag with bundles of one hundred dollar bills. By the time it got so full I couldn't get anymore in, I stuffed the remaining bundles of hundreds into my pockets. There was just enough room for them.

I secured the flap on the canvas bag and when I straightened, I felt a slight cramp in my back. "I don't want anyone to make a move for five minutes." They all looked scared. "I've got some men in the lobby who have stop watches. If one of you pokes your head out of here, you'll get it blown off."

I'd held on to the .38 all the time I was handling the money. I had kept it pointing at the employees. In one quick movement I ran my left arm through the canvas straps on the bird bag, then hooked the fingers of my right hand into the handles of the briefcase, but I was still holding on to the pistol. When I straightened up, I felt the strain of the weight and heard and felt the canvas straps that were across my arm begin to come apart. They just had to hold until I got out!

Once more I looked at the faces of the people. "I'm warning you, don't anyone try to be a hero."

I backed out of the vault and moved toward the front doors. I felt the raveled straps eating into my arms, cutting circulation; the briefcase handles were slipping from my fingers. When I reached the lobby I put the bags down so I could get a better grip, and when I straightened up I knew something was wrong.

Where were Dean and Mike?

Why hadn't one of them come to help with the heavy bags? I looked through the glass in the front doors to the spot where they had parked the getaway car. A yellow car, which I recognized immediately as one belonging to the FBI, was in the slot. I moved my eyes an inch to the left and saw a black and white police car. In the short time I looked out that window I saw other police cars pull into the parking lot to block off the whole front and side of the bank. The two words I often used when things didn't go right were, "Ah shit!" I know I said them loud enough just then for everyone in the bank to hear me.

Hell, I didn't have a chance! I dropped the bags close to the door and walked back to the vault. I spoke to the assistant manager. "What did I tell you about calling the police?"

The man turned green like he was going to be sick. "Why, how could I call the police? There's no phone back here."

"Well, come here and have a look. I want you to tell me who did call them."

I followed him to the front of the bank, grabbed his shoulder and spun him around. "You go out there and tell them to come in."

"Why, I'm not going out there," he half stuttered, "they'll shoot me."

"Well, I don't care how you do it, get them in here." I handed him my .38. "Take this along with you and throw it out the door and then stick your hand in the air. They won't shoot you."

"No, I won't do it!" he screamed, shoving the gun away.

"I'll take it and also my own," a voice said in back of us.

Both of us looked over our shoulders and watched the FBI agent walk around the end of the counter. "Hand over those guns and I will get the police in here."

I reached under my coat and pulled out the .38 Cobra I'd taken from him a few minutes ago, then handed him both guns and said, "Well, you finally got to show your ID, didn't you, FBI punk?" I watched him go to the double glass doors and poke his head out.

"I'm Freddie Cain, FBI!" he shouted. "This man inside is in my custody."

In moments the bank lobby was filled with police. After I was handcuffed I looked up and saw two TV cameras pointed at me. They were grinding away. One was from Channel 10, the other from Channel 12. I was first led to a police car where I had to wait for a few minutes, then I was transferred to a van and taken to the police station.

Cindy told me later that she had been sitting in the parking area in the service alley of the Seven-Eleven Grocery Store when Fred Wilson drove up. He said, "We've decided to abort. Things don't look right." A short time later Dean and Mike arrived. She watched them climb out and wipe down the drop car. She could see that Dean was very nervous. Both men climbed in back of the camper. Then Dean shouted, "Let's get the hell out of here!"

"Where's George?" Cindy shouted back.

There was no answer.

"I'm not going anywhere until you tell me about George."

"They got him!" Dean shouted.

"What do you mean they got him?" Cindy asked. "Did they shoot him?"

"No," Dean said, "he never had time to pull a gun. They got him as soon as he walked through the door."

Cindy couldn't believe what she was hearing. She thought that my helpers got scared and split. When she heard the news reports she realized that half what they told her were lies. She heard that both of them had gone inside with me. After I'd gone inside the vault, they left because they'd turned yellow. Mike had run out of the bank and gone to where he could see Fred Wilson sitting in his car at the drive-in window. Fred was supposed to have told him, "I don't like it, let's get out of here."

Well, Mike hurried back into the bank and told Dean what Fred had said. They walked out of the bank together, climbed in the car and left. Cindy was sure that is when some customer had called the police, and that's the reason I got caught. She drove them to where Mary Sue was waiting, and when they climbed out of the camper, neither one of them even turned to thank her; they just got in the other car and drove away.

Cindy drove to Bill Stone's house, not knowing anything else to do. She first heard publicity of my capture on the twelve o'clock news. She knew it was me they were talking about, although I'd tossed out some phony names during the first few hours before I told them the name John Webb.

Shortly after one o'clock Walter went to Bill's place and he and Cindy sat in his car and talked. He told her that he was afraid that he would be pinned in with the robbery since he'd been so closely associated with me for the past several months. He advised Cindy to leave town or she would also become involved. That afternoon she went to San Diego with some friends of ours. Her plan was to have my son, Wayne, pick her up and they could make future plans.

Wayne did pick her up and they drove to Los Angeles where she remained only eight hours before the FBI contacted her and ordered her to return to Phoenix.

When I climbed out of the police van at the station, a photographer from THE ARIZONA REPUBLIC newspaper snapped my picture, then he walked up to me and said, "Are you the bank robber?"

I kinda smiled and answered matter of factly, "Well, I thought I was."

Later that morning while I was being questioned by FBI agents, Doug Hopkins and Freddie Cain, Hopkins left the room and Cain walked over to me and said, "This is embarrassing to me, to my friends and co-workers. You understand how I feel?"

"Sure," I said, "but you didn't get arrested. Guess how I feel."

I knew he was trying to get me to keep quiet on how I'd taken his Cobra away from him and herded him into the vault with the rest of the bank employees. If his buddies found it out, he would end up being the butt of many jokes and a lot of ribbing by them if they learned the details. I wasn't going to lie for him because I didn't like him. He thought he was a real big shot, terribly impressed with his own importance. The other agent, Doug Hopkins, was the smarter of the two. He didn't try to dehumanize me, as I told Cindy later.

It was late in the afternoon before they even thought of searching me. Cain asked, "What did you do with the rest of the money? There's still eleven thousand dollars missing."

I grinned at him. "Let's play a little game. You tell me how much I had packed in those two bags and I'll produce the eleven thousand. I'm sure the news media won't give the right figures. It would make robbing banks seem too profitable."

"Our report said you had fifty-eight thousand in the briefcase and approximately one hundred and forty thousand in the bird bag. That would have been some haul if you'd gotten away."

I couldn't hide all of my grin. It was impossible trying to keep a perfect poker face.

Cain then asked, "OK, where's the rest of the money?"

"You fellows really disappoint me. I've been in your custody for six hours and haven't even been searched." I reached in my pockets and pulled out the bundles of one hundred dollar bills. Both of those agents looked plumb silly when they stared at the money in disbelief, then at each other.

Cain came to his senses first. "Just empty everything right on this table," he ordered.

"Well, I've got a little cash of my own. You don't get that, too,"

Suddenly Cain was the full fledged FBI agent and I was the criminal. "Where you're going you won't have much need for it," he said sarcastically. When I put my old friend on the table he almost came apart. "My God, you've also got a can of mace! How did you get all that in your front pockets!"

"You won't believe me when I tell you, but since you asked, my legs are like toothpicks. I can fill my big legged trousers and you'd never know there's anything in my pockets."

Hopkins smiled but Cain just glared at me. "I don't think you're in any position to joke around. Just shut up while we count the money."

They did count it and announced that there was eleven thousand and thirty-seven dollars.

"The thirty-seven dollars is mine," I said, "and I want it back."

Cain snickered, "Why don't you sue and try to get it back."

Cindy made it understood when she talked to the FBI officials that they would have to meet her at Sky Harbor Airport in Phoenix. She would catch the first flight and should be there by nine o'clock that night. But she made them wait for a couple of hours; she did not reach Phoenix until eleven. They'd given up on her so she called Agent LeBrand of the FBI and told him where she'd be staying. He called the next morning and said that he'd pick her up at noon; in the meantime he'd arrange for her to have a private meeting with me. He kept his word; Cindy and I got to spend over five hours together that afternoon. As soon as she saw me I knew she was concerned. I was gasping for breath after each spasm of coughing. They'd only given me the bare minimum of medication.

Agent Hopkins got real upset because I'd received no attention because of my condition. He even complained to the marshals and made them aware of the shape I was in. Later I was taken to the County Hospital where they gave me some treatments and medication. Cain didn't give a damn how much pain and discomfort I was experiencing — I was a no good bank robber who had made a fool out of him.

Cindy asked Hopkins if she could talk to me alone for a few minutes. The agent went to the far side of the room and turned up the volume on the intercom system so he couldn't hear what we said to each other.

The one question I asked Cindy over and over was, "Why did those three punks run out on me?"

She related their conversation in the camper and assured me that the only thing that happened was they'd turned yellow and split. We also discussed how Cain just happened to be in the bank at that particular time. Was it just a coincidence or had he been planted? When she asked me what I thought, I could only say, "It looks pretty obvious, they were just chicken shit and left me. All either Dean or Mike would have had to do was give me a warning whistle and we could all have made a quick exit."

"Well something's sure as hell fishy," Cindy insisted. "The law sure got there fast. You say they were waiting for you when you came out?"

"That's right, and I wasn't in the vault over four or five minutes. It's a good thing they caught me or I'd probably kill all three of them."

I paused to study Cindy for several moments. "I want you to make me a promise," I said.

"Sure, anything."

"First, I'm not a snitch. Second, don't you lie."

She let out a big sigh of relief. I'm sure she didn't expect either one of those statements or request. "Well, I've lived with you long enough to know you don't snitch on anyone, and if it'll make you feel better, I won't lie to them if they start asking a lot of questions."

"I've done something against God's will. I've wasted a life. Mine. That's a great sin."

34. No Nightingales In Florence

It's getting near the end of March, 1975. I've been sentenced, and in a few days I'll be shipped out to Springfield. The four-and-a-half months in the Federal Detention Center in Florence, Arizona have been the toughest of my life. Prison is a breeze compared to this place. There are thirty-two isolation cells and two dorm areas, each with sixteen double bunks. I don't know whether I've done more time in isolation or in the dorms. It really doesn't matter. At least when I'm in isolation I have a little bit of privacy.

But no matter where they put me, even when I'm in this little visiting cage, a guard checks on me every hour on the hour, day and night. I don't know which they're more afraid of — that I'm gonna kick the bucket while they're still responsible for me, or that I'll find some way to dig with my bare hands through all this concrete and steel.

Let's be realistic. It's like Black, one of the good-guy guards who worked here until he was fired, told Dobkins one morning before he sent him in to the visiting area: "If old Webb ever decided to make a run for it, he'd probably go six or eight steps before he collapsed, then we'd have to carry him back in. He sure isn't going anywhere."

Here comes my hourly check right now. That's Lieutenant Bellows — he's the guy who runs this place — popping his head through the door. "Hey, Bellows! I'm going to have them call you 'Dirty' Bellows in the book."

"If you do, I'll sue."

"You can't sue if it's true."

Say, he didn't have to slam that metal door so hard. I think I ruffled his feathers. I don't think he wants anybody to know he used to be a guard at McNeil Island when yours truly was there. If my memory hasn't gotten too faulty, I think he helped me get a couple choice hunks of meat for my cooking operation.

They've got me so doped up the last few days because of my health going rotten, it's getting harder and harder for me to think straight. I don't think I could take many more of these interviews. It's getting to me, this holding a receiver in both hands and keeping my arms bent for hours at a time. If I come out of this not paralyzed, I'll be happy. Right now my last two fingers on each hand are numb.

Like I said, doing time in this place is tough. Especially with all the bitterness I was pent up with after they caught me. It took me two months to simmer down, not because I got caught for the first time in my life in a bank, but because of New York Mike and Dean Warren. I know one thing, it wasn't very nice for them to leave me high and dry. If I'd gotten away, in the next few days I'd killed them, that's a fact. Anybody did what they did doesn't deserve to live. I probably won't forget what they did to me, and I darned sure won't care what happens to them. I won't take any action against them because of Cindy. I will not do anything that will reflect on her from this point on. I've already got her in enough turmoil as it is.

I've had three great blunders in my life. I had a blunder in the twenties, a blunder in the thirties, and a blunder in the seventies. The blunder in the twenties was the Coors caper. The blunder in the thirties was the Urschel kidnapping. Of course, my blunder in the seventies was Dean Warren and New York Mike.

Would I do the things over that I've done in my life? Look at the end result. It's not worth it. Sure, I'd do it over again. Why? Because I was made differently. But if I had known the results would have been the same, I would have gone about it another way. I could lie about it, but I would do it all over again. I wasn't born to be broke. Everybody who has known me, knows that I'm different. I might have a twisted outlook, but I'm not mentally unbalanced.

I never did anything actually just for the money — money was a fringe benefit. I didn't care whether I had a pocket full of money or just enough to live on. Maybe that's why I gave it away. The important thing to me was not so much the money as the challenge, the confrontation in getting it. It used to get me madder 'n hell for someone to call me a thief. I was definitely not a thief; I was a taker. There's a big difference. I never tip-toed in the dark behind somebody's back. I took what they had face-to-face. There always had to be that confrontation.

To the best of my ability, I figure that I was the lead man on sixty-three bank robberies. The last one — the one I got nailed for — took place about fifty years after the first one I pulled with Cotton Tabor that time we were just passing through Fort Smith, Arkansas. All in all, I've robbed banks in at least twenty states:

California, Oregon, Washington, Colorado, Indiana, Minnesota, Kansas, Ohio, New Mexico, Florida, Louisiana, Georgia, Alabama, Tennessee, Arkansas, Oklahoma, Texas, Missouri, Mississippi and Arizona. Maybe I left out a state, but I didn't add any. I'd say most of the robberies were in a fifteen-month time period up to the Urschel kidnapping. At least forty of the jobs were pulled during that period when I was rampaging every second of every day.

I even managed to have a hand in the biggest bank robbery in United States history this last October, 1974. A few weeks before the First National Bank job in Phoenix, I disappeared for two or three days and neither Cindy or anybody else knew where I was.

They wanted my advice on what was the best way to go about pulling off a "big hit" in Nevada. Well, I took a quick trip to case the place for them and give my opinion. The rest is history. The "big hit" was in Reno and they got away with over $1,200,000 in cash, plus a big bundle more in securities. It was the largest cash robbery from a U.S. bank since way back in 1931 when my old buddy Harvey Bailey robbed over a million bucks from the Lincoln National Bank and Trust Company in Lincoln, Nebraska.

The strangest thing about the Reno job, it was pulled off pretty much the way I suggested. What else should I have expected? Whether I do it or someone follows my advice, the chances are ninety-nine out of a hundred that the job will go perfectly. I only wished that I'd been able physically to have gone back to Reno and taken part in the job myself. It didn't work out that way. If I had managed to get my hands on that kind of money, I'd called it quits, settled down and lived out my years with Cindy.

At least at a certain moment in time I had those feelings, but in all honesty, who knows if I would have stopped at that point or not.

One thing that's been on my mind a lot lately is the similarity between my capture after the Urschel kidnapping and my capture in the bank in Phoenix. No shots were fired on either occasion. The only conclusion I can come to is that God had a hand in it: He wanted to keep me around for some special purpose. I guess He saw Brother Rapp way up ahead in my future and that I'd finally ask Jesus into my life.

Then I did some back-sliding all the way into this place. I've done something against God's will. I've wasted a life. Mine. That's a great sin. I know this time, if I get out, I'll go straight. I have a reason for living. But deep down I have a feeling that God has given me the last chance to witness for Him. I blew it, and I'm paying for it.

Still I've undergone some great changes. For example, last night I punched another guy in the mouth. It was a situation where I had to pull myself back by my shoelaces. The guy had taken some of my Bryl Cream. Twenty minutes after the incident I told him I was sorry. I never show my anger, but last night it showed through. It was from the results of living in this place. In the past, I'd killed guys for doing less.

The incident dealing with the Bryl Cream was a new one for me. It was the first time I'd ever apologized to anyone who had made me angry. I realized that I'd mellowed, especially when I went to bed and got to thinking about it. A few years earlier the other inmate would have been found dead somewhere in the facility. I found it disturbing to think I'd let him get away; then I realized that all the desire for killing had gone out of me.

All that bitterness has also gone out of me. I even try to be careful about making remarks like I did early last month when Dobkins passed a rumor he'd heard that Kathryn, now living in the Oklahoma City area, had been having problems with her heart and had been in and out of the hospital. I snapped at him, "Kathryn didn't have any heart trouble. How could she? She doesn't have a heart."

Of course, I still have a sort of sarcastic sense of humor. Just the other day I told Cindy, "When I die, I want you to bury me face down so all my friends can kiss me good-by."

I guess the last time I almost let my bitterness get the best of me was when Judge Walter Craig, the federal judge handling my case in Phoenix, refused to lower the $125,000 cash bond that had been held over my head. All of the others involved in the three bank robberies were out walking the streets. I didn't even have a probation report done on me until the last second. When a guy named Thomas finally took the report, it was only three days short of four months since I'd been arrested. He told me, "I don't know how we missed you."

That day I'd been brought in for additional proceedings before Judge Craig. Before I was taken in to see Craig, while I was in the U.S. marshals' holding area, my public defender, John Moran, stopped in to see me. I remarked to him almost casually, "It might be a blessing in disguise that I haven't been given a probationary report." It was just my way of saying that there was a giant loophole in my case after all. It was a nice big fat technicality, and I was primed to sink my teeth into it for all it was worth.

It was shortly after Moran left, that Thomas showed up with the report. This turn of events concerned me. I felt that Moran, going into action at this time, had sold his soul to the other side. It was a very unethical action.

Other than the fact that Moran actually did a fairly good job in explaining my health problems and my desperate need for surgical repairs, I don't think very much of the guy. He was assigned as my public defender after Tom Karas, chief public defender in the Phoenix district, pulled out of the case. Karas is a brilliant attorney; but, like me, he has to be in complete command and this was a problem between us.

During the arraignment, Karas caught FBI Agent Hopkins in a bad way on several points. He asked, "Did you search Mr. Webb?" He finally got Hopkins to admit that several hours had elapsed before I was actually searched. That's when the missing eleven thousand dollars was found in my pockets. And the van that was used to transfer me to the police station from the bank had no windows in the back. Karas asked Hopkins, "Did the van in which Webb was transported have windows in the back?"

Hopkins replied, "Yes."

Karas said, "That's all." He was laying the groundwork for later if the case went to trial. Then he'd use these points to discredit Agents Hopkins and Cain. He knew that many agents do not keep notes during questioning periods. Several months would elapse before they'd go before a jury, and then they'd try to talk strictly from memory. Karas was sharp enough that he would quickly undermine the agents' report later.

Karas even had me interviewed by a psychiatrist, a Dr. Gray, who only saw me one time for about an hour and fifteen minutes. There's no way he could have formed an accurate opinion as to my real identity, John Webb or George Kelly. From some of the questions he asked, I could tell that he obviously already checked some of the government reports on me. That would be enough to make him prejudiced about my identity from the start. If I was John Q. Public, he'd spend thirteen or fourteen hours with me and then prepare an extensive report that would shed some accurate light on the subject. I knew I'd see him just a short time, so I fed him a bunch of bull. I think Karas sensed this, and I'm sure that's one of the reasons he pulled out of the case.

Then I got stuck with Moran. Right off the bat, I didn't like him. The only thing that really sticks out in my mind about Moran is he wants my personal papers. He's a pliceman; he has political ambitions. He knew that the psychiatric report was not worth the paper it was written on. He wants to keep everything personal in case any publicity comes up so he can realize some personal gain.

If I'm just John Webb, as the government maintains, why should Moran want a personal file on me? He doesn't know for sure in his own mind if I'm really Kelly, so he wants the papers just in case. He thinks he can play anybody like he could a three dollar banjo; he can ride any monkey he wants to ride. He's hoping that I am Kelly but he's not sure, and he's not taking any chances.

I had been charged with two armed bank robberies with a third charge hanging over my head. After some behind the scenes work by one of my "great white fathers", and a series of sessions with the assistant district attorney Ron Jennings and Judge Craig, a plea bargain was arranged. In exchange for all charges being dropped against Cindy for her involvement, I agreed to a reduced charge of one count of bank larceny.

This meant that instead of ultimately facing three counts of armed robbery, each carrying a max of twenty-five years, I now faced a max of ten years. But what made the deal real sweet is that I was guaranteed an "A Number." This meant that I'd be eligible for parole almost from the moment I went to prison. In effect, my sentence became "up to ten." Here I was getting the same kind of sentence that the Watergate burglers got. They got "A Numbers", too. That's why they started popping out of prison just months after they went in. The "A Numbers" are authorized by the Justice Department in Washington, D.C. You see, it pays to have a "great white father."

Walter Maxted got probation as did Dean Warren after he was captured, I think up in Idaho. Fred Wilson got a two-year term; and the only reason he got that, he must have played tough guy during questioning. Otherwise he was a cinch for probation since Walter got off so easy.

I don't even think they tried to beat the bushes very hard to find New York Mike. I still have a sneaking suspicion he might have had a hand in my arrest. When you sit and sit in a place like this detention center, your mind thinks up all kinds of things. For example, couldn't Mike have been afraid of a drug rap about to fall on him, and volunteered the information that he could lead the law to a "big catch" in exchange for the drug charge being dropped? Then the "big catch" tuned out to be me? That would explain the FBI agent being in the bank and Mike and Dean disappearing like they did.

It could have been a set-up.

Let me get off this negative talk before you think my time has been a total loss in this place. There have been good moments, too. Cindy's visits got me through November and December into January. Her visits plus Jim's daily visits have kept me going since then. I've even had some special visits from David and Lisa, Jim's children. They're about six and four. David's old enough to understand what this place is and why I am here. But Lisa, my little doll, mainly likes to hear me sing, "I went to the animal fair." I've even sung to her on the telephone during the one call they allow me to make every week. She made me a little Valentine card and I'm not going to let it get out of my sight.

I think it's good for children to be able to come into a joint like this. It made a real impression on David. He asked me why I was here, why I dressed like I am, why we can't be in the same room, why there's bars all over, things like that. I gave him straight answers and he understood. He won't do anything to wind up like this, because he knows the end rewards just don't look very attractive.

One of the most important things that has ever happened to me is my friendship with Robert Leatherman, a nineteen-year-old man who lives in Tucson. Robert has cystic fibrosis. I say he is a man because he'd made more impact for good in other people's lives than most people ever do in a lifetime.

Jim and Cindy met Robert through the effort of Betty Janzik, a public relations lady who lives in Phoenix. Robert wanted to meet me. Since there was no way he could come to see me, Jim and Betty tried to arrange for me to see him at the hospital where he was in Tucson. Betty picked up the ball. She got permission from Pat Madrid, U.S. Marshal for Arizona, that if it was OK by William Smitherman, the U.S. Attorney for Arizona, then I'd be taken to see Robert. Smitherman gave his approval for the arrangements to be made. But the next day Betty was called and informed that the deal was off.

So Robert and I exchanged letters. He heard that I was smoking a lot of cigarettes, and he wrote me a letter asking me to quit smoking because it was hurting my health. The letter got to me, and I've cut way down on my smoking. Here's a boy who can't weigh much over fifty pounds, just some skin stretched over some bones, and he's concerned about my health. But I'm told that's the way Robert Leatherman is. He's always showing concern about the welfare of other people.

It was hearing about Robert that got me into the habit of getting back on my knees before the Lord. I think my contact with Robert was the sign to let me know I'd better get everything straight with the Lord before time ran out.

Robert is a perfect example of a true Christian. Although he's dying, he wants to follow the Bible in everything he does. He recently was baptized in a bathtub at the hospital. He insisted that he be fully immersed. Even knowing that being put into the water could kill him, he wanted this experience and he wouldn't be denied. That's real faith.

I've been praying to God, "Robert is a somebody. Grant him the right to keep breathing air on this earth, too."

When they get me back to Springfield, they're supposed to cut me open and see if they can fix up my stomach and lungs so I can stick around a few more years. The mesh lining near my stomach needs replacing where I took those bullets in the gut after the Coors kidnapping. I also have a pretty bad hernia. I'm turning blue a lot more often from asthma and emphysema attacks.

I know my body; what it can and can't do. I've looked at the situation from every angle. This is my last trip to Springfield.

A COMMENT

In the early morning hours of April 1, 1975, the man called John Webb was put in a small, tight-security van for transportation to Springfield, Missouri.

I visited with him all day, May 8, in the visiting room at the Federal Prison Hospital. He was undergoing tremendous physical strain. Cindy would have to go to the rest room and get paper towels and mop his face and hands because he was perspiring so much. He had lost a lot of weight, more than forty pounds since my first visit with him four months earlier.

He was badly shaken when I told him that Robert Leatherman had died. When he could speak, he said, "All I can say about Robert is that he's a man . . . he was more of a man than any man I've known."

He told me he had become attached to me and wanted to see me once more before he went under the surgeon's knife. He said it was his last opportunity to see me; to take back his best wishes to Ben and Naomi Jordan and to my family.

At the end of visiting hours, he got up from the couch where he'd been sitting next to Cindy on the other side of a small coffee table that separated us. He gave me a firm handshake and walked away.

I got a long distance phone call from him on July 13. He told me the chances of making it through the surgery were bad. He said that he would be dead in two weeks.

The call from Cindy woke me up. It was not yet daylight. The day was Sunday, July 27, 1975. Her voice was breaking. "He's gone. He died after midnight. He wouldn't let them do the surgery."

His body was buried in Hazelwood Cemetery under the name John Webb.

Jim Dobkins

APPENDIX

Following is the word-for-word reproduction of the entire contents of a letter sent by Rev. Harold E. Rapp, pastor of North Hollywood Family Foursquare Church, on February 10, 1988 to Jim Dobkins:

Jim:

I am writing this letter regarding a person who came to our church and gave his name as John Webb.

John and his lady, Cindy, first came to the North Hollywood Foursquare Church in the Spring of 1974. He and Cindy introduced themselves as needing spiritual help.

In my church office I prayed with John and helped him to trust Jesus Christ as his personal Savior. The experience seemed then and now to have been valid. I believe John was truly repentant.

Following the time of prayer he wanted to be baptized in water to completely follow in the Biblical footsteps of His newly found Lord.

Our church records indicate that on April 20, 1974 I baptized John Webb in water. The church issued him a certificate of the occasion.

Cindy and John spoke to me concerning performing a marriage ceremony for them. I told them that under the circumstances I knew of no reason why I could not accommodate them. So I instructed them to go to the Los Angeles County Marriage License Bureau and obtain the necessary documents. I do not remember the details of why they did not, or could not, acquire the documents. My response was that I could not perform a marriage in the State of California without following the necessary procedures. They asked if I could give a Spiritual, pastoral blessing upon their already exisitng union. In my church office I did in fact grant them a NON LEGAL yet spiritually sound blessing upon their union. I clearly let them know that the pastoral blessing upon them had NO LEGAL STANDING. It was only something within the Church and God.

I might add that I was then and now happy that I had the privilege in seeing John Webb come to a right relationship with God through believing in and trusting in Jesus Christ for his salvation.

I am also glad that I could encourage them in their union.

When John Webb and Cindy first came to our church, John asked me if he could speak with me in private. I told him certainly. The three of us, John, Cindy, and I went into my church office.

John told me that he needed my total confidence in what he wanted to share with me. I told John that clergy confidentiality was guaranteed.

John asked me if I had ever heard of "Machine Gun Kelly". I told him that probably everybody over the age of forty probably knew something of him.

John then told me that he was Machine Gun Kelly.

In my Theological and Psychological education I have long since learned to listen and to not challenge.

I listened to John without knowing in my heart whether or not to believe him. I decided that it really did not matter who he was, my God-given responsibility was to give assistance wherever possible.

John showed me his identification. A driver's license was the most important document that I remember seeing. He told me that he had been granted another name and identification to protect him after leaving prison.

He spoke of prison life with such clarity and conviction that it seemed convincing that he had been in several prisons. He did not go into any gross accounts of any of his escapades. He simply spoke of his being Machine Gun Kelly with such a naturalness that I took his words as being true. I still do.

John spoke his remorse and deep regret for his life of crime. He told me that he wasn't seeking any special help, he just wanted to have peace in his heart towards God. He wondered if God would forgive him. I assured him that God sent Jesus Christ to Calvary to bear the judgment and full penalty for all of our sins. After we prayed, John seemed changed.

Now, February 10, 1988, I still am blessed that the Lord allowed me the privilege of leading John Webb to Christ.

I believed then, and I believe now that John Webb was "Machine Gun Kelly".

Sincerely,
Rev. Harold E. Rapp
Rev. Harold E. Rapp, M.A.

Who wrote the ransom notes?

During interview sessions with Kelly, he time and again vowed that he — and not Kathryn Kelly — had written the ransom notes in the Urschel kidnapping.

Former FBI agent William W. Turner, in his book HOOVER'S F.B.I., produces evidence in the form of actual FBI file documents that support Kelly's contention that Kathryn was wrongly convicted of writing the ransom notes.

Writers Dobkins and Jordan strongly urge you to read Mr. Turner's very enlightening book.

PERSONAL APPEARANCES

Cindy Webb, widow of George Kelly, alias John Webb, is available — schedule permitting — to make personal appearances. Make arrangements by writing to:

> Cindy Webb Appearances
> UCS PRESS
> 3531 W. Glendale Ave.
> Suite 202
> Phoenix, AZ 85051

Autograph Special

Cindy Webb will be happy to personally autograph a book for you and include a brief, personal message. Send check or money order in the amount of $10 (which includes cost of book, postage and handling, and Cindy's personal message) to:

> Mail Order Dept.
> UCS PRESS
> 3531 W. Glendale Ave.
> Suite 202
> Phoenix, AZ 85051

Be sure to include your name the way you want Cindy to write it with her personal message to you. Please allow four to eight weeks for delivery.

WHO'S RAISING WHOM?
A parent's guide to effective child discipline.

Dr. Larry Waldman

$6.95   Trade Paperback   144 pgs.

A unique, easy-to-follow parenting guide that draws on the author's over 16 years' experience as psychologist and educator, and provides modification techniques that any parent can apply to better manage his or her children. Dr. Waldman thoroughly explains why children misbehave, then offers proven, step-by-step methods whereby parents can effectively deal with and <u>change</u> unwanted behavior.   WHO'S RAISING WHOM? liberally uses anecdotes from actual case histories to support and illustrate the author's points. Reading this guide is very much like personally experiencing several weeks of intensive counseling with Dr. Waldman. Includes six charts and graphs.

You can order WHO'S RAISING WHOM? direct from the publisher.   Send check or money order in the amount of $8 (includes cost of book, postage and handling) to:

> **Mail Order Dept.**
> **UCS PRESS**
> **3531 W. Glendale Ave.**
> **Suite 202**
> **Phoenix, AZ 85051**

Please allow four to eight weeks for delivery.

Books by Mail Order

MACHINE-GUN MAN can be ordered direct from the publisher. For fewer than ten books, send check or money order in the amount of $8 (which includes cost of book, postage and handling) for each book ordered. For orders of ten or more books, include payment of $6.95 for each book ordered (postage and handling will be paid for by the publisher). For orders of fifty or more books, include payment of $5.50 for each book ordered (postage and handling will be paid for by the publisher). For orders of one hundred or more books, include payment of $4.75 for each book ordered (postage and handling will be paid for by the publisher).

Send your order, along with payment (made payable to UCS PRESS), to:

Mail Order Dept.
UCS PRESS
3531 W. Glendale Ave.
Suite 202
Phoenix, AZ 85051

Please allow four to eight weeks for delivery.